Also by Edward Dolnick

*The Seeds of Life*
*The Rush*
*The Clockwork Universe*
*The Forger's Spell*
*The Rescue Artist*
*Down the Great Unknown*
*Madness on the Couch*

# THE
# WRITING OF
# THE GODS

## THE RACE TO DECODE
## THE ROSETTA STONE

## EDWARD DOLNICK

SCRIBNER

New York   London   Toronto   Sydney   New Delhi

Scribner
An Imprint of Simon & Schuster, Inc.
1230 Avenue of the Americas
New York, NY 10020

First Scribner hardcover edition October 2021

SCRIBNER and design are registered trademarks of The Gale Group, Inc.,
used under license by Simon & Schuster, Inc., the publisher of this work.

For information about special discounts for bulk purchases,
please contact Simon & Schuster Special Sales at 1-866-506-1949
or business@simonandschuster.com.

The Simon & Schuster Speakers Bureau can bring authors to your live event.
For more information or to book an event, contact the Simon & Schuster Speakers Bureau
at 1-866-248-3049 or visit our website at www.simonspeakers.com.

Manufactured in the United States of America

1   3   5   7   9   10   8   6   4   2

Library of Congress Cataloging-in-Publication Data has been applied for.

ISBN 978-1-5011-9893-9
ISBN 978-1-5011-9895-3 (ebook)

For Lynn, and Sam and Ben

Here we are then, in Egypt, the land of the Pharaohs, the land of the Ptolemies, the kingdom of Cleopatra . . . with our heads shaven as clean as your knee, smoking long pipes and drinking our coffee lying on divans. What can I say? How can I write to you about it? I have scarcely recovered from my initial astonishment.

—Gustave Flaubert, 1850

# Contents

# Timeline

**3100 BC** – Earliest hieroglyphs

**2686 BC–2181 BC** – Old Kingdom

      **2600 BC** – Great Sphinx; Great Pyramid

**2040 BC–1782 BC** – Middle Kingdom (golden age of Egyptian literature)

**1570 BC–1070 BC** – New Kingdom (wealthiest era in Egyptian history)

      **1334 BC–1325 BC** – King Tut reigns

      **1279 BC–1213 BC** – Ramesses II reigns (Egypt's mightiest pharaoh)

**332 BC** – Alexander the Great conquers Egypt

**196 BC** – Rosetta Stone inscribed

**30 BC** – Rome conquers Egypt; Cleopatra commits suicide

---

**394 AD** – Last hieroglyphs inscribed

**642** – Arabs conquer Egypt

**1773** – Thomas Young born

**1790** – Jean-François Champollion born

**1798** – Napoleon invades Egypt

**1799** – Rosetta Stone discovered

(All the ancient dates are historians' and archaeologists' best guesses)

# Prologue

Imagine an archaeologist, thousands of years from now, whose trowel clangs against something solid and hard, hidden in the dirt. In this distant age, no one knows for sure whether there once was a United States or if the name only referred to a legendary place, like Atlantis. No one speaks English. A few scraps of writing in English have survived. No one can read them.

The stone beneath the trowel looks smooth along part of its length, but a glance reveals that it is only a broken fragment of what might once have been a large block. Still, the smoothness is enough to set the pulse racing; nature seldom works so tidily. A closer look holds still more promise. *Those lines and curves gouged into the stone—could they be some sort of inscription?*

Over weeks and months, teams of researchers painstakingly trace the carved and eroded marks. They will ponder them endlessly, trying to guess a meaning in the mysterious symbols. Some are too damaged or worn to make out, and others are missing altogether.

OUR SC  E AN  SEV

Some scholars believe the message should be read the other way around:

VES  NA E  CS RUO

How would the sleuths proceed? Not knowing English, not knowing American history, would they ever manage to see that once a stone temple had proclaimed a message that began, "Four score and seven years ago"?

# THE
# WRITING OF
# THE GODS

# CHAPTER ONE

# The Stakes

In 1799, the year of the Rosetta Stone's discovery, Egypt was a sweltering, impoverished backwater. No matter. It was *ancient* Egypt that beguiled the West, and it had never lost its allure.

Herodotus, the "father of history," was the first outsider to describe Egypt's marvels. Writing in 440 BC, he entranced his readers with tales of a land whose every aspect was unfamiliar. Egypt boasted a "climate unlike any other" and a river "which shows a nature different from all other rivers." Most important, the Egyptians themselves were a people whose "manners and customs were opposite to other men in almost all matters."

Egypt was different from other countries because it was a slender strip of green surrounded by thousands of miles of desert on both sides. The Nile was different from other rivers because it flowed from south to north, which seemed contrary to nature, and, more important, because it flooded every year, even though Egypt almost never saw rain. When the floods receded, they left behind rich, black soil, perfect for farming.

The ancient world revolved around agriculture, but in all the world except Egypt, farming was a fickle business. In other lands the rains might come and bring prosperity for a season; they might fail, and then crops would wither and families starve.

Egypt, blessed by the gods, had few such worries. Despite skies that were perpetually clear, the flood had nearly always come, and it *would* always come, this year and next year and forever. Here was that rarest of gifts, a miracle with an eternal guarantee. With enemies walled off by deserts to the east and west, by the sea to the north and

1

by wild rapids to the south, Egypt sat safe and prosperous, the envy of the world.

Above all, Egypt was rich beyond reckoning. "Gold is in Egypt like the sands of the desert," a king of neighboring Assyria remarked enviously, in the era of King Tut. It was almost true. Tut was a nobody, the Millard Fillmore of pharaohs, and yet the riches buried with him dazzle museumgoers to this day. He was buried in a coffin inside a coffin inside a coffin, and the innermost of the three was solid gold and weighed 220 pounds. Inside lay Tut's linen-wrapped mummy, his head and shoulders covered by an elegant, gleaming gold mask that rested unseen for three thousand years.

Egypt was the best-known and the longest-lived of all ancient cultures. The time span is almost inconceivable. The pharaohs reigned from roughly 3100 BC until 30 BC, the year of Cleopatra's suicide. America's history extends less than three centuries. Egypt's run was *thirty* centuries.

To try to put markers on an Egyptian timeline is to risk vertigo. The Great Pyramid and the Sphinx, Egypt's best-known monuments, are older than Stonehenge. Both date from around 2600 BC (in comparison with perhaps 2400 BC for Stonehenge). By the time they were built, Egypt was already five centuries old.*

From the time of the pyramids to the reign of Cleopatra was longer than from Cleopatra to the Wright brothers. And throughout nearly all that vast expanse of time, Egypt perched atop the world.

Through the next two thousand years, from the time of Cleopatra and Caesar to our own day, Egypt's mystique would never fade. In that marvelous land, a Turkish traveler wrote in 1671, he had seen "wondrous and strange things by the hundreds of thousands. . . . Before each of them, we have been entirely beside ourselves with astonishment."

No one today spares a thought for once-mighty kingdoms like Assyria and Babylon, but Egypt still sizzles with star power. So it has al-

---

* A timeline of the world's most renowned structures would include the Parthenon, built around 450 BC; the Roman Colosseum, around 100 AD; Angkor Wat, around 1100; the Great Wall of China, around 1400; St. Peter's, around 1600; and the Taj Mahal, around 1650.

ways been, and never more so than in the last years of the 1700s, when Napoleon led an army to Egypt.

Behind the diplomatic rationales for invading Egypt was a simpler motive—Napoleon's heroes, Alexander the Great and Julius Caesar, had conquered Egypt, and therefore he would do the same. He brought with him a cadre of scientists and artists whose mission was to study Egypt and to bring it the blessings of French civilization. Their breathless accounts of the wonders they had seen would spur a frenzy that was dubbed Egyptomania.

For Europeans, *Egypt* conjured up a hodgepodge of beauty (*Cleopatra!*) and grandeur (*the pyramids!*) and mystery (*the Sphinx!*). All this was seasoned with a soupçon of shivery horror (*mummies!*) that amped up the excitement. (On his return to France, Napoleon presented his wife, Empress Josephine, with the gift of a mummy's head.)

Early on, only the most daring Europeans had ventured to this far-off land. They marveled at sights that were, by local standards, as routine as the rising and setting of the sun. "I saw the Nile, upon my first coming, full, but not overflowing," wrote an English traveler named William Bankes, in 1815. "I saw it a month afterwards spread as a sea over the whole face of Egypt, with villages as if swimming upon its surface, and men and cattle wading from place to place."

To Western eyes, everything was astonishing—the thin green thread of the Nile against a vast tan canvas, of course, but also palm trees, mirages, locusts, the endless expanse of desert sand. "To a European," wrote Bankes, "it is not another climate, it is another nature, that is before him."

That awe extended to hieroglyphs, Egypt's ancient and imposing system of writing.* Across the vast span of years before the Rosetta Stone yielded its secrets, the mystery of the hieroglyphs thrust itself in the face of every visitor to Egypt. Enticingly, maddeningly, Egypt's monuments and tombs were covered with elaborate picture-writing—an

---

* The symbols are *hieroglyphs*, not *hieroglyphics*. Egyptologists cringe at the misuse, though it is all but universal. *Hieroglyphic* is an adjective, they insist, like *artistic* or *majestic*.

"infinity of hieroglyphs," in the words of one early explorer—that no one knew how to decipher.

Temple walls carried long messages, and so did every column and beam in those temples (and every surface, including ceilings and even the undersides of beams), and so did obelisks, and papyrus sheets beyond number, and the caskets that enclosed mummies, and even the mummies' bandages. "There is hardly the space of an awl or needle-hole," a traveler from Baghdad wrote in the year 1183, "which did not have an image, or engraving or some script which is not understood."

Hieroglyphs from the Temple of Isis, Philae

Herodotus had stared uncomprehendingly at those inscriptions. Scholars who came after him—for a full two millennia—pored over inscriptions carved into obelisks that conquerors had brought home or that travelers had carefully copied. They came up empty, baffled by the mysterious zigzags and birds and snakes and semicircles.

Faced with symbols they could not decipher, they might have denigrated the mysterious markings as mere decoration. They did just the opposite.

Europe's deepest thinkers proclaimed hieroglyphs a mystical form of writing, superior to all others. Hieroglyphs did not stand for letters or sounds, like the symbols in ordinary scripts, these scholars declared, but for *ideas*.

It was not simply that hieroglyphic symbols conveyed meaning without words, like the *No smoking* signs that show a cigarette with a red slash across it. The real point was that hieroglyphs conveyed not mundane messages but profound and universal truths.

Linguists and historians insisted that these strange symbols had nothing to do with the alphabets familiar in other cultures. Those workaday alphabets, like the ones used in Greece or Rome, might suffice for love letters or tax receipts, but hieroglyphs had a loftier purpose. In effect, scholars dismissed the possibility that hieroglyphs could be used for ordinary messages or lists—*milk, butter, something the kids will eat*—in the firm belief that every hieroglyphic text was a meditation on the nature of space and time.

The beauty of hieroglyphs might explain some of this misplaced reverence. The animal symbols especially look more like small works of art than like writing; the best examples look as if they came from a naturalist's field notes.

When linguists first studied other, less imposing scripts, they tended to go wrong in exactly the opposite way—*Surely these scrawls*

*and scratches don't depict letters or words.* The scholar who coined the name *cuneiform* for one of the longest-lived and most important of all early scripts, for instance, never believed that it was writing at all. Thomas Hyde was an authority on ancient languages—he was an Oxford professor of Hebrew and Arabic—and in 1700 he published a thick book on ancient Persia. He waved aside the ornate wedge-shaped markings found on countless clay tablets throughout Persia. This was not writing, Hyde explained, despite what some scholars insisted, but merely an elaborate array of decorative wedges and arrows.

It turned out that cuneiform, in different forms, was used to write a variety of Middle Eastern languages for three thousand years. Hyde's only lasting contribution to scholarship, in the judgment of one modern expert, was providing "an outstanding example of how wrong a professor, and in his case a double professor, can be." (Cuneiform was the earliest script of all, by most scholars' reckoning. It first appeared around 3100 BC. That was slightly before the earliest Egyptian hieroglyphs, which date from around 3000 BC. The earliest Chinese writing dates from around 1200 BC.)

Another hugely important archaeological find met the same sneering dismissal at first, for nearly the same reason. The script called Linear B, a forerunner of Greek, was discovered on the island of Crete, in the 1880s, carved into huge stone blocks. Crete was a land rich in myth and history. It was Crete where the king imprisoned Icarus and Daedalus in a tower, and where father and son escaped by launching themselves into the sky on feathered wings.

Linear B, which dates from around 1450 BC, would prove to be the earliest writing ever set down in Europe. It would have been forgivable if archaeologists, dazzled by possibility, read more meaning into those symbols than truly belonged there. They didn't. When experts first examined the Linear B inscriptions they declared them to be "masons' marks."

But almost no one treated hieroglyphs with disdain. Carved into temple walls and obelisks, they were hailed as conveying peeks deep into the heart of nature. The modern counterpart would be truths like $e = mc^2$ that are written (and understood) in the identical way by physicists in Shanghai and Chicago. For nearly two thousand years, European scholars thought of ancient Egyptian priests as we think of scientists today—these sages had devised an arcane code that disclosed crucial insights to those in the know, and nothing at all to those uninitiated in its secrets.

In the words of the third-century philosopher Plotinus, "[Egyptian scribes] did not go through the whole business of letters, words, and sentences." Egypt's wise men had found a far better approach—conveying ideas by drawing signs. "Each separate sign is in itself a piece of knowledge, a piece of wisdom, a piece of reality, immediately present."

But this was guesswork, since not a single person in the world knew the meaning of a single hieroglyph. Egypt was covered with countless messages, and every one of them was mute.

It was the rise of Christianity that ensured the fall of hieroglyphs. In the early 300s, the Roman emperor Constantine converted to Christianity. That act spurred one of the most important course changes in world history. Later in the century, Christianity became the official religion of Rome. By century's end the puny new faith had grown powerful enough to outlaw its rivals.

In 391 AD the Roman emperor Theodosius the Great ordered that all Egypt's temples be torn down, as affronts to Christianity. (The penalty for worshipping the old pagan gods, even in the privacy of your own home, was death.) The last person who wrote an inscription in hieroglyphs carved it into a wall in a temple at Philae, an island far up the Nile, in 394 AD.

Edicts like the one laid down by Theodosius were new. Warfare and persecution were as old as humankind, but the issue was seldom that one side believed in the wrong gods. In the days when polytheism was all but universal, conquerors who took over new territory tended to take over the local gods, too. If you already worshipped several dozen gods, it was no problem to make room for a few more.

Then came monotheism and the belief in one true God, and everything shifted. "The Greeks and Romans had respected the old gods [before Constantine's conversion] . . . ," writes the Egyptologist

Barbara Mertz, "but monotheism is by its very nature intolerant." Hieroglyphs, as emblems of the bad old ways, came in for special condemnation. Forbidden, they were soon forgotten.

Forgotten in Egypt, at any rate. In Europe and the Arab world, the attempts at decipherment never ceased and never made headway. Think of how long that veil of ignorance stayed in place. Rome rose and fell, and still the "infinity of hieroglyphs" retained their secrets. (Rome was so obsessed with Egypt that conquerors brought home *thirteen* immense hieroglyph-adorned obelisks. To this day there are more Egyptian obelisks in Rome than in Egypt.) The Middle Ages arrived, and sky-piercing cathedrals rose across Europe—they were the first man-made structures in four thousand years to stand taller than the pyramids—and through all those years there was no progress in deciphering hieroglyphs. The Renaissance came, and with it the Age of Science and the birth of the modern world, and still . . . nothing.

The cliché has it that an unknown subject is a closed book, but Egypt was different. Egypt was an *open* book, with illustrations on every page, that no one knew how to read.

CHAPTER TWO

# The Find

No one ever set out to find the Rosetta Stone. No one knew there was such a thing, though travelers and scholars had long dreamed there might be. The stone had lain unnoticed for nearly two thousand years. It might well have stayed lost forever.

It turned up in a pile of rubble in a prosperous but out-of-the-way Egyptian town called Rashid, on a sweltering July day in 1799. France had invaded Egypt the year before. At the head of the French army was a young general, Napoleon Bonaparte, just rising to fame. Soon he would be known around the world, his name invoked with awe or whispered in horror. (In England, small children were warned that if they did not go quietly to sleep, "Boney" would snatch them from their beds and devour them.)

A team of French soldiers had been assigned to rebuild a broken-down fort in Rashid, in the Nile delta. (The French called the town Rosetta.) The fortress had once stood squat but imposing, a square eighty yards on a side with turrets, and a tower at its center. But it had been neglected for centuries, and by the time the French arrived it urgently needed repair. "I expect to be attacked at any time," the local commander wrote Napoleon, and he set his men urgently to work, converting this wreck into a proper fort with barracks and sturdy walls.

Just who spotted the Rosetta Stone will never be known. The true discoverer was quite likely an Egyptian laborer, but if so no one recorded his name. The man credited with the discovery was Lieutenant Pierre-François Bouchard, the officer in charge of the rebuilding work. Someone drew Bouchard's attention to a large, broken stone slab sitting in a heap of similar stones. Beneath the dust and dirt on the stone's dark surface, you could just make out some strange marks. *Could this be something?*

Bouchard, who was a scientist as well as a soldier, saw at once that one side of the heavy stone was covered with inscriptions. Line after line of carved symbols ran the stone's full width. That was surprising, but what set the heart pounding was this: the inscriptions were of three different sorts.

At the top of the stone were fourteen lines of hieroglyphs, drawings of circles and stars and lions and kneeling men. That section was incomplete. At some point in the past, the top of the stone and pieces on both the top right and left had been lost, and with them many lines of hieroglyphs had disappeared.

Several lines of Rosetta Stone hieroglyphs, in close-up

In the stone's middle section was a longer section of simple curves and curlicues, thirty-two lines altogether. These looked like letters from some unknown script or perhaps symbols from a code, certainly not like the pictures in the hieroglyphic section. But if these slashes and dashes were a script, they were unrecognizable; if they were merely ornamental, they looked oddly systematic and purposeful.

A section of the mysterious middle inscription, in close-up.
No one recognized the script or knew what language it represented.

The third set of marks, below the other two, posed no such riddles. This was Greek, fifty-three lines of it (with a bit broken off at the bottom right), and instantly recognizable. It was not quite *easy* to read, because it was written more like a legal document than an everyday note, but it was easy enough.

Lines from the Greek, which scholars could read, in close-up

The stone itself measured four feet by three feet and weighed three-quarters of a ton. Its jagged top showed that it was a fragment of a larger original. In Egypt, where trees are scarce, important buildings had always been made of stone. Since ancient times, that had made for a kind of slow-motion recycling, with stone blocks from one building reused in another. Or sometimes many others, over the course of dozens of centuries. (Even the pyramids were plundered and their stones reused, which is why they are no longer smooth sided.)

That seemed to have happened here. The Rosetta Stone had originally been placed in a prominent spot in a temple, on a date that corresponded to 196 BC. So the Greek text declared. Several centuries later, with the temple that had housed it demolished, the Rosetta Stone presumably lay unnoticed in a pile of rubble.

Perhaps it sat there, untouched through the generations. Perhaps it was recycled into another building, or a sequence of other buildings. No one knows. In 1470 AD—by that time it had been a thousand years since anyone in the world could read hieroglyphs—an Arab ruler began building a fort not far from where the temple had once stood.

The building supplies for the sultan's new fort included a heap of stones brought from who knows where. The laborers who wrestled the stones into place may have ignored the Rosetta Stone's inscriptions. Possibly they never noticed them. In any event, they set the stone in

The Rosetta Stone, with three types of writing. Hieroglyphs
are at the top, an unfamiliar script lies in the middle, and Greek
is at the bottom. Scholars could read the Greek but had no idea
what to make of the other two inscriptions.

position alongside countless others, an anonymous block in an anonymous wall in an anonymous fort. This was akin to using a Gutenberg Bible as a doorstop.

The first guesses were that it might take two weeks to decipher the Rosetta Stone. As it turned out, it took *twenty years*. The first linguists and scholars who saw the inscriptions set to work eagerly, buoyed by the belief that a short burst of effort would bring them their prize. They quickly grew puzzled, then frustrated, and, in short order, despairing, leaving as their only legacy a warning to others that this was a riddle impossible to solve.

Two rival geniuses, one French and one English, did the most to crack the code. Both had been child prodigies, both had an uncanny flair for languages, but they were opposites in every other regard. The Englishman, Thomas Young, was one of the most versatile geniuses who ever lived. The Frenchman, Jean-François Champollion, was a creature of singular focus who cared about Egypt and only about Egypt. Young was cool and elegantly polite. Champollion brimmed over with indignation and impatience. Young sneered at ancient Egypt's "superstitions" and "depravity." Champollion marveled at the glories of the mightiest empire the ancient world had ever known.

Intellectual battles seldom have stakes this high. With their two nations perpetually at war, the Frenchman and the Englishman were out not only to outdo each other but to win glory for their homeland. For Egypt was the mystery of mysteries, and the first person to learn how to read its secrets would solve a riddle that had mocked the world for more than a thousand years.

No one who saw the Greek text on the Rosetta Stone could miss the point. If the three inscriptions represented one message written in three different ways—and why else would they be carved into the same stone?—then in one swoop the hieroglyphs might reveal their secrets. A palace vault with a key protruding from the lock could not have beckoned more invitingly.

# CHAPTER THREE

# The Challenge

By Napoleon's day the pyramids and monuments and temples that dot Egypt had been famous for thousands of years, but scarcely anyone knew who had built them, or when, or why. They knew only that while much of the world had shivered in caves and groped in the dirt for slugs and snails, Egyptian pharaohs had reigned in splendor.

At the time the Rosetta Stone was discovered, the world had two great, globe-straddling superpowers, France and England. But at the time the Rosetta Stone was *written*, in 196 BC, France and England were home to marauding tribes whose activities extended mostly to raiding and raping. The picture had scarcely changed by 54 BC, when Caesar polished off Gaul and invaded Britain. There he found a brave but brutal foe, savages who painted themselves blue and dressed in animal skins. In that remote land, men shared their wives, Caesar sneered, "brothers along with brothers, and fathers with sons."

By Caesar's time—his affair with Cleopatra began in 48 BC—Egypt's glory days lay far in the past. But even so, Caesar's Rome fell far short of Egypt's standard, and so did Athens and every other city of the time.

In Caesar and Cleopatra's era, Egypt's capital, Alexandria, was the largest and grandest city in the world. Lined with statues, adorned with parks, bustling with shoppers and sightseers, it was Paris to Rome's Podunk. The city's broadest avenue stretched ninety feet across, room enough for eight chariots side by side. The Library of Alexandria boasted tens of thousands of papyrus scrolls, by far the largest such treasure trove ever accumulated, and this in an age when every manuscript had to be copied by hand. At its peak the library had drawn the greatest scholars of antiquity, including giants such as Euclid and Archimedes, who were wooed with lifetime appointments and lavish salaries.

But it was pomp and pageantry, more than scholarship, that the name *Egypt* conveyed. When Cleopatra traveled up the Nile, she floated in a gilded barge with purple sails and silver oars. Incense wafted through the air while flutes piped softly and young boys at the queen's side waved fans to stir a gentle breeze.

And Cleopatra came at the very *end* of Egypt's imperial run, thirteen centuries after King Tut, twenty centuries after the golden age of Egyptian literature, twenty-six centuries after the Great Pyramid.

We know that timeline now, and we know countless details about what ancient Egyptians believed, and how they lived, and what they feared, and what they hoped for. A note of caution, though. Every generalization about "Egypt" really has to do with only an ever-so-thin slice of the population. The great majority of Egyptians were illiterate peasants who lived hard, brutal, anonymous lives. "They struggled through a life of penury, privation, and physical toil, and passed away leaving no trace in this world," in the words of the historian Ricardo Caminos. "Their dead bodies were abandoned on the fringe of the desert or, at best, dropped into shallow holes in the sand, with not even the poorest gravestones to bear their names."

But even bearing in mind that giant caveat about the invisibility of the poor, we know far more about Egypt than we do about any other ancient culture. We know it because the Egyptians themselves told us—they wrote it down—and we can read their inscriptions and letters and stories. We know all that because the Rosetta Stone showed the way.

Most people miss the point of the Rosetta Stone. They know that the story has to do with texts in different languages, and they picture something like a menu in a restaurant that caters to international tourists: *roast chicken with French fries; poulet rôti avec frites; Brathähnchen mit Pommes frites.* Armed with that menu, an English speaker could make a start at decoding French or German.

That was, in fact, the expectation of the first people to gaze at the Rosetta Stone. It proved badly mistaken. Instead, the decipherers found themselves lost inside a maze, seduced by tantalizing clues and then careening into dead ends and losing hope, but then spotting new markers and dashing off jubilantly once more.

One cause of their troubles—if they'd known they might have given up before they ever began—was that the three inscriptions turned out not to be word-for-word translations of one another. They do match up but in an imprecise, baggy way, like three peoples' summaries of the same movie.

But that was only one obstacle out of many. By way of recognizing what the would-be decipherers were up against, think again of *roast chicken* and *poulet rôti*. Even if we did not speak a word of French—even if we did not know there was a language called French—we would still have some advantages over those early scholars.

We recognize the alphabet that our menu is written in, for starters, which means we can begin to sound out words. Confronted with the inscriptions on the Rosetta Stone, early linguists could only stare befuddled. How could the first Egyptologists tell if vultures and wrens, or vertical and diagonal slashes, stood for letters, or syllables, or words, or ideas? And, although we could not be sure whether to read our menu from left to right or right to left, we might guess that *poulet rôti* sounds marginally more plausible than *itôr teluop*.

For decipherers, nothing can be taken for granted. Scripts can run left to right, like English, or right to left, like Hebrew and Arabic, or top to bottom, like Chinese and Japanese. More elaborate variants have had their day, too. Some ancient Greek texts followed a back-and-forth path, like a farmer plowing a field. One line ran left to right and then the next proceeded right to left, and so on (and in each new line, the individual letters flipped direction, too). Aztec script, one historian notes, "meandered across the page like a game of Snakes and Ladders, the direction being signaled by lines or dots."

Our menu would offer us still more to work with. Sounding out *poulet*, we might draw on vague memories. *Isn't a pullet a hen or a rooster or something chicken-y?* We could continue. The little hat on the O in *rôti* might catch our eye, especially since *rôti* looks a bit like *roast*. Eventually we might find a stash of texts and inscriptions from the land of *poulet* (for, after all, our goal is to decode an entire language, not just read a menu). There we would see more of the hat-wearing *O*'s, and also hat-wearing *E*'s and *I*'s. We would find *forêt* and *bête* and *côte* and *île*, and, perhaps from context or from pictures accompanying the text, we might eventually think of *forest* or *beast* or *coast* or *isle*. At some point we might guess that the hat symbol has something to do with a missing letter *S*.

And so we could proceed, halting step by halting step. Now think of the plight of the would-be decipherers staring at the Rosetta Stone.

Its symbols corresponded to no known script, and there was no way to sound them out and listen for clues. Answers to the most basic questions seemed mockingly out of reach. The symbols marched along without a break, for instance, one crowded next to the other. How could anyone know where one word ended and the next began (if they were words at all)?

Worse still—far worse—was this: the last speakers of ancient Egyptian had died millennia ago. (Egyptians have spoken Arabic since the seventh century AD.) By way of a contemporary example, imagine trying to read Chinese if you did not speak the language. Now imagine trying to read Chinese if *no one* spoke the language.

Suppose you did somehow find a way to read the hieroglyphs. Here you'd be, sounding out words that no one had spoken since the age of the pharaohs. Then what? What would those sounds tell you?

Suppose the last English speaker had died twenty centuries ago. How would anyone ever learn that the sounds *c-a-t* pronounced in quick succession meant "furry animal with whiskers"?

What made the mystery so difficult is a big part of our story. But the flip side is just as important—this was a riddle that *looked* enticing, as if any amateur with brains and persistence might solve it. That makes for a sharp contrast with the most famous codes, like Enigma. A layman could look forever at messages that the Nazis had encrypted with the Enigma machine and never see anything but random letters, one line indistinguishable from the next. To anyone but a mathematician, Enigma is as forbidding as a cliff face.

A page of hieroglyphs, though, consists of birds and serpents and ovals and squares, and almost invites our guesses. *Did an owl mean wisdom for the Egyptians, as it does for us? The Greek text on the Rosetta Stone talks about kings; where is the king in the hieroglyphs?*

Hieroglyphs are pictures, and that fundamental observation points in two different directions at once. The first is discouraging—we're confronted with a form of writing different from nearly every other. But the second is cheerier and more important—precisely because hieroglyphs *are* pictures, this is a form of writing that looks less abstract and more approachable than nearly any other.

So our task is not as daunting as understanding Enigma. This time we amateurs *can* jump in, searching for clues in the same puzzle pieces that beckoned and mocked Young and Champollion and all their predecessors.

CHAPTER FOUR

# Voices from the Dust

The riddles of language and decoding are living mysteries—there are texts in strange scripts that no one has deciphered to this day, including one from ancient Italy* and another from Easter Island—and they speak to the deepest aspects of civilization and culture. Speaking and writing seem like two sides of one coin, but writing is fundamentally more difficult. All babies learn to speak, automatically, by soaking up the sounds all around them; no baby ever learns to read or write automatically, despite the printed words all around her.

Why that should be, no one quite knows. Perhaps it makes sense that reading should be difficult, but think for a moment how astonishing it is that learning to speak is not. Let a baby splash in a fountain of words, and she'll sort things out on her own. The novelist Nicholson Baker has done better than any linguist at making clear how much is going on inside the mind of that tiny, burbling explorer. "And you start to see that all these sounds that you can make—ngo, merk, plort—that you begin to hear, can be classified in certain ways. You're a newborn brain, you've only recently come out of solitary confinement in the uterus, and you're already a cryptanalyst in Bletchley Park. You're already parsing through, looking for similarities and differences, looking for patterns, looking for beginnings and endings and hints of meaning."

What is true of each person is true of the human race: our ances-

* Scholars have learned to *read* the script of the Etruscans, who built a thriving culture in Italy centuries before the Romans. But they do not know what the sounds meant. In effect, they can read sounds aloud, but they do not know if they have read *To be or not to be* or *All cats love Frisky Nibbles*.

tors began talking some fifty thousand years ago, but only in relatively recent times—only five thousand years ago—did some unknown genius figure out how to capture the multitudinous sounds of speech in a small array of scrawls and scratches. Or perhaps it was a sequence of geniuses, each contributing an insight or improvement.

The crucial point is that though speaking comes naturally, writing had to be invented. Speech is part of our biological heritage, like crawling and walking. Writing is a product of human ingenuity, like the telephone or the airplane. (The story of that colossal breakthrough is irretrievably lost. Ironically, no one ever wrote it down.)

So learning to read takes work. That thrusts each of us into the heart of the Rosetta Stone story, because every one of us has performed almost precisely the same kind of decoding that finally cracked the Egyptian case—every new reader struggling to bring life to the squiggles in *The Cat in the Hat* is a pint-sized counterpart of the brilliant sleuths who first wrestled with hieroglyphs. Reading *is* deciphering, and we are all linguistic detectives. Each of us has worked at Bletchley Park.

The payoff we derive from that deciphering work is enormous. The writer Alberto Manguel recalls the very moment of his breakthrough into reading. He was about four and he knew the names of the letters, when he happened to see a billboard from a car window. "What that word was on the long-past billboard I no longer know . . . but the impression of suddenly being able to comprehend what before I could only gaze at is as vivid today as it must have been then."

It was, Manguel writes, "like acquiring an entirely new sense."

The invention of writing is often classed as the greatest of all intellectual breakthroughs. "Without writing," the anthropologist Loren Eiseley once observed, "the tale of the past rapidly degenerates into fumbling myth and fable. Man's greatest epic, his four long battles with the advancing ice of the great continental glaciers, has vanished from human memory without a trace. Our illiterate fathers disappeared and with them, in a few scant generations, died one of the great stories of all time."

Countless smaller stories vanish, too, if no one writes them down.

"If humans had existed for just one day," the linguist John McWhorter points out, "then writing would have been invented about 11 p.m." If tribes fought wars before eleven p.m. on history's clock, or lovers whispered in the shadows, no one will ever know.

The memories we can hold in our head extend perhaps two generations into the past, maybe three. My grandfather lived into his nineties. We saw him often, I believe, when I was little. But now, for me, with no one left to tell his story and no letters or journals to look at, all the events of those nine decades have melted away. All that I can recall is the scratchiness of an old man's badly shaved cheeks (I didn't like kissing him goodbye) and the way his bony wrists poked out from long, floppy sleeves.

Whole swaths of culture can vanish nearly as quickly. The poet and historian Amadou Hampâté Bâ devoted a great deal of time to collecting oral tales from his homeland, Mali. "In Africa," he lamented, "when an old man dies, a library burns."

And so the story of humankind's age-old battle against oblivion is in good measure the story of writing. Which means that the saga of the Rosetta Stone is as far as could be from a narrow tale of arcane scholarship in musty libraries. On the contrary, our journey of exploration will bring us into unlikely valleys and across unfamiliar terrain. To keep our bearings, we will try not to travel too far from the Rosetta Stone itself, in the spirit of "keep the river on your right." But we are after big game—stories of archaeological swashbucklers tumbling through ancient tombs; peeks at the first-ever attempts to set down words in writing; excursions into big subjects like the struggle against death and forgetting—and it would be a mistake to forgo those adventures in favor of sticking to hieroglyphs alone.

A mistake because if we keep our eyes only on the Rosetta Stone, we miss the larger story. For the Rosetta Stone is that unlikeliest of objects, a window made of solid stone, and the view through that window tells us not only about the nitty-gritty of sleuthing and deciphering but also about the nature of language and the byways of history and the evolution of human culture.

• • •

One key point is easy to lose sight of—the invention of writing was not only one of humanity's greatest achievements but one of its most difficult as well. Think how long it took. For tens of thousands of years, our forebears drew cave paintings of stunning skill and sophistication; they fashioned stone knives so thin that you can see sunlight through the blades and so sharp that they outperform steel scalpels. No one signed those masterpieces. No one could have, because for thousands and thousands of generations no one had found a way to convert sounds into symbols.

From our vantage point downstream in time, it can be hard to recognize the hurdles that our intellectual forebears overcame. A solved mystery often looks as if it should never have been mysterious to start with. But provincialism in time is as misguided as provincialism in its ordinary sense. Until the answers are revealed, the "simplest" questions can seem baffling.

It was "a notable advance in the history of thought," the philosopher Alfred North Whitehead once observed, when some forgotten genius hit on the insight that two fish and two days and two sticks all share the abstract property of "twoness." For countless generations no one had seen it. That humble insight had tremendous consequences. Once you had grasped that the important thing was the concept 2, and not the two fish you happened to be looking at, you were well on the way to universal laws like 2 + 2 = 4. You had set out on the road to science.

All deciphering stories sit inside a thicket of these simple-afterward-but-mysterious-before questions. This is especially true in the case of the Rosetta Stone, because the hieroglyphs' eye-catching appearance led everyone astray. But *every* deciphering story requires a deep dive into the mysteries of language, and languages are frustratingly diverse and endlessly intricate. Languages do have various features in common, since they all describe our one shared world, with its mothers and brothers and sun and moon and rushing rivers and crawling babies. But they look and sound astonishingly different.

To step off a plane in Beijing or into a classroom at Gallaudet is to plunge into helpless bewilderment. And no wonder, for languages are built of puffs of air (or hand gestures), and an architecture of words can take on far more fantastic shapes than anything built of bricks or wood.

The upshot is that the work of deciphering is both hugely difficult and hugely important. Written down, the tiniest events and the grandest sagas have a chance at immortality. Love letters have surfaced after thousands of years, and receipts for the sale of a dozen footstools, and epic tales of heroes and ogres in deadly combat.

In the case of Egypt, the deciphering of hieroglyphs gave voices to pharaohs and schoolboys and merchants and travelers who died thirty centuries ago. In other, wetter lands such messages would have long since disintegrated, but Egypt's hot, dry climate serves as a kind of inadvertent time capsule. Messages cut into monuments long ago, or drawn on temple walls, remain sharp and distinct to this day. Countless papyrus texts survive, some carrying the print of a scribe's inky finger or a teacher's scrawled corrections on a student's work.

The details and colors on the walls of Egypt's tombs are as vibrant today as when the tombs were sealed shut thousands of years ago.

Visitors from rainy climes are always astonished at how very dry Egypt is. In the dazzling city of Luxor, for instance, the average annual rainfall is 0. So it has been since ancient times. "Neither rain, nor any sign of rain, is shown in the paintings of the tombs," the English archaeologist Flinders Petrie pointed out a century ago. "No wide hats, no umbrellas, no dripping cattle, are ever represented."

In Egypt our word *perishable* scarcely applies. A flower from a funeral wreath made three thousand years ago might still be identifiable. A loaf of bread older than Greece and Rome might show a baker's thumbprints. Egypt's heat and dryness would have mummified bodies, too, and without any need for lengthy, difficult procedures. Indeed the whole complicated embalming process that we identify so closely with ancient Egypt was built on a Catch-22.

Egyptians believed in life after death. Mummification was so important because you needed a lifelike body in order to carry on. Embalming was a difficult, time-consuming art that employed hooks for dragging the brain out through the nose, and special knives for slicing open the abdomen to remove internal organs, and specialized techniques for drying tissue. And yet when a dead body was simply set down in a shallow pit in the desert, as had traditionally been the fate of the poor, the hot sand and the blazing sun mummified it naturally.

The rich insisted on grander send-offs. But the very act of shutting bodies into dark, still coffins made necessary the whole range of techniques needed to stave off rot and decay.

So in ancient Egypt, artifacts endured almost by default. In a culture obsessed with continuity, that was vitally important, and it was that power to transcend time that made writing special above all other arts. Hieroglyphs were the writing of the gods, ancient texts decreed, and then the gods had bestowed this marvelous gift on humankind. From its earliest days, Egypt had recognized the possibilities.

One temple inscription from about the same era as the Rosetta Stone praised the gods who "created writing in the beginning" and thereby "caused memory to begin." Thanks to this divine gift, "the heir speaks with his forefathers," and "friends can communicate when the sea is between them, and one man can hear another without seeing him."

Engraved inscriptions dealt largely with kings and gods, but messages on papyrus tended toward the mundane and practical. "Please make me a new pair of sandals," reads one note from around 1200 BC.

Another from the same era asks, "Why haven't you answered my message? I wrote to you a week ago!"

One junior scribe complained to his supervisor, in around 1240 BC, that he was mistreated and taken for granted. "I am like a donkey to you. If there is some work, bring the donkey. . . . If there is some beer, you do not look for me, but if there is work you do look for me."

An aggrieved mother railed against her ungrateful children, and her bitterness speaks to us undiluted by the intervening eons. "I am a free woman of the land of Pharaoh," she declared in her will, in around 1140 BC. "I brought up eight children and gave them everything suitable to their station. But I have grown old, and they have not looked after me. Whoever of them has aided me, I will leave my property. But he who has neglected me, I will not aid him."

Perhaps the biggest single stash of ancient writing turned up in 1897, when two English archaeologists found several thirty-foot-tall mounds of papyrus scraps covered in sand (and mixed with random debris) in the desert south of Cairo. The scraps had originally come from rubbish heaps in the once-thriving city of Oxyrhynchus. (The name means "city of the sharp-nosed fish.") Safeguarded by the desert's dryness, the ink had retained its blackness for two thousand years.

Half a million fragments survived, some as small as a postage stamp, some as big as a tablecloth. Most provided glimpses of everyday life. A wealthy couple sent a thousand roses and four thousand narcissuses for the wedding of a friend's son. A man named Juda fell off his horse and needed the help of two nurses just to turn over. Scraps from marriage contracts, horoscopes, and steamy novels turned up, and so did an unknown play by Sophocles and snippets of poems by Sappho.

Many ancient Egyptian texts have an unsettling, almost-familiar-but-not-quite quality. Writers describe emotions that we recognize at once but make their points with images that remind us, with a jolt, that we are far from home. A poem from the era of King Tut, around 1300 BC, described the obstacles that confront a pair of young lovers: "My beloved is on yonder side / A width of water is between us / And a crocodile waits on the sandbank."

Sometimes the writing reveals an altogether strange and forbidding world. Egyptians believed, for instance, that when a person died, the gods placed his heart in one pan of a scale and a feather, representing truth, in the other. If the heart and the feather balanced, the person had lived a truthful life and had a chance at a kind of heaven. Fail the test, though, and the result was not hell and everlasting flames, but disappearance! The telltale heart was thrown to a part-hippopotamus, part-crocodile creature that gulped it down. *Poof!*

The "Weighing of the Heart" ceremony. The ibis-headed god of writing,
Toth, stands at the right, poised to record the test's result.

The most compelling voices might have cried out yesterday. One Egyptian scribe scrawled his frustration on a piece of papyrus that survived to find its way to the British Museum. "Would I had phrases that are not known," he wrote, "in new language that has not been used, not an utterance which has grown stale, which men of old have spoken." The lament was written in about 2000 BC. It predates Homer by a thousand years.

But what if the writing survives, but the knowledge of how to read it does not?

# CHAPTER FIVE

# So Near and Yet So Far

I f you pull the camera back far enough, all cultures look the same.
People meet and fall in love; they boast and puff themselves up; they
mock their rivals; they pray to their god, or a host of gods; they fear
death. The details make all the difference. Aztecs ripped the beating
hearts out of captives taken in battle, to placate their gods; Jains sweep
the sidewalk to safeguard any bugs they might step on.

A drawing by an Aztec artist depicts a priest
removing a sacrificial heart.

We know a great deal about ancient Egyptians, because they left so
many texts. The temptation is to think we know far more than we do.
"The beer-swilling artisans, the persnickety letter-writers, the elegant
ladies, the ambitious bureaucrats and dedicated hunters—all come

across (we delude ourselves) as the sort of people we know and whom we could have met," writes the historian Peter Green.

But this was, Green says, correcting himself, an "exotic (not to say freakish) culture."

That back-and-forth dance—*these were people like us; these were bizarre strangers*—goes a long way toward explaining ancient Egypt's allure. Egypt occupies a sweet spot in our historical imagination. Near enough to draw us in, it is far enough away to fascinate.

We can imagine inserting ourselves into the Egyptian past, and when we do, like all armchair time travelers, we wave the dark realities aside. Danger and hardship are the first to go. No one daydreaming herself back to the dawn of time pictures herself writhing, helplessly mangled, in the jaws of a tyrannosaurus; no one imagines sweating his life away in a pharaoh's work gang, hauling blocks of stone up a dirt ramp.

How to account for Egypt's enduring appeal, when we dismiss every other ancient culture as too dusty and dreary for words? To say that Egypt's most famous images have become iconic is just to argue in a circle.

One part of the answer may have to do with a simple matter of scale. We never entirely outgrow our six-year-old selves, and sheer size never loses its fascination. Hence, dinosaurs again. Every natural history museum in the world draws crowds who gape at room-filling, ceiling-scraping skeletons. So it is with the pyramids, where colossal size (and simplicity of design) is the essence of the story. The Sphinx is even better, not merely massive (each mighty paw is bigger than a school bus) but mysterious, as well.

Mysterious but not utterly out of reach. We know a fair bit about Egyptians' everyday lives, far more than we know about other ancient cultures. Much of the reason, oddly, is that we know so much about the Egyptian picture of the afterlife. Egyptians took for granted that you *could* take it with you. You would live eternally in your familiar body, and you would carry on eating and drinking and enjoying life. And so the Egyptian picture of death provides us a vivid picture of Egyptian life.

Tombs were stuffed with chairs and beds, loaves of bread, jars of wine, joints of meat, clothes, toys, makeup, jewelry. "It was," one historian writes, "as if they were packing for a trip to a place they had never visited and weren't sure what to bring, so they brought everything."

Egyptian culture was fixated on death, to an astonishing degree. Everything we associate with Egypt—pyramids, mummies, the tombs, the gods, the Book of the Dead—had to do with warding off death, or conquering it, or navigating the afterlife. Prayers and hundreds upon hundreds of spells obsessively echoed the death-is-not-the-end theme. Pharaohs were sent into the afterlife with a magic incantation: "You are young again, you live again, you are young again, you live again, forever."

So preoccupied were the Egyptians with death and the afterlife that Egyptologists to this day battle about what it all meant. *Why* were Egyptians obsessed with living forever? Was it because they found death too terrifying to contemplate, or was it that they were so enamored of life that they could not bear to acknowledge its end? The Egyptologist John Wilson summarizes what is perhaps the prevailing view. "The Egyptians relished their life. They clung to life, not with the desperation that comes from a horror of death, but with a happy assurance that they had always been victorious and so would defeat mortal change itself."*

The afterlife as Egyptians pictured it was as down-to-earth as a heaven could be. The whole point of mummification was that you

---

* Some archaeologists believe that we overestimate how much thought Egyptians gave to death. In ancient Egypt, towns typically rose up on wet, fertile ground, while tombs and cemeteries were relegated to the desert's edge. As a result, the most abundant and best-preserved relics are those associated with death. "This has given us a very distorted view of the culture," writes the Egyptologist Richard Parkinson. "Imagine if only municipal cemeteries were preserved from Victorian Britain." (Historical terms like *Stone Age* may reflect a similar misreading. We talk about the "Stone Age" because stone relics are the only ones that made it to our day. For all we know, our Stone Age forebears made daily use of wooden dishes and leather shoes.)

would need your body in the afterlife; the mummy-making process was the way to keep your physical self intact so that you could carry on as you always had.[*]

The Christian heaven was far more austere, with no place for food, drink, or sex. (Instead, Saint Augustine explained, there would be hymn singing. "All our activity," he wrote, "will consist in singing 'Amen' and 'Alleluia.'") Still, the West's everyday picture of heaven, where we hug long-lost friends and throw sticks for beloved dogs, is not so different from the Egyptian version.

We could point to a dozen such cultural resemblances. An ancient papyrus, which touted cures for gray hair, baldness, and impotence, was a close cousin to the spam that clogs inboxes around the world. An essay written in 2400 BC passed along detailed, and still relevant, advice in the how-to-get-along-with-your-boss genre. "If you are a guest at a table of one who is greater than you, laugh when he laughs. That will please his heart, and what you do will be acceptable."

Egyptian folktales featured princesses locked in towers, and heroes granted three wishes, and even a distraught king who sent messengers across the land to locate the woman whose beautiful slipper he'd happened to find. "From the early centuries of the Christian era up to the middle of the nineteenth century, there was not a single man on earth" who could read these stories, marvels the Egyptologist Barbara Mertz, and yet, she notes, somehow their key bits ended up in "Rapunzel" and "Cinderella."

We share other beliefs and acts across the gulf of time. Protesters still burn effigies of their enemies, for instance, and sports fans burn the jerseys of superstars who desert them for a different city. King Tut would have understood perfectly. "Tut's sandals are decorated with prisoner figures," the Egyptologist Robert Ritner observes, "his cane handles with bound enemies, his shields with defeated foes, his footstools with bound prisoners. Simply by making a state appearance, and

---

[*] Pop books notwithstanding, Egyptians did not believe in reincarnation. If they'd thought that the soul could find a home in a new body, there would have been no reason to bother with mummifying the old one.

with no special ritual, the king throttles and crushes underfoot the potential enemies of the state."

Egypt's continuing allure has still other sources. The Egyptian story seems ongoing in a way that isn't true of other ancient civilizations. Many of the most astonishing archaeological discoveries date from relatively recent times. The statue that may be the most admired of all, showing Queen Nefertiti, turned up only in 1912. It lay on the floor of a sculptor's studio, upside down and half-covered in rubble. King Tut's tomb was discovered just a century ago, in 1922. One of Egypt's most dazzling treasures, the 144-foot-long wooden ship built for the pharaoh of the Great Pyramid, was found more recently still. Khufu's ship, as it is sometimes called, may have been intended to carry him to the afterlife. Archaeologists found the ship in an underground chamber next to the Great Pyramid, in 1954.

Many Egyptologists believe there is far more still to come. To cite one example from countless possibilities, scarcely anything is known about perhaps the most esteemed of all Egyptian artists, a painter dubbed "the Michelangelo of the Nile" by one eminent historian. He is known for the tomb paintings he created for an official named Nebamun. They depict dancers and banquets and hunting scenes, in sinuous, lifelike detail and in dazzling colors.

Dancers and musicians, in a wall painting from Nebamun's tomb

Nebamun was a nonentity, and everything about his tomb is a mystery. No one knows the painter's name. No one knows why a midlevel administrator ranked such a tribute. No one knows where the tomb was located. (A Greek grave robber found it in the 1830s and made off with the panels. He sold them to a collector but then decided that he'd been underpaid. He died two decades later, still bitter, never having revealed his secret.) To this day, no one knows if Nebamun's missing tomb holds additional treasures.

If Europe were as thick with unknown wonders as Egypt likely is, there would still be Sistine Chapels hidden under sand and mud, waiting to be unearthed by some boy chasing a dog that had disappeared down a hole.

The beauty of lapis lazuli necklaces and golden bracelets in ancient tombs, the elegance of the sculpted head of Nefertiti, the hominess of board games and spinning tops, all speak across the ages and seem to draw us close.

But look again. Peter Green is right to remind us of Egypt's "freakish" side. Constant exposure has made Egypt's main attractions so familiar that they no longer register as weird. The Great Pyramid is a monument to absolute power that can seem not so different from Versailles—any of the pharaohs could be Louis XIV in a kilt and sandals. Mummies are horror movie clichés.

But even the most familiar features of the ancient landscape prove exceedingly strange in close-up. We tell ourselves that we understand the notion of kings and one-man rule and despots who build monuments to themselves. But the Great Pyramid is a monument unlike any other, a stone mountain towering into the sky and absurd in its presumption.

Forty stories high, it is made up of more than two million stone blocks. Each weighs two tons, on average, and stands about waist-high and several feet across. The blocks fit together so neatly that you could not slip a knife blade between any two. Building that mountain took two full decades of brutally hard work. A bit of arithmetic spells out just how much labor the pyramids required—on average, workers had to slide a two-ton block into place every five minutes, day and night, for twenty years.

Perhaps ten thousand men at a time labored away, playing the role of ants stumbling ceaselessly under giant loads.* The work was not only endless but also dangerous. Stones had to be hauled into place hundreds of feet above the ground. When blocks slipped, they crushed arms and legs and smashed skulls. Even in the best of circumstances, the unremitting labor took a toll. Archaeologists have unearthed workers' skeletons; they are marked by deformed bones and twisted spines.

All this labor was carried out using scarcely any technology beyond human muscle power. The Egyptians built the pyramids without even making use of the wheel—they had no carts, no wagons, not even any cranes or pulleys. The pyramids were a triumph of social engineering—organizing that workforce was a colossal feat—but not of engineering in the usual sense.

This was not a question of ignorance but of conservatism. Egyptians knew about wheels, which had been in use in neighboring empires for five centuries. They chose not to use them. (About a thousand years after the pyramid era, they began building war chariots.) We might think we understand the appeal of tradition and the fear of change, but Egyptian culture was conservative to a degree we can scarcely fathom.

Art highlights the point. The same drawings turn up again and again in temples built two thousand years apart. Here the pharaoh grabs his enemies by the hair with one hand and raises the other to strike a mighty blow, and there—a thousand miles and a thousand years away—the identical image recurs.

---

* The laborers were free men. Contrary to what "everyone knows," the pyramids weren't built by slaves. And the pyramids were built a thousand years before the era of Moses and the plagues and the parting of the Red Sea, even presuming that there is historic truth to the biblical stories. So the belief that Hebrew slaves built the pyramids under a foreman's lash is, so to speak, doubly false. The mistake arises partly from old-fashioned Hollywood movies like Cecil B. DeMille's *The Ten Commandments* and partly from a hundred stray bits of our common culture. At Passover seders every year, for instance, Jews recall that they "were all slaves to Pharaoh in Egypt." Maybe they were—historians tend not to think so, although there are dissenters—but whatever they were doing in Egypt, it was not constructing the pyramids.

Near Egypt's southernmost border, a carving depicts the pharaoh surveying a line of hapless prisoners bound together by their necks and with hands tied behind their backs. Across the land, on one looming wall after another, the same image reappears. This was art as propaganda, like a drawing of Uncle Sam with rolled-up sleeves and a rifle grasped in a brawny hand. But it is as if the same drawing had been used to inspire soldiers from Valley Forge to Vietnam and for another twenty centuries beyond.

"What they did is, they repeated the same thing over and over, for three thousand years," says the Egyptologist Bob Brier. "It wasn't considered great to be an innovator in art. If it ain't broke, don't fix it. If you wanted a statue of a god, you didn't have some sculptor come up with a new idea. You got out the old statue and you said, 'Copy it.'

"When you go into a museum," Brier continues, "you can look at a statue from 2500 BC, and 1500 BC, and 500 BC, and they're not really different. And that's why you can recognize Egyptian art at a glance, because *it didn't change.*"

We might think we know all about mummies, but that story, too, is deeply strange. Egyptians mummified not only human beings but animals, and the animals outnumbered the humans by many millions. Cats and dogs were mummified, and so were gazelles and snakes and monkeys, not to mention ibises, shrews, mice, and even dung beetles.

A few of those animals were beloved pets, mummified so that they could romp through the afterlife alongside their owners. Typically, though, they were sacred animals; exactly what their purpose was remains murky. "These animals performed the same function that a lighted candle does in a church," writes the Egyptologist Salima Ikram. "They acted as the physical manifestation of a prayer addressed by the pilgrim to the divinity for eternity."

The demand for animal mummies was nearly insatiable. In modern times, scientists have unearthed vast animal cemeteries. At a burial ground called Saqqara, a single cemetery yielded four million ibis mummies. A nearby cemetery contained seven million dog mummies. In 1888, an Egyptian farmer happened on a graveyard containing countless ancient, mummified, linen-wrapped cats. "Not one or two here and there," the *English Illustrated Magazine* reported, "but dozens, hundreds, hundreds of thousands, a layer of them, a stratum thicker than most coal seams, ten to twenty cats deep." Modern commerce and ancient doctrine joined forces. Soon after that accidental discovery, a ship containing nineteen tons of cat mummies was steaming its way to Liverpool, where merchants planned to peddle the dried-up bodies as fertilizer.

The worship of animals reached "grotesque" proportions, in the judgment of the Egyptologist Henri Frankfort; it was the "most baffling, most persistent, and to us most alien feature" of Egyptian religious belief. It would have been one thing, Frankfort went on, if Egyptians had chosen to exalt the mighty lion or the imposing eagle, but so often the Egyptians had chosen to venerate "quite insignificant creatures like the centipede or the toad."

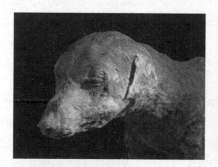

The dog (who has lost his wrappings) was a royal pet buried in a tomb in the Valley of the Kings. Cat mummies and ibis mummies numbered in the millions. The box shows a tiny statue of a shrew (most of his tail is missing, but you can see the tip extending just past the edge of the box). A mummified shrew rested inside.

• • •

So *that* was different. But, on the other hand, the Egyptians were like us. From the moment it became plain that there was a market for mummified creatures, con men began stuffing bandages with rags and bits of bone, shaping the packages to look like cats or falcons, and then charging the gullible top prices for these makeshift companions for eternity.

Tomb robbing, too, goes back to the earliest days of Egyptian history. As soon as Egyptians took to filling tombs with gold and jewels, thieves took to helping themselves to the loot. Worse still, the more elaborate and lavish the preparations for the afterlife, the more likely that thieves would get word of treasures just waiting to be plucked. "That men who believed as the Egyptians did were ready to rob a fellow creature of eternal life in order to steal his amulets," laments the historian and novelist Mary Renault, "throws a depressing light on human nature."*

But it is human nature, so malleable and so fixed and so endlessly various, that intrigues us. The "poetry of history," Simon Schama once remarked, is that "it is about people who in many ways are just like us, but also couldn't be more different."

The moral for us is that the decipherers' quest was even more difficult than it might appear. Their challenge was not merely to make sense of a host of strange symbols and a dead language but to navigate a strange and bewildering culture. (If the Rosetta Stone had included vastly more text than it did, then decipherers might have been able to decode it without bringing in clues from Egyptian culture. But they needed more material to work with.)

The focus on culture and history makes for a crucial difference between the task of decipherers like Champollion and Young and that of their codebreaking counterparts like the sleuths at Bletchley Park. Cryptographers in wartime faced colossal pressures, but at least they had a well-defined problem to tackle. Their mission was akin to solving

---

* Why steal? Egypt was a cashless society that ran on barter, not coins or paper money. But thieves appeared in history long before the invention of money. Black markets thrived even in barter-based economies. All that was necessary was that one person value what another possessed.

a mega Rubik's Cube, while the clock ticked and the world burned. The challenge for decipherers was more like time-traveling to the Silk Road in 700 AD or to Egypt in 2600 BC and trying to fit in with the locals.

Put another way, wartime codes were akin to puzzles, which meant they were based on tricks and mechanical procedures. Discover the trick and you were well on your way to cracking the code. But the decipherers' task was to unravel a mystery that had evolved and grown like a living organism.

Both challenges were formidable, but the codebreakers' task was not quite as daunting. Codes are hard on purpose; languages are hard by accident (and harder still if everyone who once knew how to read them has long been dead). Information has been concealed in one case and misplaced in the other.

Accident and happenstance turn out to create more problems than even the most cunning plans. Accidental losses can be sweeping—gods whose mere names struck terror into the hearts of trembling worshippers may end up entirely forgotten. But even a tiny bit of forgotten lore can pose bewildering riddles. Will archaeologists thousands of years from now manage to guess that once upon a time *blue* meant *sad* or that *head over heels,* which seems to refer to a perfectly ordinary state of affairs, meant *madly in love*? Will future scholars figure out what a cat could have wanted with a tongue? Or why shoulders were cold and herrings red?

Decipherers like Young and Champollion had to be improvisers almost before they were anything else. An ancient text might have been anything—a tax bill, a prayer, a poem. For decipherers, that infinity of possibilities makes for extra difficulty but extra fascination as well. "There is always the excitement of the chase," says Peter Parsons, one of the great authorities on the papyrus scraps found heaped up at Oxyrhynchus. "Open a box of unpublished papyri, and you never know what you may find . . . Your new papyrus may offer you unknown Greek poetry; it may offer unique evidence for the inflation of donkey prices at the height of the Roman Empire."

Military messages are simple by comparison. Codebreakers in wartime play their games on a narrow field. They can be sure that an intercepted message is not a sonnet or a sales receipt. *Attack at dawn*, it might say, or *Retreat at once*. Nor is there likely to be any mystery about what language a message is written in—the Nazis communicated in German, the Japanese in Japanese. (Imagine how much harder crossword puzzles would be if the answers could be in any language, including dead ones.)

Even with the aid of heavy hints like these, codebreaking is daunting work. The serial killer called the Zodiac sent the police a mocking, encoded message in 1969, and fifty-one years passed before a team of computer scientists cracked it, in 2020. Everyone who tried to decipher the Zodiac's cipher—newspapers splashed it on page 1—knew perfectly well to look for words in English, and they had some idea, from other taunting notes, of the sort of words to look for. And many would-be decipherers could enlist battalions of computers in the hunt.

The task was astonishingly difficult, even so, because there was no telling how Zodiac had scrambled his message (did it run backward? Did it run diagonally and skip every other letter?) or how he had matched symbols to letters (did a solid square mean A? Did it mean A the first time it appeared and J from then on?). The team that eventually proved successful spent endless hours coaxing their computer programs to test yet another arrangement of the message's symbols, yet another assignment of symbols to letters. Nothing. Nothing again. Hundreds of thousands of experiments and still nothing. Finally, on a December morning in 2020, two phrases—*trying to catch me* and *the gas chamber*—clicked into place, like tumblers on a combination lock.

That was only a start, but it seemed plain that the cryptographers were well on their way. And, indeed, the code was broken in another two days, though the Zodiac himself was never caught.

The first lines of the Zodiac cipher, which begins,
"I hope you are having lots of fun trying to catch me."

Despite everything they're up against, codebreakers have still another advantage over decipherers. They know at once if they have gone
wrong. If their decoding produces a string of nonsense, they know
they need to try again. But one early translation of an Egyptian obelisk,
from pre-Rosetta days, began, "The supreme spirit and archetype in-
fuses its virtues and gifts in the soul of the sidereal world." Every word
of that supposed translation turned out to be fantasy—the hieroglyphs
simply gave a pharaoh's name—but no one knew that for 150 years.

The best examination of the difference between codebreakers and
literary decipherers comes from a pair of writers particularly well
placed to explore the subject. Whitfield Diffie is a cryptanalyst married
to an Egyptologist named Mary Fischer. The decipherer's task, they
agree, is far harder. "It is easy to trace with one's fingertips the signs in-
cised on the Rosetta Stone," they write, "but it is another matter to trace
the minds that composed them."

The problem is that you need to understand those minds, at least to
some degree, to have any hope of understanding their writing.

## CHAPTER SIX

# The Conquering Hero

At a huge celebration in Paris on December 10, 1797, a frenzied crowd gathered to celebrate Napoleon's latest triumphs. He had just won a series of military victories in Italy, and he returned to France a superstar. Throngs of onlookers shouted in jubilation. Speakers smothered Napoleon in praise. "Nature exhausted all her powers in the creation of Bonaparte," one official proclaimed, and he went on to declare that the only question was whether Napoleon was more like Socrates or more like Caesar.

That was a view entirely in line with Napoleon's own thinking. He was literally a conquering hero and ambitious almost to the point of madness. Though only twenty-eight, he tormented himself with the knowledge that Alexander the Great had amassed *his* vast empire by age thirty. Time was pressing. What next?

This painting shows Napoleon, at age twenty-seven, leading his troops to a victory over the Austrian army. It was 1796, two years before his invasion of Egypt.

Perhaps an invasion of England? Napoleon spent two weeks in February 1798 in French port cities personally interviewing sailors, smugglers, and fishermen to size up the odds. Reluctantly he decided to look elsewhere.

Soon he had made his decision. "Tiny Europe has not enough to offer," he proclaimed. "We must set off for the Orient; that is where all the greatest glory is to be achieved."

Every archaeological discovery is a tangle of long-shot coincidences, lucky stumbles, and missed chances. The Dead Sea Scrolls, for instance, turned up in 1947 on a day like any other, when a Bedouin shepherd looking for a stray goat happened to see a hole in a cliff face. The cliff was dotted with caves, but most of the entrances were at ground level. This opening was smaller than the others and higher on the cliff wall. The boy flung a stone into the darkness. Back came not the solid thunk of a stone hitting a wall, as anyone might have expected, but a brighter, higher-pitched plink, as of a rock smacking a clay pot.

And so it proved. Inside the cave the young shepherd found an array of large clay jars, some of them with mysterious scrolls inside. They turned out to be Hebrew manuscripts a thousand years older than any known biblical texts. The pots and their ancient texts had sat in the dark, undisturbed and unread, for two thousand years.

The discovery of King Tut's tomb, perhaps the most spectacular find in the history of archaeology, was just as fluky. It might never have come to pass if an English aristocrat named Lord Carnarvon (who lived in Highclere Castle, now famous as Downton Abbey) hadn't been advised by his doctors that English winters were too harsh for his weak lungs. They recommended he visit Egypt, at the time a fashionable destination for the wealthy but frail.

Carnarvon followed the advice. But shooting parties and formal dinners soon lost their allure. Carnarvon cast about for new diversions. He crossed paths with Howard Carter, an accomplished but down-on-his-luck archaeologist who was trying to scratch out a living by peddling watercolors and guiding tourists. The two teamed up, Carnarvon as patron and Carter as explorer. On a November day in 1922, they cast their startled gaze upon a gold-filled burial chamber that had been sealed shut thirty centuries before.

In the case of the Rosetta Stone, the unforeseeable circumstance that set the whole story in motion was Napoleon's lust for glory.

For would-be empire builders, Egypt had long made a conspicuous target. It was weak, and it was well located, at the crossroads of Europe, Africa, and the Middle East. In 1798 France and England were in the midst of a series of confrontations that spanned half the globe. "The first world war began in 1793," the historian John Ray observed, "and lasted until the Battle of Waterloo in 1815."

England already had India. Perhaps France could grab up Egypt, as a counterweight? No one could quite agree on what France would do with such a possession. Would Egypt serve as a base from which to attack the British in India? Perhaps it would become the prize colony in an overseas empire? Or an international trading hub that would fill French coffers?

Such questions turned out not to matter much. Best to seize opportunity today and sort out the details tomorrow, especially because personal ambition played as large a role in the tale as global politics. For Napoleon, whose dreams always merged gain for the nation with glory for himself, Egypt proved a temptation impossible to resist. India had been a glittering prize; Napoleon saw Egypt as an equally gaudy jewel that he could snatch for his own crown.

On May 20, 1798, he sailed forth at the head of the largest naval fleet ever assembled, to conquer Egypt.

Crucially for our story, Napoleon's plans for Egypt extended beyond conquering new territory. He brought with him some 160 dazzlingly talented scientists, artists, and scholars; their role would be not to fight but to study and draw and record and measure every strange sight they saw (there was as yet no such thing as photography). But these *savants*, as they were called, would do more than document Egypt's ancient wonders. Just as important, Napoleon insisted, they would perform a civilizing mission, bringing to backward, ignorant Egypt all the modern ways of the world's most sophisticated culture, France.

When they set out from France, neither the savants nor the soldiers had any idea that Egypt was to be their destination. Napoleon had kept that information from all but a select few. (He had not even confided his plans to France's minister of war.) The savants knew only that they had been chosen to participate in something new and secret and, no doubt, glamorous. Fueled by excitement, they had gambled that any excursion with Napoleon would lead to greatness.

Napoleon had a genuine interest in science and technology, and the savants were his pets. Several of the most eminent among them had been selected to travel with him aboard *L'Orient*, the flagship of the fleet and the largest warship in the world. On evenings when the voyagers were not seasick (Napoleon suffered, too, and his bed was on wheels as a supposed remedy), the savants dined alongside Napoleon and his officers. Napoleon presented a topic for the evening—*What do dreams mean? What is the ideal form of government? Are there living beings on other planets?*—and he took the leading role at this seagoing salon, while insisting that here he was merely another philosopher. Drinks were poured, the lanterns on the table flickered, and the talk lasted deep into the night.

The English, in the meantime, had no inclination to stand on the sidelines and applaud Napoleon's verve. The Royal Navy, the mightiest in the world, intended to intercept and defeat the French fleet before it ever reached Egypt. Each superpower was commanded by a figure of almost legendary stature. The British were led by Horatio Nelson, one-eyed, one-armed, and indomitable, the French by Napoleon, still only twenty-eight years old, never yet defeated in battle, and a military genius whose talent was fully a match for his ambition.

The clash between France and England began thrillingly, with a life-and-death game of hide-and-seek that played out across the Mediterranean. Napoleon had planned to embark for Egypt from Toulon, on France's southern coast, on the morning of May 13, 1798. (He would be joined at sea by forces that had embarked from other ports.) In spite of the secrecy that surrounded their mission, the French had assembled an enormous fleet that numbered 180 ships and 40,000 soldiers.

Unbeknownst to Napoleon, Nelson, taking advantage of spies and guesswork, lay in wait a dozen miles out to sea from Toulon. But on the night of May 12, a storm blew up, scattering Nelson's ships across hundreds of miles of open sea. For a week, the French sat stuck in port waiting for the gale to blow itself out. When the weather finally cleared, the French took impatiently to sea, never knowing that Nelson had been swept out of their way.

The two fleets would barely miss one another twice more. The closest call came in a heavy fog off Crete, on a dark night in June. In the murk, Nelson's ships fired their guns at regular intervals, as a signal to one another, so that they could keep together. The French, safeguarded by the gloom, sailed silently by, so near that they could hear the muffled roar of the English guns.

Dawn the next day found each fleet alone on the empty sea. Gambling that Napoleon's plan was to invade Egypt—even now, no one was sure what he was up to—Nelson hurried to catch him. But he moved *too* quickly. When the English reached Alexandria, the French had not yet arrived. Bewildered and furious, Nelson set out to sea once again, to renew his search. The British sailed away from Alexandria on June 30, 1798. The French arrived there the next day.

As mighty as Egypt had once been, that era had vanished long before. Now the country was poor and neglected, nominally ruled by Turkey but in fact controlled for five hundred years by a fierce sect of Muslim warriors called Mamelukes. The arrangement worked well for the Mamelukes, who gouged the Egyptian peasantry without mercy, and for the sultan of Turkey, who pocketed a share of these "taxes." But for Egypt itself, neglected when it was not exploited, the results were dismal. "The country that had once built the pyramids," the historian Paul Strathern laments, "had yet to see the introduction of the wheelbarrow."*

Against this dreary backdrop, the Mamelukes stood out like splen-

---

* How the richest nation in the ancient world fell so far in modern times is a long, complex tale. Foreign conquest and the Black Death of the mid-1300s (which killed perhaps 40 percent of all Egyptians) played enormous roles.

did figures from another age. Magnificent horsemen, they rode to war in boldly colored silks, in reds and blues and yellows, in turbans decked with egret feathers or in helmets that glinted in the sun. Each horseman carried a small arsenal of weapons, half a dozen altogether, including rifles, pistols with jewel-encrusted handles, spears, axes, ivory-handled daggers, and scimitars.

When the Mamelukes swooped down on a foe, they drew weapons in turn from holsters and scabbards. They fired rifles when they first drew in range, then turned to pistols as they closed in, then flung a spear or an axe, then slashed at the enemy with a scimitar, or even two at once, with their horse's reins clenched in their teeth.

Since the Crusades they had exulted in a reputation for valor and impossible-to-resist ferocity. "Let the Franks come," one Mameluke leader threatened, referring to the French. "We will destroy them beneath our horses' hooves." Mamelukes' boasts were as vivid as their costumes. "I will ride through them," the same warrior announced, "and sever their heads from their bodies like watermelons."

But the Mamelukes had never faced a modern foe. On July 21, 1798, they confronted the French a few miles from the pyramids. Twenty-five thousand French soldiers met an army of perhaps thirty thousand Mamelukes, the Frenchmen sweltering in woolen uniforms, the Mamelukes dazzling in swirling silks.

"Soldiers, forty centuries of history are looking down on you," Napoleon told his troops. The chronology was accurate—forty centuries was, if anything, a bit of an underestimate—but the geography was off. If a soldier had squinted toward the horizon, he could just about have made out the pyramids in the distance. Still, one Egyptologist notes, accuracy is not everything; *the Battle of the Melon Field* does not have the right ring.

The Battle of the Pyramids, as it is known instead, proved utterly one-sided. The Mamelukes charged the French lines, shrieking their battle cries, pennants flying, cloaks fluttering, sabers flashing, hooves pounding. Spectacular, chaotic, and doomed, this was "the last great cavalry charge of the Middle Ages," in the words of one historian.

The French had formed into battle squares, defensive formations in which rifle-wielding soldiers formed a hollow square six men deep, with artillery at the corners. (Forming squares was urgent business, but it had one diverting feature. The soldiers, who were always happy to mock the savants for their uselessness, delighted in the order, "Donkeys and savants into the middle!")

For the defenders, the challenge was to keep their nerve. Fire too soon and the attacking wave would scarcely slow; fire too late and the enemy's wounded, terrified horses would collapse onto the defenders' ranks, opening gaps in the line for other fighters.

As the Mamelukes neared, the French held their fire, their rows of bayonets a steel hedge. The Mamelukes spurred their horses onward; *now* the French fired, in volleys that cut down the attackers like scythes through tall grass. All was mayhem, as cannons roared and horses shrieked and wounded men in close quarters thrust at one another with daggers and bayonets.

In two hours it was all over. Perhaps twenty French soldiers had been killed compared with some two thousand Mamelukes. Bravery was a fine thing, but tactics and technology were better still. Decades would pass before the Charge of the Light Brigade, when six hundred cavalrymen rode headlong to their deaths, straight into an array of waiting cannons. But the judgment of a French officer who watched that doomed attack would have applied to the Mameluke charge as well. "It is magnificent, but it is not war."

The French exulted in their victory (though most of the Mamelukes had ridden away and would fight again, and from here on they would use hit-and-run tactics rather than head-on assaults). Napoleon had arrived in Egypt only three weeks before, and all was proceeding exactly as planned.

Ten days later, disaster struck.

# CHAPTER SEVEN

# The Burning Deck

The French had left their entire fleet of battleships anchored in Aboukir Bay, just off Alexandria. The thirteen ships hugged the shoreline, in an ideal position to confront any enemy. Too near the shore for anyone to sneak past them on the landward side, the French moved their cannons to the ships' sea-facing side, and waited.

But the French had miscalculated, and the mistake would prove deadly. On August 1, 1798, Nelson sailed into Alexandria. The British attacked the French fleet almost immediately and, daringly, astonishingly, from both sides at once. Improvising on the fly, the British had gambled that they could find deep water on the French ships' *shoreward*, and undefended, side. It worked, and the French found themselves caught in the crossfire of an enemy attacking from two sides simultaneously.

In brutal, close-range fighting, with ships burning and cannons pounding and masts crashing to the decks, both sides battled into the night. All wars are gruesome, but close combat in wooden ships held special horrors. When enemies met at sea, they had room to maneuver, and even, perhaps, to flee.

Not here. On the French ship *L'Orient*, fire had broken out, and the commander, Admiral Brueys, had lost his legs to a cannonball. Brueys remained on deck, tourniquets on his stumps, giving orders from a chair, until another cannonball blasted him apart and killed him. In the meantime, Nelson was hit in the forehead by a piece of flying metal. A flap of skin fell over his one good eye, blinding him. "I am killed," he whispered as he was carried to the ship's surgeon.

By now the fire on *L'Orient* was out of control, burning so fiercely that sailors aboard *English* ships felt the flames.* The fire reached the ammunition storeroom, which contained thousands of tons of gunpowder. *L'Orient* exploded, blasting the immense ship into pieces and producing a thunderclap that could be heard twenty miles away.† For several minutes, mangled bodies, broken masts, burning sails, and cannon fragments rained from the sky. Eight hundred of *L'Orient*'s one-thousand-man crew were killed.

France had begun the day with thirteen warships. By the following morning, eleven had been captured or destroyed. "Victory is not a name strong enough for such a scene," Nelson declared as he scanned the carnage. Napoleon, who had not been present at the battle, did not receive word of France's defeat until two weeks later. He took the news calmly. "It seems you like this country," he told his staff on August 15, 1798. "That's very lucky, for now we have no fleet to carry us back to Europe."

The French were stranded. Nelson exulted. "The French army is in a scrape," he wrote. "They are up the Nile without supplies." There would be no relief. The Royal Navy controlled the Mediterranean, which meant that no food or weapons could come by sea, and nature and hostile locals would do the rest. "Their army is wasting with the flux [dysentery]," Nelson went on, "and not a thousand men will ever return to Europe."

But at the very time when the military situation looked bleakest, life for the savants took a turn for the better. On August 23, 1798— this was a mere three weeks after Nelson had destroyed the French fleet—Napoleon presided over the savants' first formal meeting. They

---

* With *L'Orient* on fire, French sailors jumped overboard and swam for their lives. One who remained was a nine-year-old midshipman whose father had been wounded and carried to the ship's infirmary. The son refused to leave the burning deck without his father's say-so. Until a generation or two ago, all schoolchildren learned his story ("The boy stood on the burning deck / Whence all but he had fled; / The flame that lit the battle's wreck / Shone round him o'er the dead"). The singsong rhymes distance us from what was a scene of unrelieved horror, with howling men and blood-slick decks and a helpless ship aflame.

† In 1998 French underwater archaeologists found fragments of *L'Orient*'s mast and its thirty-six-foot rudder.

gathered in a sprawling building in Cairo that had been a Mameluke palace. Napoleon dubbed the savants' new headquarters the Institute of Egypt, in homage to the Institute of France, in Paris.

The original institute had long stood near the peak of French intellectual life. It served as honorary home to the nation's leading artists, writers, and scientists; election to its ranks was one of the greatest honors a Frenchman could achieve. Napoleon had been voted a member in 1797, and he relished the tribute. (He often signed official dispatches, "Bonaparte, Member of the Institute, General-in-Chief.")

The reconfigured palace would become headquarters for the savants, with a library, workshops, a printing press, a zoo, a museum, and sections devoted to mathematics, physics, the arts, and economics. (The mathematicians met in what had been the palace harem.) Here the savants listened avidly to reports on mummies, and the science behind mirages (everyone who set out into the desert had been tormented by visions of shimmering lakes), and the meaning of hieroglyphs, and the purpose of an ostrich's tiny wings.

In hindsight, one subject stands out. At the institute's first meeting, a brilliant mathematician named Gaspard Monge had been elected president. (Remarkably, Napoleon had opted for the post of vice president.) Monge gave a brief talk setting out the scholars' mission as he saw it. As they investigated Egyptian life in its various aspects, Monge told his fellow savants, they should devote themselves especially "to the study of ancient monuments, to explaining these mysterious signs, these granite pages on which an enigmatic history is inscribed."

The military picture, in the meantime, grew worse. With his fleet destroyed, Napoleon had turned his thoughts to fighting on land. Once again, he seems to have modeled his plans on those of Alexander the Great—he would march on India, like his great predecessor.

This was jaw-droppingly ambitious (for starters, India lay some three thousand miles to the east), but in Napoleon's mind that may have counted as a plus. The French assault began with a plunge deep into Syria, Egypt's nearest neighbor to the east. What had been bad turned disastrous.

At Acre, a Turkish stronghold, Napoleon launched assault after assault. His rival was a warlord nicknamed "the Butcher" for such gruesome acts as plastering prisoners inside fortress walls with only their heads protruding, "the better to enjoy their torments." Eventually the prisoners died, one appalled eyewitness recalled, but their skulls remained in place as mute warnings. (Even the Butcher's allies were perpetually in danger. His own chief of staff had suffered, as punishments for various misdeeds over the years, the loss of his nose, an eye, and an ear.)

Acre was a walled city perched on the sea, and this was siege warfare of the grimmest kind. The French blasted the city's thick walls with cannon fire, while the Turks, and their British allies in ships just offshore, blasted back. When the cannon fire forced a breach in the walls, the French gave the order to charge. The troops stormed forward, some carrying ladders, while the defenders shot down at them and flung grenades and poured down boiling oil.

After sixty-two futile days and at a cost of two thousand men killed and wounded, the French abandoned the siege and left. Acre marked Napoleon's first defeat in a land battle.

The army staggered back across the desert toward Cairo, tormented by thirst and the scorching sun, racked with dysentery and stricken by bubonic plague (for every six French soldiers who contracted plague, five died). Napoleon had seen enough. He would spend the summer casting about for a rationale for leaving Egypt.

In that summer of 1799, everything happened at once. While Napoleon did his best to spin the Syrian fiasco into a tale of splendid victory—he arranged a celebratory parade in Cairo, complete with military bands and brand-new uniforms for the troops—Pierre-François Bouchard and his men were racing to rebuild the fort at Rosetta.

Early in July, someone told Bouchard about the strange stone they had found. A more conventional officer might not have spared time to ponder an oddly marked hunk of rock, especially at a time when everyone was racing to prepare for an enemy assault. But young Bouchard was emphatically not just another fighting man. Only twenty-eight, he had dual credentials—he was one of Napoleon's savants and also a soldier. The two groups heartily mistrusted each other. With impeccable military *and* scientific credentials, Bouchard was one of the few at home in both camps.

He had been a technology buff since his school days. Before coming to Egypt, Bouchard had fought in Europe with a brand-new branch of the French army, the balloon corps, whose job was to float high above the battlefield and report (by signal flag) on the enemy's troop movements. He had also studied mathematics and engineering and found time to work alongside some of France's most eminent scientists.* No one could have been further from a "shut up and dig" construction boss.

And so, though it was a fluke that the Rosetta Stone had turned up at all, it was a near certainty that, if such a prize *was* found, it would be pounced on with glee and fascination. Bouchard recognized at once that he had found a treasure.

Bouchard sent news of the find to his commanding general, Jacques Menou, who immediately had the stone brought to his tent. Soldiers and savants scrambled into action, cleaning the stone, scouring the grounds for its missing fragments, tackling the passages in Greek.

To this day, the missing bits of the Rosetta Stone remain lost. But the Greek inscription was nearly intact, and the translators dove in eagerly, hoping for grand, resounding phrases and trumpets and fanfare. They found no such thing.

The inscription had been carved, the text declares in its opening lines, on a date that corresponded to the year 196 BC. The message was mundane, crammed with tributes to "the youthful king who has arisen in the place of his father." This was Ptolemy V, who had been named king eight years before, at the age of six.

* It did not always go well. While still in France, Bouchard and Nicolas-Jacques Conté, a brilliant inventor, had worked together to find a new coating for military balloons. They accidentally set off an explosion that nearly cost Bouchard vision in his right eye and destroyed Conté's left eye altogether. Both men carried on undeterred. Ever after, Conté cut a dashing figure with a dark band of cloth low across his forehead and covering his left eye.

His father had been a nightmare, a "young degenerate" in one modern historian's judgment, who had taken over a mighty kingdom and frittered away its power. In a reign of not quite twenty years, marked by "love of ease, wine, lasciviousness, and literary dilettantism," Ptolemy IV had given orders that his uncle, brother, and mother be killed. His young son survived the purge, but the Rosetta Stone never hinted at any of this dark backstory. Instead, the stone's inscription hailed the teenage ruler, "whose power is great, who has secured Egypt and made it prosper, whose heart is pious toward the gods, the one who prevails over his enemy, who has enriched the lives of his people."

In truth Ptolemy's hold on power was precarious. Enemy armies had attacked Egypt from outside; rebels had attacked from within. The temple priests, always a formidable power bloc, had lately been hinting that the time might be right to rethink the status quo. Historians would later label this era "the Great Revolt." Egypt was not yet weak, but it was troubled.

Most of the trouble arose from a single root: the ruling family were outsiders. They were not Egyptian but Greek. Alexander the Great had conquered Egypt in 332 BC; after his death, one of his generals became pharaoh, and Ptolemy was a descendant of that general. "A small class of Greek officials, merchants, and soldiers ruled the roost," one historian notes, "while the mass of Egyptian peasantry tilled the fields, as they had always done." The royals spoke Greek and carried out all official business in Greek. They married other Greeks, not Egyptians. None of them read or spoke Egyptian. The very hieroglyphs on the Rosetta Stone that declared Ptolemy's virtues would have been, so to speak, Greek to him.*

The reason for inscribing the stone in the first place was to assert that all was well in the land of Egypt. The pharaoh, though assuredly young, was a mighty ruler and a descendant of mighty rulers. The priests, the message went on, supported him wholeheartedly. Priests

---

* None of the rulers in the Ptolemaic line bothered to learn the local language. On the evening before one battle, Ptolemy IV (the father of the Rosetta Stone's Ptolemy) delivered a speech meant to rally the troops in "band of brothers" fashion. But the speech fell flat because an interpreter had to translate the pharaoh's Greek into Egyptian.

and pharaoh together continued to perform the age-old religious rites in honor of the gods, with zeal and devotion.

The Rosetta Stone was almost too heavy to budge, but it was in effect a propaganda poster plastered to a wall. The scent of a deal hangs over the stone's text. First comes a recitation of the pharaoh's good deeds. To American ears, the litany sounds like the flip side of the list of King George's misdeeds in the Declaration of Independence. Instead of reading about the king's "imposing taxes on us without our consent" and "abolishing our most valuable laws," we are reminded of how the pharaoh "has reduced some [taxes] and abolished others completely, in order to give prosperity to the army and the rest of the population during his reign."

Nor was that all. "He released those who were in prison, and those who had been charged for long periods of time." And he had triumphed on the battlefield. He had subdued rebel forces, who had been "doing damage to the temples and abandoning the ways of the king and his father." Then, commendably, "he impaled them on the stake."

The praise poured on, line after line. The translators grew worried. What they had hoped for was a bold assertion—*Here is a wondrous proclamation, in different scripts and different languages!* Instead, they found only bombast and chest-thumping. One phrase after another had now yielded its meaning, but with no payoff. What did all this boasting and swagger have to do with the stone's other inscriptions?

Then came the answer. So great were the pharaoh's deeds, the inscription declared in its last lines, that they should be known to all. "This decree shall be inscribed on a stela of granite"—on a stone slab— "in the writing of the words of the gods [hieroglyphs], the writing of documents [this was evidently the mysterious middle section of text], and the writing of the Ionians [Greek], and it shall be displayed in the temples of the first rank, the temples of the second rank, and the temples of the third rank, alongside the statue of the king who lives forever."

*One message, written three ways.* (And, evidently, there had originally been many "Rosetta" Stones, scattered across Egypt.)

The race was on!

# CHAPTER EIGHT

# Monsieur Smith
# Makes His Exit

The first order of business was to spread the news of the discovery. At Rosetta, Bouchard assigned another of the savants, a twenty-five-year-old mathematician named Michel Ange Lancret, to send word to his fellow scholars at the Institute of Egypt, in Cairo. Lancret played it cool. Citizen Bouchard—in the wake of the Revolution, all titles had been banished in favor of *citizen*—had made a "discovery at Rosetta of some inscriptions that may offer much interest."

On July 29, 1799, the institute began the day's session by reading Lancret's letter aloud. No detailed record of the meeting survives, but the savants' presentations ranged all over, as usual. The zoologist Geoffroy Saint-Hilaire described a freshwater puffer fish he'd found in the Nile. The mathematician Gaspar Monge gave a brief lecture on a problem in advanced geometry. A botanist, an architect, and a poet all had their say.

A visiting dignitary sat through it all, unimpressed. His interpreter had whispered along with the talks as best he could, but the guest of honor shrugged off everything he had heard, though he perked up a bit at the mention of the puffer fish. Even then, his enthusiasm was short-lived. "What! So many words for a single fish?"

The first newspaper description of the discovery appeared in the *Courier de l'Egypte*, a paper published for the French army in Egypt, on September 15, 1799. The stone was a handsome black slab—"*une pierre d'un très beau granit noir*"—with three distinct inscriptions written in three parallel bands, including fourteen lines of hieroglyphs. "This stone is of great interest to the study of hieroglyphic characters," the *Courier* reported, with commendable restraint. "Maybe it will even provide the key at last."

The story ran on page 3. This sounds like bad news judgment, but the Rosetta Stone was not the only big story in that edition of the paper. On page 2, the *Courier* printed a remarkable dispatch, in just four detail-free sentences. Napoleon had left Egypt and returned to France! "His absence should not cause worries either to the French or to the Egyptians," the *Courier* told its readers, in an attempt to paint the astonishing news as nothing out of the ordinary. "All his actions aim at nothing but the happiness of both."

By the time the newspaper ran its story, Napoleon had nearly reached home. He'd slipped away late in the day on August 23, 1799, to a rendezvous point near Alexandria, without confiding in any of his fellow officers. A ship lay waiting just offshore. Only at the last minute did Napoleon's second-in-command, General Jean-Baptiste Kléber, learn—from a note—that he and the rest of the army had been abandoned.

The tone of Napoleon's message to Kléber was casual and hasty, less like a general's proclamation than an excuse from someone wriggling out of an invitation to a weekend in the country. "The news from Europe has caused me to decide to leave for France." That was all. Napoleon would never see Egypt again.

(The departure itself was carefully planned. Napoleon had cooked up a story for his mistress, to keep her from guessing he was leaving without her. Just as important, he'd sent a chest laden with goodies— wine, coffee, sugar, and liquor—to the ship that was waiting to take him to France. The chest bore a bland label meant to throw any snoops off the scent: "*Pour Monsieur Smith*.")

France, during most of this era, had heard scarcely any news about how its army had fared in Egypt. As soon as Napoleon returned home, he ordered a series of medals commemorating his Egyptian "victory."

One showed him in a Roman toga, flying above the pyramids. The caption declared, "The Hero Returns to His Country." Another showed him in a chariot drawn by two camels, above a slogan proclaiming, "Egypt Conquered."

This was nervy, but it worked. "Bonaparte arrived triumphantly from Egypt," one historian marvels, "and no one asked why his army wasn't with him."

The soldiers left behind in Egypt could only sputter. From the beginning, Kléber had regarded the whole Egyptian venture as both pointless and reckless. (Napoleon, he wrote in his diary early on, was "the kind of general who required an income of 10,000 men a month.") Now, furious at what he saw as cowardice on the part of "that Corsican runt," Kléber shouted his contempt. "That bugger has deserted us with his breeches full of shit. When we get back to Europe we'll rub his face in it."

So much for glory.

Napoleon had brought three of the most eminent savants back to Paris with him. That left the army, and all the rest of the savants, still in Egypt. For the soldiers, Egypt meant exile; for the savants, it was exile with a loophole. There was no denying that they had been abandoned, but the not-quite-saving grace was that they had an intriguing and almost unknown country to explore. They set to work reluctantly but doggedly.

Unlike the soldiers, the savants were volunteers. (To the soldiers' fury, Napoleon had arranged for them to have military pay even though they had no military responsibilities.) They were painters, mathematicians, mapmakers, doctors, astronomers, naturalists, engineers, and architects, many of them renowned to this day; there were no Egyptologists, for such a specialty did not yet exist. But there was Joseph Fourier, the mathematician (present-day graduate students in physics and math study Fourier series and Fourier transforms); and Vivant Denon, an artist and writer whose drawings of Egypt were destined to enthrall the world; and Claude-Louis Berthollet, one of France's most eminent chemists;* and Nicolas-Jacques Conté, an inventor so brilliant and re-sourceful that Napoleon would proclaim him capable of re-creating "the arts of France in the deserts of Arabia."

The best-known savants were in their forties and fifties, but most were far younger. The typical savant was boyish and eager—their aver-age age was only twenty-five—and the youngest were still students, in their teens, selected for their brilliance. From the moment of their ar-rival in Egypt, they had begun dashing around the country like school-boys on the world's best field trip.

Often the savants had no choice but to go where the army went, like embedded journalists today. They bent over their sketchpads, ab-sorbed in their work and heedless of bullets whistling by.

Napoleon had pictured a twofold mission for the savants that in-cluded both recording Egypt's ancient wonders and propelling it forward into the modern age. In Napoleon's view, Egypt had con-siderable room for improvement. Egyptians were "stupid, miserable, and dull-witted," he complained, and "in the villages they don't even have any idea what scissors are." For soldiers in particular, Egypt was a wasteland with "no wine, no forks, and no countesses to make love to."

The savants couldn't do much about the scarcity of countesses, but Napoleon had pictured them tackling an array of engineering pro-jects—devising schemes to purify water from the Nile, for instance, and finding better ways to make beer, and build bridges, and construct water mills. But with Napoleon back in France, the savants had room to improvise, and they focused their attention on documentation rather than engineering.

They scrambled up pyramids and wandered through ancient courtyards, drawing temple ruins and copying inscriptions. Hundreds of miles up the Nile, they explored tombs and temples that Europeans had scarcely heard of.

---

* *The* most eminent, Antoine Lavoisier, had been guillotined a few years before, for running afoul of the French Revolution. "It took them only an instant to cut off his head," another scientist lamented, "but France may not produce another such head in a century."

Savants clamber over the Sphinx to take measurements. The drawing
is by Vivant Denon, an artist and diplomat whose sketches helped
trigger a European-wide craze for all things Egyptian.

This was not glamorous work, for modern-day Egyptians had
not the least reverence for the relics of a long-gone, pagan culture. A
once-magnificent temple at Edfu, for instance, served as a garbage
dump. Trash and sand reached nearly as high as the ceiling. "Every
morning peasants heaved buckets of ashes from cooking fires and
donkey, camel, and horse manure through the window holes," writes
the historian Nina Burleigh, "as the savants stood nearby with their
sketchbooks and measuring devices."

Sketch of Edfu, by Vivant Denon

Conditions elsewhere were even worse. In tombs and temples across Egypt, the savants "tripped on fresh corpses and mummies and slipped in centuries of bat guano," Burleigh writes, "in rooms so dark they couldn't see their own hands. Working by torchlight was dangerous in itself, since the long-enclosed areas were highly flammable, packed with wood, ancient paint, and mummy tar."

They worked on, undaunted. Perhaps the most ardent explorer of all was Denon, the artist, even though at age fifty-one he was one of the oldest of the savants. An aristocrat who had managed to survive the Terror, Denon was handsome, witty, and seemingly indestructible. He had been the Chevalier de Non before the Revolution, then Citizen Denon during the tumultuous 1790s, and Baron Denon after Napoleon's rise to power.

Denon had talent and charm to spare, but he had never quite settled on a career. (He was, in one historian's attempt at a summary, "a diplomat, artist, and pornographer.") He was, as well, a close friend of Napoleon's wife, Josephine, and he had managed to parlay that friendship into a prominent role with the savants when Napoleon assembled his army of invasion.

In Egypt, the dilettante came into his own, repeatedly risking his life to record sights new to Western eyes. Even veteran soldiers marveled at Denon's bravery as they watched him sketching away on horseback, his drawing board balanced across his saddle, oblivious to the rifles firing all around him. (He would publish a fat volume packed with drawings in 1802, soon after his return to France. *Travels in Upper and Lower Egypt* provided Europeans their first peek at Egypt's marvels, and the book was a giant hit.)

Denon made a point of slathering Napoleon with praise, but he did not romanticize the horrors of combat. "War, how brilliant you shine in history! But seen close up, how hideous you become, when history no longer hides the horror of your details."

Brave as Denon was, sometimes it was not courage that was called for but diligence. Denon excelled then, too. In addition to drawing temples and monuments, he made a point of copying the writing on their ancient walls. "I have discovered in myself the willpower required to remain passive while simply drawing hieroglyphs," he wrote, as if surprised at his own patience. He had faith that someday these inscriptions would yield their meaning. In the meantime, he copied away, with care but without any hope that he himself would be the one to sort out the mystery. "Mine is an ardent piety, a blind zeal ultimately to be compared only to that of vestals of old who prayed, believed, and adored in a foreign language they did not understand."

By one tally, one-fourth of the savants died in Egypt; the total included five men killed on the battlefield (though they were noncombatants) and fifteen who fell victim to plague and dysentery. Even so, their morale was generally high. Certainly the savants were in better spirits than the soldiers, who blamed them for the entire misbegotten expedition. Good men were dying in the desert, the soldiers grumbled, so that a handful of useless intellectuals could ponder heaps of broken stones.

But it was that handful who would make history. The drawings they made in their three years in Egypt, especially their copies of hieroglyphs, would prove invaluable. Napoleon's army numbered forty thousand men, the savants not even two hundred. The army is forgotten. The savants swung open a gate that had been closed for two thousand years.

# CHAPTER NINE

# A Celebrity in Stone

The savants began by taking the first careful look at the Rosetta Stone, but they made no headway beyond translating the Greek. The hieroglyphs "consisted of fourteen lines," the *Courier* reported, "but some have been lost because the stone is broken." That was accurate, if unhelpful, but it was better than the description of the mysterious lines between the hieroglyphs and the Greek. "The intermediary inscription, in characters thought to be Syrian, consists of thirty-two lines."

That guess proved wrong. It would turn out that the middle inscription was not Syrian at all, but Egyptian. The script was a sort of shorthand that had developed because hieroglyphs were too elaborate for everyday writing.

Thus, the Rosetta Stone had *three* inscriptions—hieroglyphic, demotic (the name for the shorthand script), and Greek—but carried messages in only *two* languages: Egyptian and Greek. A rough modern-day equivalent would be a three-part note: first, several lines elegantly written in swirling calligraphy, in English; next the same message in hasty handwriting, also in English; and, last, the same message once again, this time in Greek letters and in the Greek language.

Stymied by the Rosetta Stone but eager to get on with their drawing and mapping, the savants made the most of their enforced exile. Almost at once, they happened on two tantalizing finds. In the autumn of 1799, in a town called Minuf in the Nile delta, two young engineers spotted another stone with bilingual inscriptions, like the Rosetta Stone. But it proved to be so badly eroded that they copied the few words they could make out ("of the young king, always," in Greek) and then moved on. The stone was a slab of black granite about a foot high and a yard long; it sat in front of a nondescript house, and the occupants used it as a bench.

A year later, another savant found still another almost-Rosetta. It was black granite also, and slightly bigger than the Rosetta Stone. Like the real thing, it carried inscriptions in hieroglyphs, demotic, and Greek, but it, too, was so badly worn that it was useless. It had turned up in a mosque in Cairo, where it served as a doorsill.

The French army, in the meantime, wanted nothing more than to leave Egypt behind. General Kléber, who had taken over for Napoleon, had been trying to negotiate a peace treaty with the Turks and the British. Kléber was popular with the troops and a certified military hero besides, but he saw no point in further battles in Egypt. When his diplomatic chores permitted, he spent his time trying to seduce Napoleon's mistress. (This was the young woman whom Napoleon had ducked out on. Pauline Fourès was a Frenchwoman married to a French lieutenant. She'd come to Egypt in the first place by sneaking aboard her husband's ship disguised in a soldier's uniform.)

But in June 1800, Kléber was assassinated in Cairo by a Syrian named Suleiman al-Halabi. The attacker was quickly caught, tried by a special court consisting entirely of Frenchmen, and convicted. When it came to sentencing, the judges deferred to local custom. The sentence called for Suleiman's right hand to be burned to the bone and then for him to be impaled. Suleiman sat silently while an official roasted his hand over red-hot coals. (He protested only when a coal rolled onto his elbow, pointing out that the sentence had specified that his hand alone would be burned.)

Next a nine-foot spike was hammered up Suleiman's rectum as far as the breastbone, and the stake, bearing its prisoner, was planted in the ground. Suleiman took four hours to die. Throughout the ordeal he maintained his silence except to cry out, once, "There is no god but Allah, and Muhammad is his prophet."*

---

* After Suleiman's death, his skeleton and skull were sent to the Museum of Anatomy in Paris. There they featured in an exhibit on phrenology; museums of the day collected the skulls of criminals and traitors in order to study the telltale bumps that indicated a tendency to murder and fanaticism.

Kléber's successor was an unfortunate choice, a general named Jacques Menou. (It was Menou who had first taken custody of the Rosetta Stone, in his role as commanding officer of the fort at Rosetta.) At fifty-one, Menou had seniority in his favor but little else. In contrast with the dashing Kléber—"the god Mars in uniform," according to Napoleon—Menou was fat, bald, and unkempt, and he strutted about in a self-important way that made him unpopular with both soldiers and savants.

He wanted nothing to do with peace negotiations. "I shall defend myself to the last extremity within the walls of Alexandria," he wrote to Napoleon, by way of criticizing another officer for his lack of zeal. "I know how to die, but not how to capitulate." He learned quickly. On September 2, 1801, just over a year after taking command, Menou surrendered to the British.

Now it was time to agree on peace terms. The British insisted that, as victors, they were entitled to all the booty the French had gathered in Egypt. From the start Menou had regarded the Rosetta Stone as his private property. Once he had taken over from Kléber, he had insisted on sleeping with it under his bed. (By some accounts, the Rosetta Stone lay hidden not under Menou's bed but under a pile of his belongings in a warehouse, concealed by mats.)

The British demanded that Menou hand them the Rosetta Stone. He exploded in rage. To call on him to give up his personal belongings was scandalous. "Never has the world been so pillaged!"

The British negotiators smiled. Menou's tantrum "diverted us highly," one of them wrote, "as coming from a leader of plunder and devastation." Menou persisted, asserting his rights in a series of indignant letters to Lieutenant-General Sir John Hutchinson, the British commander in chief.

Hutchinson responded with polite malice. "When I demand the Arabic manuscripts, statues, and several collections and antique objects, I am only following the fine example you set for Europe . . . In all the countries where the French have waged war, they have seized everything that seemed to them suitable to take."

This was harsh but true. To choose one instance from many, two of

the best-known savants, Monge and Berthollet, had spent time comb-
ing Italian museums and churches in 1797, after the French conquest,
selecting paintings for the Louvre. (Napoleon applauded "the good
harvest" and noted cheerily that nearly "everything of beauty in Italy"
would soon be headed to France.) Many of the savants' selections remain in place to this day, in the Louvre's Renaissance galleries.

But the savants in Egypt were as furious as Menou. They had criss-
crossed a hostile land to make their maps and drawings; they had
dodged bullets; they had clambered up ladders and crawled inside
sweltering, foul, bat-infested tombs to copy inscriptions.

The savants pleaded with Menou to back them. He didn't try hard.
The savants could not bear to give up their precious finds? What had
those smug eggheads ever done for him? "I have just been informed
that several among our collection-makers wish to follow their seeds,
minerals, birds, butterflies, or reptiles wherever you choose to ship
their crates," he wrote to Hutchinson, the British commander. "I do
not know if they wish to have themselves stuffed for the purpose, but
I can assure you that if the idea should appeal to them, I shall not prevent them."

Three of the savants visited Hutchinson to make their case in
person. "You are depriving us of our collections, our drawings, our
maps, our copies of hieroglyphs," shouted the naturalist Geoffroy Saint-
Hilaire, "but who will give you the key to all of this? . . . Without us,
these materials are a dead language from which you will hear nothing."
Hutchinson listened, unmoved.

The savants left. By the next day, Geoffroy had grown even angrier.
"We shall burn our riches ourselves," he yelled to Hutchinson's repre-
sentative. "You want fame. Well, you can count on history remember-
ing this: you too shall have burned a library in Alexandria."

The British ended up compromising, a bit. The savants could keep
their drawings and collections. The British would take the big items,
seventeen in all, weighing a total of fifty tons. The prizes included statues of gods with animal heads and an immense sarcophagus that was
supposedly Alexander the Great's, which had been found in a mosque

in Alexandria, where it served as a public bath. The greatest prize of all was the Rosetta Stone.

A British officer, the grandly named Tomkyns Hilgrove Turner, took possession of the stone and escorted it to England aboard HMS *L'Égyptienne*. (This was a French ship, as the name indicates, which meant that the captured trophy traveled to its new home aboard a captured ship.) Turner delighted in his role as a supporting actor in the drama. The Rosetta Stone was "a proud trophy of the arms of Britain," he proclaimed, "not plundered from defenseless inhabitants, but honorably acquired by the fortune of war."

And so the Rosetta Stone sits triumphantly in the British Museum today, and not in the Louvre. In British eyes, no home could have been more appropriate. The museum had boasted, back in 1761 in its first-ever guidebook, that its collection was "a lasting monument of glory to the nation." Here was a fitting trophy for that starry collection.

Look closely at the Rosetta Stone today, and you can just make out the capital letters painted on its sides. "Captured in Egypt by the British Army 1801," the left side declares, and, on the right, "Presented by King George III."

From the outset the public clamored to see the Rosetta Stone. (And to touch it, when the attendants weren't looking. "It's one of the museum's great embarrassments," a British Museum Egyptologist says, "that we issued postcards for many decades saying the stone was black basalt." A recent cleaning revealed that the Rosetta Stone is gray, not black, and not basalt at all. It turned black because the oil from countless fingertips had combined with a layer of protective wax that has since been removed.)

How to account for the fascination with a nondescript hunk of rock? Not for its message, which is mundane. Unlike history's other famous documents—unlike the Magna Carta, say, or the Declaration of Independence or the Bill of Rights—the Rosetta Stone's importance is *not* in what it says. What elevates the Rosetta Stone to world-class status is the way that message was presented.

And, perhaps, because of the way it was discovered. The Rosetta Stone is the ultimate message in a bottle, adrift on the waves of time for more than two thousand years before it was finally found. It was not *intended* as a message for a far-off audience; the idea was that it would be read at once, where it stood. But its discovery so many centuries after the disappearance of Egyptian culture makes it seem almost like the first-ever communication from an alien world.

The popularity of the Rosetta Stone has never diminished, as a visit to the British Museum gift shop confirms at once. Rosetta-themed trinkets outsell all other goodies. Visitors can take home Rosetta Stone jigsaw puzzles, coffee cups, earrings, cufflinks, iPhone cases, ties, T-shirts, aprons, playing cards, chocolates, tea towels, mousepads, umbrellas, luggage tags. For many decades, for as long as anyone at the museum can remember, its postcard has been the number-one seller in the gift shop.

Of the millions of objects in the British Museum collections, it remains the single most popular. "The Rosetta Stone is as much the prize possession of the British Museum," writes the classics scholar Mary Beard, "as the *Mona Lisa* is of the Louvre."

For laymen the Rosetta Stone's celebrity is a draw in itself—fame is a magnet, no matter its source. For would-be decipherers in the 1800s, the excitement was easier to explain. Now, at last, hieroglyphs would yield their secrets.

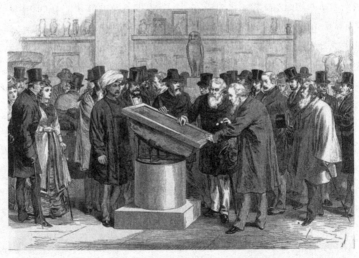

Scholars studying the Rosetta Stone in 1874

# CHAPTER TEN

# First Guesses

Even in the years before anyone had heard of the Rosetta Stone, hieroglyphs were so tempting a prize that scholars devoted decades of their lives to them. This endless digging in the dark yielded, at most, a spark here or there.

In 1798, one of Europe's most eminent linguists published a seven-hundred-page tome summarizing everything he had learned in a lifetime's study of Egyptian writing. Georg Zoëga was an authority on Egypt and on linguistics. In his magnum opus he noted, with dismay, that he had made only a start at deciphering hieroglyphs. He added, with pride, that he had done as much as anyone possibly could have. One year later, a French soldier stumbled over the Rosetta Stone.

Zoëga, a Dane, was a scrupulous scholar. From its earliest days, Egyptology had been a subject where nearly everything was speculation and almost nothing was solid fact. Zoëga refused to play that guessing game. Not knowing what to make of hieroglyphs, he did the best he could, which was to classify them.

He counted 958 different symbols. Here was a group of birds, here were insects, and humans, and human-animal hybrids, and plants, and tools, and abstract shapes. This was valiant and painstaking work, but it was almost poignant in its narrowness. The erudite scholar had no choice but to play the role of an illiterate man trying to make sense of a huge collection of postage stamps. Here were red ones and blue ones and some with portraits and some with animals. *But what were they for?*

Zoëga did rack up some genuine insights. He found, for instance, that although a hieroglyphic inscription could run either right to left or left to right, you could tell where a particular line began by looking at pictures that looked to one side or the other. Wherever there was a figure in profile, like a bird or a cat or a man, it always faced toward the beginning of the line. (Decipherers can test such guesses in various ways. If a text's left-hand margin is tidy and uniform but its right-hand margin shrinks and grows haphazardly, for instance, then the writing likely proceeded left to right. This is not especially subtle detective work, but without this opening step you could not tell if you were trying to decode the word *language* or *egaugnal*.)

Hieroglyphic writing could run left to right or, as in this example and the Rosetta Stone, right to left. Drawings in profile always faced toward the beginning of the line.

Zoëga saw, as well, that his tally of hieroglyphs told a story. What kind of writing system used 958 different symbols? If each symbol stood for a word, then the count was far too low. No language could get by with fewer than a thousand words. (A typical five-year-old knows ten thousand words.) But if each hieroglyph stood for a letter, then the count was far too *high*. Alphabets typically have dozens of letters, not hundreds. Anything much bigger would be unwieldy.

The only possibility, Zoëga concluded, was that hieroglyphs must be some kind of hybrid system. Perhaps a drawing sometimes stood for a word and sometimes for a letter, or a syllable, or a sound. That was a brilliant guess. But, having seen that far ahead, he gave up.

"Further goals I have thought best left to posterity," Zoëga wrote. He held out one faint hope. Someday, in the future, "when the numerous ancient remains still to be seen in Egypt have been accurately explored and published, it will perhaps be possible to learn to read the hieroglyphs."

That future came along one year later, with an accidental discovery in an obscure Egyptian fort. Zoëga never managed to see the Rosetta Stone's inscriptions, let alone the stone itself. "I would treasure an exact copy of it," he wrote despondently to a friend in 1800, "but in the present circumstances I know of no means to procure it."

The problem was war. Europe had been in turmoil since shortly after the French Revolution, when Europe's monarchs had banded together to fight France, in fear that if the people in one country could rise up and chop off a king's head, then other kings and other necks were in danger, too. The flames of war flared up and died down starting in the 1790s and continuing for a quarter century. Peace would not come until 1815, when Napoleon was defeated at Waterloo. By the end of the Napoleonic Wars, the death toll had reached four million—three million soldiers and one million civilians.

Against such a backdrop, any degree of international cooperation was remarkable. The record was surprisingly good. Some scholars, like Zoëga, missed out, but copies of the Rosetta Stone did reach many others. The savants led the way. They had improvised several ways to print directly from the stone as soon as they had it in their hands. As early as 1800, scholars in Paris had set to work examining the inscriptions.

When the Rosetta Stone reached London, in 1802, a group called the Society of Antiquaries took charge of making copies. Within months, they sent plaster replicas of the stone to linguists in Oxford, Cambridge, Edinburgh, and Dublin, and they distributed copies of the inscriptions to Paris, Rome, Berlin, Holland, Sweden, and even Philadelphia.

In these early years, would-be decipherers confronted two problems. The first was that, even if they did have access to the Rosetta Stone, it was unlikely that its fourteen lines of hieroglyphs would provide all the clues they needed. Decipherers and codebreakers need reams of text in order to tell patterns from coincidences. A spy might guess that *xyyxjb* in a message stood for *attack* (because many English words have a double *T* and because the *X*'s occur in the right places), for example, but it might just as well be *google* or *effect*. Without more intercepted messages, you could never know.

Decipherers' tools are intuition, experience, and deep knowledge, but they could never even get started without the archaeologists and explorers who bring back inscriptions from musty tombs and half-buried temples. This makes for odd partnerships. *Will Shortz, meet Indiana Jones.*

For some scripts, the scarcity of examples can be a deal-breaker. No one has ever deciphered a form of writing found exclusively on Easter Island, for instance, partly because only twenty-odd "texts" survive. The script, called Rongorongo (the name means, roughly, "to recite" in the local language), is attractive but enigmatic; the characters look a bit like birds and flowers that have been flattened between the pages of a book.

Until the 1800s the inscriptions were plentiful, usually carved into pieces of wood. But then raiding parties in search of slaves and other disasters nearly emptied Easter Island, and all knowledge of how to read Rongorongo vanished. Most of the wooden messages were thrown onto fires, for heat. Ever since, forlorn scholars have been left to pore over the tiny number of relics that remain—a tattoo copied long ago from a man's back, for instance, and a string of characters carved into a human skull.

An inscription in Rongorongo

The Rosetta Stone has distressingly few hieroglyphs because it is broken at the top. (Judging by the length of the other two inscriptions, about half the hieroglyphs are missing. Thomas Young sent a letter to an Egyptian explorer in 1818, begging him to search for the lost fragments, "which, to an Egyptian Antiquary, would be worth their weight in diamonds." They have never been found.) This is where the disorder in Napoleonic Europe came in. With travel and communication cut off, scholars had no access to papyrus texts in distant cities, or travelers' drawings with their lines of hieroglyphs, or collectors' statues and sculptures with their inscriptions. They could do little but stare endlessly at the same few lines of inscrutable inscriptions.

The early decipherers faced a second problem. Confronted with the stone's two unfamiliar inscriptions, they had to pick one to start with. For reasons that seemed perfectly reasonable at the time, they all made the wrong choice.

One inscription was incomplete and strange looking—this was the hieroglyphic—and the other was nearly complete and looked like an ordinary script—this was the middle section, the so-called demotic. Out with hieroglyphs, then, and on to demotic.

That decision immediately led to another. Since demotic looked like an ordinary script, and since ordinary scripts were based on alphabets, the first order of business was to figure out the demotic alphabet. It seemed like a good idea. It was, in fact, a jump from the starting line straight into a ditch.

Demotic would prove to be a place to explore at the end of the quest, not the beginning. Years of hard work would eventually unveil it as a pared-down, built-for-speed shorthand based on the hieroglyphic script but far more abstract and elusive.

Hieroglyphic characters were pictures, many of them rendered with meticulous care. Those pictures had evolved into simplified but still recognizable forms, and those bare-bones drawings had in turn given rise to the lines and slashes of demotic script, which barely hinted at their original versions. Though no one could have known better, demotic was *not* an alphabet.

The first accomplished linguist to take on the Rosetta Stone was a French academic named Silvestre de Sacy, a professor of Arabic in Paris. De Sacy began by looking for proper names in the demotic inscriptions. He knew that the Greek text referred to Ptolemy again and again, eleven times in all. The first step, then, was to look for a string of symbols in the demotic that turned up several times, in about the right positions. (The counts might not match exactly, because the demotic might sometimes refer to Ptolemy as *the king* or some such phrase.) You could do the same thing with other names, like *Alexander.*

De Sacy found the matches he was looking for. So far, so good. Then he made a mistake. Greek writing was based on an alphabet, de Sacy knew, and he had managed to match names in Greek with strings of symbols in Egyptian. The number of characters in the two names matched, or almost matched. This was coincidence, although de Sacy did not know that. What could be more natural than to conclude, as de Sacy did, that ancient Egyptians, like ancient Greeks, had made use of an alphabet?

Then he turned from names to words that occurred repeatedly in the Greek, like *god* or *king*, and tried to match them with strings of characters that turned up several times in the demotic. Tentatively, he built up his alphabet, with particular characters in demotic corresponding to particular letters in Greek.

De Sacy's approach was serious and methodical, but—since demotic was not in fact alphabetic—he was doomed to failure. In 1802, he gave up. "The hope I had at first entertained," he wrote dejectedly, "has not been realized."

A Swedish diplomat named Johan Åkerblad tried next. Åkerblad had been a pupil of de Sacy's and was an authority on ancient languages. He followed the same strategy as his ex-mentor, trying to match Greek names with strings of demotic characters and then moving on to matching ordinary words. By virtue of persistence or perhaps just good fortune, he fared better than de Sacy in finding matches.

Ironically, Åkerblad's successes set him up for failure because they reinforced his mistaken belief that the demotic script was alphabetic. (In the end it would turn out that demotic was a hybrid, like "I ♡ NY" but more complicated. Some symbols did indeed stand for letters, but others did not. The mistake that de Sacy and Åkerblad made was akin to guessing that ♡ was a letter that it vaguely resembled, perhaps *M* or *V.*)

Soon Åkerblad, too, gave up. For a dozen years, so did everyone else. Beset by war and stymied by the riddle of the stone, Europe's linguists sat stalemated. "Seven years having now elapsed since the last communication on the subject," one scholar wrote despairingly in 1812, he saw "little reason to expect" any progress.

Ironically, the years of false starts and dashed hopes saw a wave of fascination for all things Egyptian. The sulking of frustrated scholars did nothing to slow it. Architecture, fashion, even hairstyles remade themselves in line with the new craze. "Everything now must be Egyptian," one English writer complained in 1807. "The ladies wear crocodile ornaments, and you sit upon a sphinx in a room hung round with mummies, and the long black, lean-armed long-nosed hieroglyphical men are enough to make the children afraid to go to bed."

Napoleon's savants had inspired much of the excitement, with their tales and drawings and looted souvenirs. The public's obsession grew through the early decades of the 1800s, spurred in part by one of the most elaborate and well-publicized series of books ever published. The series, titled *Description of Egypt* and produced by the savants, attempted to embrace all that those scholars had learned. Like other vast projects, this one fell years behind schedule. Its final volumes did not appear until 1828, about twenty years late. Earlier volumes had appeared piecemeal, when they were ready.

To this day, few books have matched the scope and ambition of these handsome volumes. (Napoleon had authorized the government to cover the production costs.)* Thousands of engravings stretched across enormous pages that measured about three feet wide and two feet high. Two volumes of maps accompanied ten volumes of text and drawings.

Purchasers had the option of buying a specially made chest of drawers to house the opus, with narrow shelves for the picture volumes, ver-

---

* Napoleon kept a close eye on certain aspects of the project. The preface, written by the savant Fourier, declared that all Egyptians kept the name of Bonaparte alive in their hearts. Napoleon amended the text to read, "the immortal name of Bonaparte."

tical slots for the text ones, and an adjustable top that formed a display rack. A sculptor had worked with a cabinet maker to decorate the case with temple columns and lotus flowers, in Egyptian mode.

But when it came to the Rosetta Stone, the editors of *Description of Egypt* confessed that they had not been able to move the story along. They had reproduced the stone's inscriptions "with religious care," but their meaning remained out of reach. The editors made do with a series of precise measurements instead. "The stone is black granite; its average thickness is 0.27 meters, the width of its lower part 0.735 meters." This was true but beside the point, as if a biographer assessing Abraham Lincoln's place in history described him as a 48-long.

Åkerblad, the Swedish linguist who had proclaimed himself defeated by the Rosetta Stone a few years before, spoke up again. He declared himself bewildered by *two* mysteries. The first was the Rosetta Stone itself; the second was why everyone had given up on trying to decipher it.

"At its first discovery," Åkerblad wrote, "the monument of Rosetta appeared to attract the attention of all the learned throughout Europe." Since then it had been "neglected in an inconceivable degree."

A bit of that professed puzzlement was just good manners. Åkerblad knew perfectly well that his own failure, and de Sacy's, had intimidated other, lesser figures. By temperament, scholars generally are uncomfortable at center stage. That is all the more true of specialists who have chosen to spend their careers in quiet solitude, in dusty archives deciphering dead languages.

To announce a breakthrough in the riddle of the Rosetta Stone, though, would have been to *demand* a spotlight. Most scholars took a brief look, gulped in dismay, and skittered back to more congenial ground.

But in the very year of Åkerblad's lament, 1814, the era of neglect would come to an end. With the professional linguists on the sidelines, the field was open to outsiders. From here on, two unlikely geniuses would take over.

# CHAPTER ELEVEN

# The Rivals

The two heroes of our story had almost nothing in common except that both were geniuses and both had a gift for languages. Even their genius came in two distinctly different forms. Thomas Young was one of the most versatile thinkers who ever lived, eager to tackle any challenge from any direction. Jean-François Champollion was utterly single-minded, unwilling to focus his gaze on any topic but Egypt.

Both Young and Champollion had displayed their linguistic talents early on. (Champollion was the younger of the two, by seventeen years.) By the time they reached their teens, each had knocked off too many languages to list—Greek and Latin, for starters, along with deep dives into Arabic, Hebrew, Persian, Chaldean, and Syriac.

What would have been arduous labor for nearly anyone else seemed like play to these remarkable boys. At thirteen Young found a book that included versions of the Lord's Prayer in a hundred different languages. Contemplating and comparing the unfamiliar swirls and loops, he recalled in adulthood, provided him "extraordinary pleasure."* Champollion, at fourteen, once found himself alone and restless; he begged his older brother to send him a book of Chinese grammar, for distraction.

Neither man came from easy circumstances, and Champollion's finances would remain precarious throughout his life. He was the child of an unlikely match, a father who was a bookseller and a mother who could neither read nor write. His hometown was a backwater in

---

* From his school days on, Young took notes on his reading. He often wrote in Latin, although when he read Greek or French or Italian authors, he wrote his notes in those languages.

southwestern France called Figeac. During the Revolution, boisterous crowds had filled the town square and roared their approval as the guillotine's blade plummeted toward its latest victim. As a small child, Champollion lived within steps of the execution site; the sound of the baying crowd filled the toddler's ears.

Young's family was only marginally better off. In an autobiographical essay, he described his parents as "rather below than above the middle station of life," and he was the oldest of ten children. But then everything changed. When Young was a university student, an uncle died and left him his London house and an inheritance of £10,000 (in the neighborhood of $1.5 million in today's money).* That fortune, on top of Young's income as a physician, would free him from money worries for the rest of his life.

Young and Champollion differed as much in character as in income. Young was so remarkably even-tempered that one lifelong friend marveled that he had never seen him angry. Champollion was a perfect hero for the Romantic age. Prone to ecstatic outbursts and black moods, subject from boyhood on to fainting fits, he was moved to rebellious rage by the merest hint of bureaucratic foot-dragging. Depending on his mood, every day's events marked a triumph for the ages or a catastrophe.

Young was a creature of wry understatement, raised eyebrows, sly digs. Seldom boastful, he was often dismissive, as if amused by the earnest efforts of slower, clumsier thinkers. Champollion's style was altogether bolder. "Enthusiasm, that is the only life," he proclaimed, and he lived up to his credo. Young read the savants' accounts of Egypt and shook his head at the "ridiculous deities" and "superstitious rites." Champollion pondered the mighty works of the pharaohs and declared that, in comparison with ancient Egyptians, "We Europeans are merely men of Lilliput."

Champollion leaned left politically—Young had far less interest in politics—and he was fervently antimonarchy and antichurch. (He

---

* This same uncle had rebuked Young for his "prudery" when, as a teenager, he swore off sugar because it was a product of slave labor.

agreed with Diderot that it would be a happy day "when the last king is strangled with the guts of the last priest.") And no kings were ever so self-indulgent as the pharaohs, no priests so sure of their grip on power as Egypt's priests. But such considerations did nothing to dampen Champollion's ardor. Egypt was not a model; it was a marvel. It was, above all, the natural home of all that was colorful, strange, and exotic.

From childhood on, Champollion had thrilled to accounts like those in Herodotus of a topsy-turvy land where bakers kneaded dough with their feet rather than their hands, and mourners shaved their eyebrows when a pet cat died, and crocodiles were kept as pets and adorned with earrings and bracelets fashioned from pure gold.

Jean-François Champollion (*left*) and Thomas Young (*right*)

In their closest relationships, Champollion and Young offered still more evidence of their contrasting personalities. Champollion had an older brother who was his lifelong ally and, early on, his intellectual mentor. The two nearly always lived near each other and exchanged flurries of letters on the rare occasions when they were apart. Champollion's love and gratitude spill off the page. "You have long since demonstrated that you and I are one person," he wrote his brother in 1818, after yet another mishap and yet another rescue. "My heart tells me that we will never be two separate people."

Young never gushed. He was deeply devoted to his wife, for instance, but when he wrote his autobiography (in the third person), he passed over his marriage in a single sentence: "In 1804 he married Miss Eliza Maxwell, second daughter of J. P. Maxwell, Esq. of Cavendish Square."

Both men saw early on that they would need heaps of hieroglyphic texts if their deciphering efforts were to succeed, but even here their approaches diverged sharply. Champollion burned to get to Egypt so he could see the wonders of that extraordinary land with his own eyes. What could be better than to copy inscriptions himself and collect his own texts? Young had no taste for such labors. Why not hire "some poor Italian or Maltese to scramble over Egypt" instead?

Champollion was perpetually in a hurry, always furious with the simpletons who knew no greater pleasure in life than to dawdle in his path. (Perhaps his bad health made for this lifelong sense of urgency.) He believed fervently in the maxim that whatever is worth doing is worth overdoing. Though born in a provincial town to parents barely getting by, he became a university professor at age nineteen. "He shot out of the darkness into the light like an arrow," one biographer marveled.

Young, though just as ambitious, always gave the impression that he had all the time in the world. Perhaps he did. Young turned his thoughts to Egypt and hieroglyphs for the first time in the summer of 1814. By then he had racked up a dazzling record in science and medicine. He was forty-one. Champollion would *die* at age forty-one.

Thomas Young's cool façade concealed a hot heart. He seldom raised his voice, but that was a matter of style rather than temperament. "Scientific investigations are a sort of warfare," he confided to a friend, and the enemy camp included "all one's contemporaries and predecessors." Though he was raised as a Quaker, Young admitted that he took delight in vanquishing his foes. "All this, you see, keeps me alive."

Champollion relished a contest, too, and he was not as coy as Young about his love of combat. He was "a virulent polemicist," in the judgment of his biographer Jean Lacouture, "at times viperish, an implacable arguer, intolerant." No doubt Champollion would have disputed *that* judgment, too. It was not that he was belligerent, but, after all, a person must defend himself. "Fortunately, I was given a beak and claws," he liked to declare in the aftermath of a clash with a rival.

From the age of ten or eleven, Champollion focused his formidable talents on Egypt alone. (He followed the lead of his older brother, who was himself a student of languages with a passion for Egypt and the Rosetta Stone.) By his teens, an interest had become an obsession. Champollion published his first paper, on place names in ancient Egypt, at age sixteen. The idea was that the names of towns, rivers, and other geographic features might provide clues to the language of ancient Egypt, because names can be slow to change. (Champollion's strategy was akin to that of present-day linguists who look to names like *Massachusetts* and *Minnesota* for glimpses of Native American languages.)

The teenager presented a lecture on his findings to a society of scholars and capped his performance by informing his audience that one day he would decipher the hieroglyphs. At eighteen, he began earnestly studying Coptic. This was not the language of Egypt under the pharaohs—that language was dead and forgotten—but one that came along later. Coptic had only a brief run as Egypt's language, but the gamble was that it had inherited many features from its predecessor.

The heyday of Coptic dated from around the third century AD until shortly after the Arabs conquered Egypt in 642 AD. Within the following few centuries, Islam would displace Christianity and Arabic would displace Coptic. By the 1600s, a once-thriving language had become a relic. In 1677 one German traveler claimed he had met the last living Coptic speaker, in a village in Upper Egypt.*

---

* Johann Vansleb roamed widely through Egypt, but it would be a mistake to put too much stock in his eyewitness accounts. He described a bird "so strong that some say it can carry up a Man into the Air," for instance, and he explained in great detail how crocodiles mate belly to belly. (Once on their backs, they are helpless to turn over, Vansleb wrote, but all is not lost because crocodiles are as chivalrous as they are fierce. "The Male takes care when he hath performed his duty to turn her again upon her Belly, for fear of the Hunters.")

But that dead language will play a crucial role in our story, and we should pause a moment to look at it. By the time the Rosetta Stone turned up, Coptic had disappeared nearly as completely as ancient Egyptian. A few scholars could still read it, and Coptic remained the official language of Egypt's Christian Coptic Church. (To this day it can be heard in Coptic churches, like Latin in Catholic churches.) For decipherers desperate for some way to probe Egypt's secrets, the vital question was whether Coptic was a descendant of ancient Egyptian or merely its successor. Champollion cast a hearty vote for *descendant* and plunged into the study of this lost language, in the fervent belief that it would bring him closer to the real goal, Egyptian.

Coptic had one crucial feature that set it apart from Egyptian. It was written not with hieroglyphs but using the Greek alphabet, augmented by half a dozen symbols for sounds not found in Greek. So Coptic looked like Greek, and it included a fair number of Greek words besides. As a result, most scholars believed that Coptic and Greek, rather than Coptic and Egyptian, were kin. Champollion had important allies who shared his contrary view, including both Åkerblad and de Sacy, but he was in a distinct minority.

Since Coptic was written with Greek letters, the knowledge of how to read it had never been lost. That proved vital, because Champollion's guess would prove correct—Coptic *did* derive from Egyptian, and it did provide a bridge that offered access to that ancient language. But by the time Young and Champollion came along, the West had only a handful of Coptic manuscripts. If not for a few bold collectors and travelers, they might have had none at all.

Perhaps the most important collector was an Italian aristocrat, Pietro della Valle, who had set out in 1614 on what would become a multiyear trip through the Middle East as a way to recover from a broken heart. (He had narrowed his choices, after his breakup, to travel and suicide.) Trained as a composer, Della Valle lived an odd and remarkable life. He was the first modern visitor to identify the ruins of Babylon and the first to bring clay tablets inscribed with cuneiform writing to Europe.

In 1615, in Baghdad, he fell in love with a young woman named Sitti Maani. Soon after, the young couple traveled to Egypt, where Della Valle happened to see several examples of Coptic writing. He concluded (mistakenly) that he had discovered a new language and a new script and (also mistakenly) that the Coptic alphabet was as old as the hieroglyphs. These false hopes inspired him to purchase several Coptic manuscripts.

Then, in 1621, Sitti Maani died in childbirth. The heartbroken Della Valle vowed that he would carry her body back with him to Rome, to be buried in a grave site he had already decided on. He ordered a specially designed, airtight casket. Then he wandered his way home over the course of the next five years, toting his wife's body, two mummies he had purchased in Egypt, and his Coptic manuscripts.

Those manuscripts included a Coptic-Arabic dictionary and a book (in Arabic) on Coptic grammar. The collection ended up, eventually, in the Vatican Library in Rome. Without the information in those musty texts, the Rosetta Stone might not have yielded up its secrets.

Champollion seems never to have doubted that Coptic would be crucial to his deciphering work. When he was just eighteen, he wrote excitedly to his brother, "I give myself up entirely to Coptic . . . I wish to know Egyptian like my French, because on that language will be based my great work on the Egyptian papyri."

He followed up almost immediately with another letter to his brother. "I dream only in Coptic . . . I am so Coptic that, for fun, I translate into Coptic everything that comes into my head. I speak Coptic all alone to myself (since no one else can understand me)."

Champollion befriended a Coptic priest who helped him with the language. What he liked best of all was attending church and letting the sounds of the Coptic mass wash over him He noted cheerily, too, that he was ahead of his rivals. He had it on good authority that "Åkerblad didn't know much Coptic."

The bulk of Champollion's work on Coptic took place in the National Library in Paris. There he dove into the heaps of books that Napoleon had snatched from the Vatican Library in Rome, as part of the spoils of war. The stash of Coptic books included the ones that Della Valle had lugged home along with his wife's corpse.

A decade later, after Napoleon had been defeated and the looted texts returned to the Vatican, one scholar found Champollion's scribbled notes in the margins. "I think there are few Coptic books in Europe he has not examined . . . There is no book in the Vatican in that language that has not remarks of Champollion in almost every page, which he made when the manuscripts were at Paris."

Young's research style was entirely different. Champollion chose a single field and never thought of working anywhere else. Young leapt from subject to subject with the ease and nonchalance of a mountain goat traversing a cliff. Even colleagues who worked alongside him marveled at his range. "He knew so much," wrote Sir Humphry Davy, the best-known British scientist of the early 1800s, "that it was difficult to say what he did not know."

Young had known everything, it seemed, from earliest childhood. By the age of two, he would later recall, he had "learned to read pretty fluently." By six his reading was broad and miscellaneous. He had read the Bible and *Gulliver's Travels* and *Robinson Crusoe*, and poems by Pope and Goldsmith, and a book about a child prodigy named Tom Telescope who explained "the Newtonian System of Philosophy, Adapted to the Capacities of Young Gentlemen and Ladies." In his university days, he was so dazzling a figure that his fellow undergraduates dubbed him "Phenomenon Young."

Decades after Young's death, the renowned physicist Hermann von Helmholtz found himself stymied by the question of how the eye sees colors. Looking into the scientific literature for hints, Helmholtz found that Young had solved the problem years before. No one at the time had understood him. So far-seeing was Young, wrote Helmholtz, that this was the typical pattern—his best ideas lay buried and forgotten in scholarly journals (like hieroglyphs in a papyrus scroll), awaiting the time when a new generation would be able to decipher his cryptic words.

Those breakthroughs covered a vast range. A physician by training, Young was the first to discover how the eye changes focus depending on whether objects are near or far.* From there he moved on to the work on color vision that Helmholtz rediscovered. (Almost in passing, Young would later explain why it is that soap bubbles shimmer with iridescent colors.) He was the first person to use the word *energy* in its scientific sense, as in *atomic energy.* Curious about sound, he created a new way to tune keyboard instruments and devised a theory about the total number of sounds that the human tongue and voice box can produce. (He came up with forty-seven sounds and invented a universal alphabet to represent them.) Distracted one day by a pair of swans swimming in a pond, he began thinking about how ripples spread across water. Soon his thoughts turned from waves on water to waves in general. In time, Young proved that light is a wave as well as a particle.

This was not merely a revelation in itself but a rebuke to Isaac Newton, who had insisted that light is a particle. Newton was considered an almost godlike figure, and to challenge him was shocking. And yet Young took on the great man (at age twenty-seven) as if nothing could have been more natural.

The episode is worth a moment's attention, because it testifies simultaneously to Young's intellectual powers and to his audacity. More than that, Young's triumph reinforced his faith that he could tackle any mystery whatever and solve it by sheer force of intellect. (Reluctant though he was to toot his own horn, Young recognized his gifts. Talents like his, he admitted in his autobiography, had "a natural tendency to produce, in a person who has any consciousness of his own power, a sentiment not very far from conceit and presumption.")

What had led him to success in medicine and physics would surely carry over to languages and deciphering, as well. Others might have tried and failed, Young wrote to a friend, but their misfires served not

* Young always preferred working on his own, even if that meant experimenting on his own eyes. It is impossible to read his accounts of his research on vision without wincing. To measure the size of his eyes, for instance, Young blunted the two ends of a compass and then worked one compass point to the back of his eye and the other to the front. "With an eye less prominent," he noted, "this method might not have succeeded."

as a warning but as an invitation. So what if hieroglyphs had baffled the world for fourteen centuries? *Let's have a look.*

The wave/particle dispute that Young took on so blithely could scarcely have been more fundamental; it had to do with the structure of the world. In particular, the question was how light works. If there's a candle a few feet from you, you see it plainly, and if someone walks into the room and plants himself in front of you, the candle disappears from view. But that is not how sound works. If a piano player sits down a few feet from you and starts playing "Happy Birthday," you hear the song clearly, and if someone walks into the room and stands in front of you, you still hear the piano perfectly well. Before Young came along, the reason for the difference seemed easy to explain: light travels in straight lines, so obstacles can block it; sound travels in waves, so it can bypass objects it encounters, just as waves of water can flow around objects that happen to stand in their way.

Newton had made that argument. Take a cardboard tube and hold it to your eye, Newton had said, and you will see light. Make a sharp bend in the tube, though, and you can't see anything. But you can *hear* through a bent tube nearly as well as through a straight one. This proved, Newton concluded, that light was composed of particles and sound was composed of waves. QED. Then came Young.

Young explained to the world that Newton's argument did not show what Newton thought it did. Light and sound are not fundamentally different. Both are waves, but light waves are tiny in comparison with sound waves. As a result, you can block a light beam with your hand, but a boulder just offshore does *not* block the water rolling in toward the beach. For this demonstration alone, Young would rank high in the pantheon of physics.

"There are two kinds of geniuses," the twentieth-century mathematician Mark Kac wrote, in discussing Richard Feynman, "the 'ordinary' and the 'magicians.' An ordinary genius is a fellow that you and I would be just as good as, if we were only many times better. There is no mystery as to how his mind works. Once we understand what they have done, we feel certain that we, too, could have done it. It is different with the magicians."

Young fell into the magician camp, seemingly able to direct his talents to any mystery that caught his eye. He turned to Egypt not out of innate fascination but to answer the most tempting riddle of the age. Champollion was "merely" a brilliant thinker who had steeped himself in all things Egyptian since boyhood. Young wanted to solve a puzzle. Champollion wanted to unveil a culture.

# CHAPTER TWELVE

# Thomas Young
# Is Almost Surprised

In 1813, Thomas Young read something that caught his eye. As he often did, he had taken on as a diversion what would have been, for most people, a labor of Hercules—he was writing a review of a three-volume opus on the history of language, in German, that dealt with such questions as the relationship of Sanskrit to European languages. A brief passage stood out. The writing on the Rosetta Stone, Young read, was "capable of being analyzed into an alphabet consisting of little more than thirty letters."

By this time, though Young did not know it, every attempt to take on the Rosetta Stone had fizzled. Then, in May 1814, a friend of Young's happened to show him a papyrus he had purchased on a trip to Egypt. The papyrus, which was badly damaged, was covered with mysterious symbols. It had been found in a tomb in the city of Luxor (known in ancient times as Thebes), inside a mummy's casket.* Intrigued by the notion of a mysterious alphabet and a script that no one could read, Young decided he would have a look at the Rosetta Stone.

He liked to spend summers at his country house tackling whatever

---

* Young's friend William Rouse Boughton had purchased the papyrus while traveling in Egypt a few years before. "In the course of the year 1811," as Rouse Boughton told the story, "I had the good fortune to meet with a mummy." With the mummy was "some writing upon papyrus in a state of perfect preservation." Rouse was so pleased with his purchase that he had someone make him a tin box for the papyrus, to protect it, and sent it home by ship. Things did not go well. The precious text was "unluckily soaked by salt water," though Rouse Boughton noted gamely that the fragments had "not lost all their value."

project had lately drawn his notice. He settled down with a copy of the inscriptions on the Rosetta Stone and with essays by de Sacy and Åkerblad describing their work. "You tell me that I shall astonish the world if I make out the inscription," he wrote to a friend named Hudson Gurney. The two had been close since boyhood, and Young came closer to letting down his guard with Gurney than with almost anyone else. Surely Gurney had overstated the challenge? "I think it on the contrary astonishing that it should not have been made out already."

Young set to work scrutinizing the Egyptian characters in search of patterns. Like his predecessors, he began with the demotic text rather than the hieroglyphs. Like his predecessors, he had made a choice that doomed him from the start.

He proceeded methodically, with the intense focus that marked all his investigations. One string of symbols occurred "twenty-nine or thirty times"; the only Greek word that occurred so often was *king*, which Young found thirty-seven times. He found fourteen instances of a different string in the Egyptian; that tally matched fairly well with eleven mentions of *Ptolemy* in the Greek.

Young tried another plan, which again reflected his methodical, almost scientific approach. He began by burrowing into the Greek text. The first step, he explained, involved "marking, on a straight ruler, the places in which the most characteristic words, such as *god*, *king*, *priest*, and *shrine*, occur." Armed with information about the distance between words in Greek, or about the distance of those words from the beginning or the end of the Greek inscription, Young looked for strings of characters in the other inscriptions in roughly the expected locations.

This was painstaking but uncertain work, because there was no way of knowing how Egyptian grammar worked. Perhaps the most important words in a sentence came at the beginning or at the end, or perhaps the word order followed some more arcane rule. All this was made worse because so much of the hieroglyphic text was missing. You could experiment endlessly, but nothing was guaranteed.

Each time he made a guess, Young pasted the matching strings of characters onto a large sheet of parchment. Just above them, he added the corresponding word in Greek, in his tiny and meticulous hand-writing. We can almost hear him humming contentedly. "Certainly the labour of a few days" ought to crack it, Young wrote Gurney.

But it didn't. "I have been a month upon this," he confessed in frustration at summer's end, and he had little to show for his labors. For the most part he had simply rediscovered what Åkerblad had already found. This was, Young grumbled, "intolerably provoking."

For a man with a track record that consisted entirely of triumphs, this was not merely irritating but almost unfathomable. Confronted for once with a mystery he could not unravel, Young found himself contemplating a meta-mystery—how could his powers have failed him? "The difficulties have been far greater than there was any reason to expect," he told Gurney, with dismay and wonder, "and I am almost surprised that the labor I bestowed on them has effected so little."

Young wrote to de Sacy, the recognized authority on ancient languages. He knew that de Sacy and then Åkerblad had taken on the Rosetta Stone, but that had been a dozen years ago. What had happened in the meantime? "I am very anxious to know if Mr. Åkerblad has continued his attempts to decipher it."

De Sacy replied reassuringly. He and Åkerblad had turned to other things—the mystery was still open—and in any event he had "always entertained grave doubts" about Åkerblad's claim to have found the basics of a demotic alphabet.

But then, just when Young might have sighed in relief, this ominous note—"I ought to add that M. Åkerblad is not the only one who flatters himself that he has read the Egyptian text of the Rosetta Stone. M. Champollion, who has just published two volumes on the ancient geography of Egypt and who is active in the study of the Coptic language, claims also to have read the inscription."

This may have been the first time that Young had heard Champollion's name. Whether Champollion had heard of Young by this time, or heard whispers that Young had set out in pursuit of the Rosetta Stone, no one knows. In any event, de Sacy's news was not quite accurate. In truth, the summer of 1814 found Champollion as frustrated as Young. "I am always working on my inscription from Rosetta," he wrote a friend, "and the results are not coming as quickly as I would have wanted."

Then came a bizarre coincidence. At almost exactly the time that Young received de Sacy's letter with its news of a French decipherer, Champollion made his first contact with Young—by mistake! Champollion had written a letter asking for information about the Rosetta Stone. As the result of a misunderstanding, he sent it to Young. This was a complete fluke, as if Sherlock Holmes had needed information about a case and accidentally sent his request for help to Professor Moriarty.

What happened was that Champollion sent his letter about the Rosetta Stone to the president of the Royal Society, in London. He had two copies of the inscriptions, he wrote, but in a handful of places they didn't match. "I am convinced that I would already have settled the reading of the entire inscription," Champollion wrote, "if I had had under my eyes a plaster cast made from the original." Could the society help him with his predicament?

But the Royal Society didn't have anything to do with the Rosetta Stone. Champollion should have directed his letter to the Society of Antiquaries, a completely different organization. Champollion's letter made its way to the Royal Society's foreign secretary, the person in charge of correspondence with scientists from abroad. The foreign secretary was an English scientist named Thomas Young.

Suddenly Champollion seemed to be popping up everywhere Young turned. He had received de Sacy's warning letter and then Champollion's accidental letter. Now his friend Gurney wrote with alarming news. Had Young heard that a Frenchman, one Champollion, had tackled the Rosetta Stone? Young replied at once: "Your first letter disturbed my rest with impatience to see Champollion's work."

Young reassured Gurney (or himself) that he was ahead of the pack—he had deciphered many more words than de Sacy and Åkerblad had ever managed. Even so, he fretted about Champollion. He concluded his note to Gurney with a request that he send him Champollion's book on Egypt's geography, and the italics in his plea serve to underline his jumpiness. "You will easily imagine that I am not a little anxious to see what *he has done*."

Thwarted by the Rosetta Stone itself, Young retreated a step. Rather than deal exclusively with the inscriptions on the stone, he would delve into Egyptian writing generally, looking for patterns or anything else that might give him a way to get started.

It was Young's versatility that first caught the eye, but it was the combination of doggedness and all-around brilliance that truly made him "Phenomenon Young." From a distance he might have looked like a dilettante, as he dashed every which way. His notes and papers make plain how false that impression was.

Alone and out of sight, in between dashes, Young worked relentlessly. Like many decipherers, he had endless patience and an exceptional visual memory—he would have been brilliant at jigsaw puzzles.[*] Young had tackled deciphering projects before the Rosetta Stone, and many of his ventures had involved week upon week of poring over faint and damaged texts in ancient languages, trying to guess what letter a tiny curl might once have belonged to or what words had halfway disappeared in the course of a thousand years, ravaged by time and worms.

This sort of work is immensely difficult. In one notorious case, from 1904, a British scholar published a much-acclaimed translation of a Latin text that had newly been found in Bath, England. The writing, scratched into a lead tablet, was faint and incomplete, and the translation was hailed as a coup for scholarship. *Just think—from a few faint lines and scratches, to have deduced whole letters and words!*

Ninety years later, an Oxford historian reexamined the evidence. The original translation, it turned out, was completely wrong, an exercise in self-delusion based on hopeful guesses and dubious assumptions. The 1904 decipherer had been holding the tablet upside down.

Young had too good an eye to blunder like that. But it's always the

---

[*] A colleague of the great decipherer Michael Ventris—we will meet Ventris in chapter 15—marveled that Ventris had "made himself so familiar with the visual aspects of the texts that large sections were imprinted on his mind simply as visual patterns, long before the decipherment gave them meaning."

case that the day-in, day-out work of deciphering involves an endless series of judgment calls. Especially when it comes to handwritten scripts,
the telltale clues are so subtle that they are nearly impossible to spell
out, which is why computers have yet to displace human codebreakers.

(Outsiders have set themselves the task of watching decipherers
at work, in hopes of explaining their strategies. They tend to give up,
more bewildered and less enlightened than when they began. One
great pioneer in the study of cuneiform, for instance, had a knack for
piecing together fragments of broken clay tablets. "A given tablet might
have been broken into a dozen or more pieces," his biographer tells us,
"now widely dispersed among the hundred thousand fragments in the
museum's collection.")

Young had learned to absorb countless patterns in an almost subliminal way. When he turned his focus to ancient Egypt, he drew on
skills he had developed a decade before. He'd been working then on
deciphering papyrus texts that had been nearly destroyed in 79 AD,
when Mount Vesuvius erupted and buried Pompeii and Herculaneum
in lava. This was agonizingly slow work. The sheets of papyri had lain
buried under 120 feet of ashes, sand, and lava, and the heat of the explosion had fused them into black lumps. Simply teasing the sheets
apart was a feat.

Young found that copying the faint characters by hand, ever so
slowly and carefully, somehow stimulated his memory. "Those who
have not been in the habit of correcting mutilated passages of manuscripts," he wrote, "can form no estimate of the immense advantage
that is obtained by the complex sifting of every letter which the mind
involuntarily performs, while the hand is occupied in tracing it."

Now Young applied the same technique to stacks of Egyptian inscriptions, from the Rosetta Stone itself, from papyrus scraps brought
back from Egypt by collectors, from strings of symbols carved into
statues, from writing that the savants had copied from temple walls.

These inscriptions were in different scripts (both hieroglyphic and
demotic), which made Young's task all the more difficult, but other-
wise the assignment he had set himself was roughly akin to looking
at handwritten notes from a diary, a photograph of neon signs on the

Strip in Las Vegas, and a scrap of newspaper with the ornate *New York Times* nameplate in giant letters, and guessing which symbols matched up. If all knowledge of our alphabet had disappeared long ago, how long would it take to see that a lowercase *t* is the same letter as *T*? Or that *Y* and 𝖄 are the same but that *i* and *j* are different?

One strategy helped Young considerably. Often the same drawings turned up in different places; as we have seen, Egyptian culture was so deeply conservative that it used and reused its favorite images over the course of thousands of years. In some fortunate cases, Young found identical images accompanied by texts in different scripts. (A modern counterpart would be finding photographs of the same scene in an American newspaper and a Chinese one, each with an accompanying caption.)

Here Young's gift for pattern recognition kicked in, and he pointed out what no one else had ever seen. The demotic characters—some of them, at any rate—bore a too-close-to-be-coincidence resemblance to hieroglyphs. This was a remarkable achievement. Demotic looks like "row upon row of agitated commas," one modern Egyptologist observes. "It is perfectly dreadful stuff to read."

The similarity in appearance of hieroglyphs and demotic was real, but it was subtle. (In Young's proudly understated formulation, there was no "very striking analogy" between the two forms of writing.) But Young had seen the truth even so. Demotic and hieroglyphs were *not* distinct scripts (like the Roman alphabet, with its familiar *abc*, and the Greek alphabet, with its *αβγ*), but two versions of the same thing (like the Roman alphabet and the shorthand alphabet).

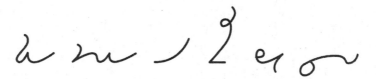

"Four score and seven years ago" in shorthand

In the summer of 1815, Young wrote to de Sacy once again. De Sacy had searched in vain for an Egyptian alphabet. Now Young proposed to explain what had gone wrong. "I am not surprised that, when you consider the general appearance of the [demotic] inscription, you are inclined to despair of the possibility of discovering an alphabet capable of enabling us to decipher it," he began.

Then he added, with a flourish that was uncharacteristic of him, "If you wish to know my 'secret,' it is simply this—that no such alphabet ever existed."

Why was that announcement so momentous? Because if demotic writing was not alphabetic, then it was built on some strange and unsuspected foundation. And if demotic writing was strange—and if hieroglyphs and demotic were two variations on a single theme—then hieroglyphs, too, had something bizarre at their core.

But everyone knew what hieroglyphs were—they were timeless truths written in stone. If Thomas Young was right, perhaps that assumption was wrong, too.

# CHAPTER THIRTEEN

# Archimedes in His Bathtub, Thomas Young in His Country House

Every diamond heist, every bank job, every jailbreak, hinges on the discovery of some vulnerability, no matter how tiny. Perhaps there is a corner of a hallway not covered by security cameras, or a guard with a drinking problem.

For codebreakers, decipherers, and sleuths of all sorts, the game starts with finding not a weakness, necessarily, but a quirk, a puzzle piece that's ever so slightly off. The most innocuous-looking clue can lead to pay dirt. The Nazis believed their Enigma code was unbreakable; it nearly was, but for one glitch. Enigma took the letters in a message and, using a secret recipe, changed them to other letters (an *a* might become a *p*, say). The glitch was that the recipe never permitted a letter to remain unchanged (an *a* could never stay an *a*). That tiny quirk helped to defeat Hitler.

Sometimes the first step is simply a matter of spotting something odd. Watergate started when a security guard noticed a door with a piece of tape over the latch, to keep it open. The story of penicillin began when a scientist returned from vacation and looked at the petri dishes where he had been growing bacteria. Several of the dishes had been contaminated with yeasts and molds that had drifted in from somewhere. But one contaminated dish had something odd about it— surrounding the newly arrived mold was a clear spot where no bacteria had survived! Alexander Fleming, an ever-so-understated Englishman, responded not by shouting *Eureka!* but by murmuring, "That's funny."*

Crucial clues can be tinier still. A year or two ago, a scandal over college admissions broke when someone noticed, in an essay supposedly written by a high school student, two spaces (rather than one) after every period. No young person would do such a thing; two spaces were a sure sign of an overzealous parent who had learned to type back in typewriter days. "It is in the negligible," the writer and director Jonathan Miller once observed, "that the considerable is to be found."

But discovering a starting place can take endless scrutiny. Every crossword fan knows the dismal feeling of reading the same clues over and over again, searching for even one plausible answer. Thomas Young, trying to find a toehold for his assault on hieroglyphs, struggled and stumbled. When progress finally came, it arrived, unannounced, in the unlikeliest guise.

In the summer of 1816, Young happened to read a magazine article explaining the rudiments of writing in Chinese. "The Chinese article is by Barrow, Secretary of the Admiralty," Young wrote his friend Hudson Gurney, and he was "excessively delighted" with what he had learned. He had never thought about that "unique language," and he'd had "no conception of its nature before."

A lifetime civil servant—Barrow did not give up his job until age eighty-one, at which point he was given his old desk as a retirement gift—Barrow looked bland and forgettable. He was not. He was a man of formidable talent whose curiosity ranged nearly as broadly as Young's. Officially he was second secretary to the British Admiralty, which meant that he helped to shape policy for the Royal Navy, but in reality he was a resourceful and innovative problem-solver who could always be counted on when everyone else had thrown up their hands.

---

* If not for another fluky bit of fortune, Alexander Fleming's research career might never have begun. Fleming happened to be a skilled shot with a rifle. After medical school, he had intended to go on to a career in surgery. But a hospital with a research program had a rifle club, and they recruited Fleming to join them because of his prowess as a marksman. He would remain at St. Mary's Hospital in London for his entire career.

When the British were trying to decide where they could safely stash Napoleon after Waterloo, it was John Barrow who proposed that he be exiled to Saint Helena, one of the most remote islands on earth. When a publisher ran out of book ideas for a series on naval history, it was Barrow who combed through official records and wrote up a true story that he called *The Mutiny and Piratical Seizure of HMS* Bounty.

He had learned Chinese as a young man, during a stint as tutor to a child prodigy who spoke five languages. (When it came to Chinese, pupil and tutor exchanged roles.) A decade later, in 1793, Barrow had accompanied the British ambassador on an ill-fated voyage to China, serving as interpreter. The ambassador arrived bearing gifts meant to wow the emperor with the marvels of British technology—telescopes, elaborately decorated rifles and pistols, a hot-air balloon (with a pilot at the ready)—but the Chinese dismissed visitors and gifts alike. "We have never valued ingenious articles," they declared, "nor do we have the slightest need of your country's manufactures." Nor, for that matter, did the emperor see the slightest need for an ambassador. Such a visitor would be "not in harmony with the regulations of the Celestial Empire."

The British were sent back where they'd come from, but Barrow's fascination with all things Chinese did, at least, find a receptive audience in Thomas Young. As he read Barrow, it dawned on Young that the Chinese system of writing, with its thousands of characters, could deal perfectly with every imaginable task—except one.

How would you write a foreign name in Chinese? Take *Napoleon*. There's no problem in translating ordinary words into Chinese and then writing them down—the Chinese language has words for *house* and *duck* and *basket*, so you can easily write them. But Chinese had no word for *Napoleon*. Why would it?

The Chinese solution, Young learned, was simple enough. To write a foreign name in Chinese, you picked characters that had the appropriate sounds, and you ignored their meaning. This is roughly what we do when we spell out names in *Whiskey, Bravo, Tango* fashion. Thus, a man named Wood trying to place an order over a crackly phone line might resort to, "It's Wood. That's *Whiskey Oscar Oscar Delta*." No one cares that whiskey is a drink.

So, at last, Young had his starting point. He knew that non-Egyptian names—most prominently *Ptolemy*—popped up throughout the Greek text on the Rosetta Stone. And he knew that the hieroglyphic inscription was a translation of the Greek. That meant that names like *Ptolemy* had to be hidden throughout the hieroglyphic text, too, like nuggets of gold in a riverbed.

If he could find those foreign names, and if the Egyptians had hit on the same solution as the Chinese—as Young fervently hoped—then he would soon know how to read a handful of names written in hiero-glyphs. Those would be the first hieroglyphs to yield their meaning in fifteen centuries.

More than that, Young would have taken the first steps toward resur-recting the *sounds* of Egyptian, since *Ptolemy* and *Alexander* and other names presumably sounded more or less the same in every language.

Young plunged ahead. Where to look for names? In the fourteen lines of hieroglyphs on the Rosetta Stone, he focused on half a dozen ovals that each encircled several hieroglyphs. *Perhaps these ovals were special?* The savants in Napoleon's army had noticed them, too—they called the ovals *cartouches*, French for *cartridges*, because they bore a resemblance in shape to rifle cartridges—but they hadn't known what to make of them.

Three of the Rosetta Stone's cartouches were identical, and the other three started out in exactly the same way as the others and then added several more symbols.[*]

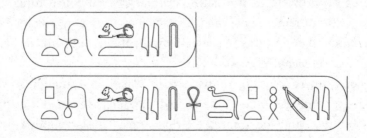

* For the sake of convenience, these cartouches are drawn to read from left to right. The originals read right to left, but that makes comparison with Greek and English more difficult.

Young guessed that the cartouches played a double role. First, they signaled that the hieroglyphs they enclosed were noteworthy in some way (as italics or bold type instructs us to pay particular attention to certain words). Second, they carried instructions to sound out their hieroglyphs phonetically.

The cartouches were the most eye-catching feature of the Rosetta Stone's hieroglyphic section, and the name of the king was the stand-out feature of the Greek section. What could be more natural than to hope that the hieroglyphs in the cartouches spelled out the name *Ptolemy* (or, as it was written in Greek, *Ptolemaios*)?

Young found the name *Ptolemy* in Greek (it was actually written
*Ptolemaios* rather than in the Anglicized form we're more accustomed
to). Look for ΠΤΟΛΕΜΑΙΟΥ (in the third line, beginning
with the fourth character).

The number of letters in *Ptolemaios* matched—or matched with a little fiddling—the number of hieroglyphs in the cartouche. (In Greek, each letter is sounded individually; there are no silent letters. Greek speakers pronounce the *P* in *Ptolemy*.) But the hieroglyphs posed challenge upon challenge: Where one hieroglyph sat atop another, were the two signs separate? If so, which came first? Or were they two parts of a single symbol? And did you read the hieroglyphs left to right or right to left? Young made the same guess that Zoëga, the Danish linguist, had proposed earlier: the figures in profile faced the start of the line, as if telling you where to begin reading.

With no choice but to hope that he'd guessed right, Young set to work. If *Ptolemaios* corresponded to the hieroglyphs in the first cartouche above, then you could begin to construct a table by matching sounds in Greek with pictures in Egyptian:

P = ☐ T = ⌒ O = ⟏ L = 🦁 M = ⬯ E = 𓏥 S = 𓊽

Here was a name, *Ptolemy*, written in hieroglyphs. The Rosetta Stone had sat mute for nearly two thousand years. Now Thomas Young had leaned close and heard it speak.

The longer string in the second cartouche above, he suggested, might refer to Ptolemy with an honorary title tacked on at the end. Perhaps it read "Ptolemy the Most High" or some such.

Promising as all this seemed, these guesses might have been only a pipe dream. If fate had been kinder, Young's path ahead would have been easier. If the Rosetta Stone had been intact, for example, he might have counted the *Ptolemy*s in the Greek text and the cartouches in the hieroglyphs and seen if the numbers matched. But the stone was broken. If the stone had been intact, Young might have found cartouches that spelled out other names than *Ptolemy*. But all six cartouches were nearly identical.

If all knowledge of Egyptian grammar and vocabulary had not been lost millennia before he came along, Young could have looked at the first words in a Greek sentence and compared them with the corresponding words in Egyptian. But who knew if the two languages put words in the same order? For that matter, the hieroglyphs marched along without any breaks. How could you even pick out individual words, let alone deduce anything about structure and syntax?

Even so, Young's hunch that the Rosetta Stone's cartouche contained the name *Ptolemy* was truer than he knew. In ancient Egypt, the cartouche's oval shape had told a story of its own. A cartouche depicted a rope with its ends tied together. That endless loop represented the sun in its path around the sky; by encircling the pharaoh's name, the cartouche served as a reminder that his rule extended to the sun's farthest reaches. The image served ancient Egyptians, the historians Lesley and Roy Adkins explain, much as the cry "Long live the king!" served the English.

We know this because Egyptologists eventually managed to read the texts that said so. We can imagine future generations equally oblivious to symbols that *we* take for granted. Will archaeologists centuries from now grasp that a lightbulb over a person's head once meant *Eureka*?

The strategy of starting with foreign names, when you begin trying to decipher an unknown language, seems almost obvious in hindsight. That is often the fate of good ideas, which lose their luster (like magic tricks) the moment they are explained.

Nowadays starting with names is standard practice for decipherers. Names are special, whether they refer to people or to places. When you move between languages, there is no reason that ordinary words with the same meaning should look alike. *House* and *maison* and *casa* look different, and that is no surprise. But the names *Albert Einstein* and *Amsterdam* should appear much the same whether in the *New York Times* or *Le Monde* or *El Mundo*.

Even where scripts are different, a name might offer a decipherer some hints. In Russian *Albert Einstein* is *Альберт Эйнштейн*; *Leo Tolstoy* is *Лев Толстой*. Young's bright idea was that, even if you were dealing with scripts that were not just different but *completely* different, like Chinese or Egyptian, names might still offer a starting point.

Young seems to have come up with the idea on his own, and he was certainly the first to apply it to the Rosetta Stone, but others had thought of it before him. Champollion had figured out the significance of names half a dozen years before, in 1810, and without the Chinese detour. Simply as a matter of logic, he had noted, if Egyptians had a way of using hieroglyphs to write foreign names, then certain hieroglyphs *had* to correspond to sounds. But then he'd hurried off to other topics.

The first person to have pointed out the value of names in deciphering ancient languages was Gottfried Leibniz, one of history's most daunting geniuses (and Isaac Newton's great rival). This was in 1714, a full century before Young, but Leibniz was nearly always miles ahead of everyone else. He was the first to envision the computer, for instance, though he lived in a world without electricity.

In any event, Leibniz was a sort of Young-before-his-time—both men are the subjects of biographies titled *The Last Man Who Knew Everything*—and it is only fitting that their thoughts ran on similar lines. (So daunting a figure was Leibniz that even supremely able thinkers quailed when they contemplated his abilities. "When one . . . compares one's own small talents with those of a Leibniz," wrote Denis Diderot, the philosopher/poet who had compiled an encyclopedia of all human knowledge, "one is tempted to throw away one's books and go die peacefully in the depths of some dark corner.")

Leibniz had a long-standing obsession with devising a universal language. So did many thinkers in his era, all of them inspired by the triumphs of the Scientific Revolution. An arrow shot into the air in China followed the same arc as one in England. That was not news; what was marvelous was that a Chinese mathematician and an English one could describe that arc in the same equation using the same mathematical symbols. And surely, if a newly invented mathematical language could describe the myriad wonders of the natural world, then a sleek, pictorial language could replace the cacophony that had bedeviled the world since Babel.

Thus the fascination with Egyptian hieroglyphs, which in the judgment of Leibniz and his contemporaries represented an early attempt at capturing deep truths in universal symbols. It was in the course of pondering the nature of such a universal language that Leibniz happened on his insight about deciphering foreign names.

But Leibniz didn't have the Rosetta Stone.

Young did, and his reading of *Ptolemy* would prove correct. It was only one word, but for fifteen centuries there had been no words at all. From one word to an entire language is a vast distance. But from zero words to one is much further, and Young had bridged that chasm.

# CHAPTER FOURTEEN

# Ahead of the Field

In the years from around 1814 to around 1820, Young had the Rosetta Stone largely to himself. These were bad years for Champollion. His health had never been good—throughout his life he suffered unpredictable bouts of dizziness, fever, fainting spells, and coughing fits that made it nearly impossible to catch his breath—and lately things had taken a turn for the worse. In the meantime, the fall of Napoleon meant the return of the French monarchy and new opportunities for those in favor with the regime. That was bad news for antiroyalists like Champollion.

Despondent and broke, he confessed his fears to his brother, in a letter written in 1814. "My fate is clear. . . . I will try to buy a barrel [to live in] like Diogenes . . . I firmly believe that I was born at a bad time and that nothing that I want the most will ever succeed."

In 1816, both brothers were booted out of their faculty jobs at the University of Grenoble, on the grounds of political unreliability, and sentenced to internal exile in their hometown, Figeac. Distraught, Champollion contemplated the prospect of abandoning the scholarly life and taking up law instead. "You will tell me that it is like a priest becoming a miller," he told his brother, "but what does that matter if the priest has not eaten and they have flour at the mill?"

Still, Champollion kept his eyes on the prize. Throughout this bleak stretch he continued to concentrate on studying Coptic, in the firm belief that it would someday prove the key to the hieroglyphs. "Every day my Coptic dictionary is getting thicker," he wrote in 1816. "The author, meanwhile, is getting thinner."

In the meantime, Young forged ahead, even though the Ptolemy cartouches were the only ones on the Rosetta Stone. For the most part, he relied on his gift for pattern recognition, looking for strings of hieroglyphs that seemed to match recurring words in Greek. The Greek text referred again and again to such words as *king* and *day* and *month* and *god*, and Young found hieroglyphs, or short strings of hieroglyphs, in about the right places.

With the aim of deciphering hieroglyphs generally, and not just those on the Rosetta Stone, Young continued to gather inscriptions from all over. He found symbols that seemed to correspond to *one* and *two* and *ten*. He noticed, too, that some cartouches had the same pair of hieroglyphs at the end—a semicircle above an oval—and he proposed that this was a sign for *female*, perhaps indicating a queen or a goddess.

Most of these guesses proved correct, but it's important to bear in mind that matching was not the same thing as reading. Young had managed to identify certain strings of hieroglyphs, but the principle behind them still eluded him. In the same way, a toddler today might learn to recognize the word *dog* (perhaps because it appeared under pictures of dogs in her books) even if she didn't know how to sound out the letters.

Young found the word *pharaoh* in hieroglyphs, for instance, but he didn't know that he'd found it. He believed he'd found the word *temple* or, perhaps, *great house*. And indeed he had.

But he didn't know that the first symbol meant *great*, and he had no idea that it was pronounced *per*, nor did he know that the second one meant *house* and was pronounced *aa*. Nor could he have known that the Egyptians referred to the king as the *great house*—the *per-aa*, or *pharaoh*—in much the way that we might say, *"The White House announced . . . ,"* when we mean, *"The president announced . . ."*

Young sometimes blundered. In a cartouche from the temple at Karnak, in Thebes, he felt certain that he'd spotted the name of a queen, Berenice. The temple had inscriptions both in Greek and in hieroglyphs, and Young had also spotted the name *Ptolemy* in Greek. (This was not the Ptolemy of the Rosetta Stone, who was Ptolemy V, but an ancestor, Ptolemy I.)*

Young saw, as well, two cartouches with hieroglyphs. The hieroglyphs in one cartouche matched the *Ptolemy* hieroglyphs on the Rosetta Stone.

That was just what Young had hoped and expected. That left the second cartouche, which contained a string of some half-dozen hieroglyphs. The last two symbols were the semicircle and oval that Young had already identified as meaning *queen*.

Here, then, were two cartouches, one for Ptolemy and the other for his queen. Young knew from ancient Greek texts that Ptolemy I had married a Macedonian noblewoman named Berenike (sometimes written *Berenice*). Two cartouches, two noble names. Puzzle pieces seldom line up so tidily.

Berenike was no Cleopatra, but she was, by the standards of antiquity, a celebrity. She and Ptolemy had been depicted on a coin, and the Greek poet Theocritus, who lived around 270 BC, had sung the praises of "fair Berenike" and "renowned Berenike." She was, Theocritus had written, the best of wives. "Never woman gave man so great delight as Ptolemy took in his love of that his wife."

---

* Ptolemy I features in one of the most famous anecdotes in the history of science. Euclid, the father of geometry, taught mathematics in Alexandria during Ptolemy's reign. Frustrated that he could not grasp the theorems and proofs in Euclid's masterpiece, the *Elements*, Ptolemy asked if there was an easier way. "There is no royal road to geometry," Euclid told his sovereign.

Best of all, from Young's point of view, *Berenike* was a foreign name. That meant he could apply his sound-out-the-hieroglyphs trick. (Young assumed that the names of native Egyptian pharaohs were written in hieroglyphs, too, but he thought that *those* hieroglyphs stood for ideas rather than sounds. His notion was that idea-hieroglyphs had meanings but didn't correspond to sounds, in roughly the way that a smiley face or a skull and crossbones functions for us.)

Young had already read one royal name, *Ptolemy*. Now he would add another name to his collection, along with several new hieroglyphs.

Unfortunately *Berenike* had almost no sounds in common with *Ptolemy*, so Young had to start from scratch. This was akin to filling in a crossword answer in a new part of the puzzle, where there were no intersecting answers to build on.

The first hieroglyph in the *Berenike* cartouche looked like some type of container. Young's heart soared, because the Coptic word for basket was *bir*, which sounded like the beginning of Berenike's name. *Perhaps the hieroglyphs were a sort of rebus?* A hieroglyph near the end of the string, just before the semicircle above an oval, was a bird. Young took it to be a goose, and he noted that according to some sources the Coptic word for *goose* began with a *K*.

With the first and last sounds of *Berenike* now in hand, Young worked his way along, assigning the intervening hieroglyphs in the cartouche to the intervening letters in Berenike's name (and leaving out one bad fit as "superfluous").

This was not outright cheating, but it was wishful thinking. "The warmest advocates of Dr. Young," one nineteenth-century biographer wrote, "must admit that this analysis . . . was more creditable to his ingenuity than to his judgment."

The problem was that the basket turned out to be an incense burner, and the goose an eagle. (The confusion over the birds was not Young's fault. He had been victimized by the equivalent of a typo; the person who copied the inscription had drawn a goose where the original had an eagle.)

Young had stumbled into the right answer—the name in the cartouche was indeed *Berenike*—but this was as if a detective chasing a suspect in a red pickup truck had pulled over a yellow sports car instead and, by a fluke, found the very thief he'd been pursuing.

To make a mistake was no scandal. Every decipherer goes wrong countless times. (Even crossword puzzlers use pencil rather than ink.) And Young's coups far outnumbered his false steps.

Many were so subtle that it is impressive that he unearthed them at all, let alone so early in his deciphering career. Young saw, for instance, not just that the semicircle and oval hieroglyphs conveyed information—*this is a woman's name*—but that the Egyptian approach was different from the one used in English in old-style words like *actress* and *poetess*.

In Egyptian, the symbols were not part of the word that preceded them, and they were not pronounced. (Nor was there any indication, like underlining or an accent mark, that distinguished them from ordinary hieroglyphs.) The reader simply noted the information conveyed in the symbols, in roughly the way that a modern reader would note the italics in *Chicago* and would know that this was a reference to the movie rather than the city.

Young's approach to deciphering was every bit as important as the advances themselves. In the hands of all his predecessors, "translation" had been an anything-goes game where any string of hieroglyphs might yield any meaning whatsoever. Deciphering hieroglyphs was an exercise with no rules and no limits, like finding shapes in the clouds. ("Do you see yonder cloud that's almost in shape of a camel?" Hamlet teased Polonius, before forcing him to agree that on second thought it was more "like a weasel" or perhaps "like a whale.") But Young's puzzle-solving strategy relied on specific guesses that could be tested, not taken on faith.

Most important of all, Young had made a conceptual breakthrough. By deciphering *Ptolemy* on the Rosetta Stone, he had shown that hieroglyphs sometimes stood for sounds.

That simple statement had enormous implications. If hieroglyphs were sounds, then they were not ideas. Which meant that every authority for fifteen centuries had gotten the story wrong.

That was a huge step forward, but Young's focus remained entirely on names—rather than words—and on foreign names at that. He had yet to consider an astonishing, and much broader, possibility. Perhaps the ancient Egyptians had also used hieroglyphs to spell out ordinary Egyptian words? In that case, the lions and birds and snakes would have served as everyday tools for setting down everyday words rather than as exotic gear used only for rare cases involving the strange names of foreign rulers.

In hindsight the move from names to words looks like a baby step. At the time it required a mental leap. Geniuses though they were, neither Young nor Champollion saw their opportunity. Neither man saw yet how near he was to sounding out words. If you could sound out a word today, then perhaps you could sound out a few more tomorrow. And eventually, if all went well, a great many more. You could resurrect a dead language.

They had nearly bumped into the prize, but so far no one had seen it.

In December 1819 Young wrote up his findings in a major article for the *Encyclopedia Britannica*, titled "Egypt." The *Britannica* of that era was top-flight, with writers as prominent as Sir Walter Scott (who wrote an entry called "Chivalry") and John Stuart Mill ("Government"). Young wrote anonymously, as he preferred, but he told his friend Gurney that "everybody whose approbation is worth having will know the author."

He discussed the Rosetta Stone and explained cartouches, and the importance of foreign names, and told the story of how he had deciphered *Ptolemy* and *Berenice*, and listed the hieroglyphs that he had managed to match with sounds.

The *Britannica* article served as a kind of marker, and it left Young well ahead of any rivals. "Young had by far exceeded everything that Champollion had ever published on hieroglyphs (which was virtually nothing)," the Egyptologists Lesley and Roy Adkins observed, "and it seemed that with such a lead he could not be overtaken."

# CHAPTER FIFTEEN

# Lost in the Labyrinth

Thomas Young gave every appearance of never breaking a sweat—one college chum marveled that "there were no books piled on his floor, no papers scattered on his table, and his room had all the appearance of belonging to an idle man"—but in truth he worked steadily and unsparingly. A plaque in Westminster Abbey in his honor runs through a long list of achievements and declares, correctly, that Young was "patient of unintermitted labour."

But even the most talented decipherers spend most of their time forlorn and frustrated, wandering lost in the dark and yet feeling certain that crucial clues lie hidden just *this* close. To live in that netherworld between hope and despair, trapped almost-there-but-nowhere-close, is thrilling but maddening. "Don't be discouraged about the Egyptian text," Champollion's brother wrote to him in 1804, after his first attempts on the Rosetta Stone had turned up nothing. If he could crack just one tiny part of the puzzle, the whole thing would open up. "A letter will lead you to a word, a word to a sentence, and a sentence to all the rest, and so everything is more or less contained in a single letter."

And so you can never pause to rest.

Obsessiveness is key. One of the most brilliant decipherers who ever lived, an Englishman named Michael Ventris, played the lead role in perhaps the most daunting linguistic triumph of them all. In the 1950s, without the help of anything like the Rosetta Stone, Ventris deciphered Linear B. This was the earliest known form of Greek, from a thousand years before the era of Socrates and Plato. If the Trojan War really did take place—archaeologists have never settled on an answer—Linear B might have recorded the language that Odysseus and Achilles spoke.

The first Linear B texts were discovered in Crete. This was the island home, at least in myth, of King Minos and the labyrinth with the man-devouring Minotaur at its center. For all connoisseurs of deciphering and codebreaking, the story of the labyrinth has, tucked inside it, one special bonus. According to the myth, Minos's daughter Ariadne gave Theseus a ball of string—a *clewe*, in Middle English—so that, after he had slain the Minotaur, he could follow the string and find his way back out of the labyrinth. Eventually the word *clewe* became *clue*, still retaining its original sense of a hint to unraveling a mystery. The usage is so deeply embedded in the language that to this day we talk about "following the thread" of a difficult explanation.

Ventris was a linguistic magician who was as adept as anyone has ever been at unraveling archaeological riddles. He was brilliant, and just as important, he was relentless. During World War II he served as a navigator for the Royal Air Force. When he flew back to base from bombing raids over Germany, one journalist wrote, "Ventris would set course and then, clearing a space on the navigator's table, happily set to work on his Linear B documents, while the aircraft groaned its way home, searchlights stretched up their probing fingers, and bursts of flak shook the bomber."

Oblivious to mere gunfire, Ventris viewed the job of navigator, one friend remarked, as "a desk job really, in the middle of the plane." The danger was more than offset by the lure of the mystery. Several years after the war's end, Ventris finally made his breakthrough. "About two o'clock in the morning the door burst open," a colleague recalled, "and Michael came pounding in and said, 'Do you want to be the second person in four thousand years to read this script?'"

In deciphering and codebreaking, even the tiniest steps forward come with great difficulty, no matter how glaringly obvious they might appear in hindsight. Historians hail the breakthrough of an English bishop named William Warburton, who wrote about hieroglyphs in 1744. Warburton's great coup was seeing that hieroglyphs were words, not disguises; their role was to *say* something. Hieroglyphs, Warburton proposed daringly, were "intended to preserve the memory of the actions and thoughts of people, not invented with the view of keeping them secret, as has been believed until now."

Even for geniuses, the going is frustratingly slow. Champollion tried deciphering an Egyptian papyrus, in 1808, and finally confessed to his brother that the symbols had thwarted him. "I have studied them, pondered for entire days, and I have understood nothing." In a lecture two years later, in 1810, he proudly proclaimed, "It is my conviction that a single hieroglyph, that is to say in isolation, has no value, but that they are arranged in groups which I can already distinguish with ease."

This was true and crucial, but think of how much labor it had taken for Champollion to advance this tiny distance from the starting line. It was as if, after thousands of hours spent poring over books and magazines written in English, you announced that a single letter—*B*, for instance—meant nothing on its own. But there were whole strings of letters you had come to recognize. You might have found *big*, perhaps, or *table*, or *Mobil*, though without the slightest idea what they might mean.

Stories of invention or discovery always get the balance wrong, because a true picture would linger on false starts and futile wandering, and not on the ever-so-rare breakthroughs. No reader could put up with so disheartening a tale. After the truth has finally been found, Einstein once remarked, "the happy achievement seems almost a matter of course, and any intelligent student can grasp it without too much trouble. But the years of anxious searching in the dark, with their intense longing, their alternations of confidence and exhaustion, and final emergence into light—only those who have experienced it can understand that."

Few people are tempted to spend their lives on so wearying a quest. And when you turn to deciphering and codebreaking riddles in particular, as opposed to scientific mysteries in general, the job requirements grow more stringent still. Now, in addition to brainpower and doggedness, you need two traits seldom found together.

What is essential, the historian Stephen Budiansky writes, are "an almost infinite tolerance for drudgery and repetitive detail" along with "the exact opposite" of those traits, a gift for making sudden and startling leaps of imagination. "The ideal cryptanalyst is Beethoven with the soul of an accountant; or vice versa."

Two of the best-known cryptographers, the husband-and-wife team of William and Elizebeth* Friedman, wrote an essay that highlighted a related point. (Together the two deciphered thousands of encrypted Nazi transmissions during World War II.) Deciphering was a mix of science and art, the Friedmans explained, but a decidedly odd mix. "In no other science are the rules and principles so little followed and so often broken; and in no other art is the part played by reasoning and logic so great."

As if it were not rare enough to combine a flair for science and a taste for art, codebreakers and decipherers need still another unusual trait. They have to be, in the words of Stephen Budiansky, almost paranoid. "Not 'paranoid' in the sense of having a persecution complex, but paranoid in the sense of believing that hidden in some almost irrelevant detail lay a grandiose truth; paranoid in the sense of believing that one could see what everyone else had failed to see."

Here, perhaps, was a point of similarity between Champollion and Young. Each man had a serene faith that he was one of nature's elect, privy to secrets that others could not see. Each had utter confidence in his own talent, coupled with a deep belief in the proverbial wisdom that "he travels fastest who travels alone."

According to Champollion family legend, lovingly retold through the years, a local healer told his mother when she was pregnant with Jean-François that she would give birth to a son "who would be a light of centuries to come." At age eleven, according to another family tale, Champollion met the savant Joseph Fourier, who showed him several hieroglyphic inscriptions. At that moment, Champollion would later claim, he vowed that someday he would become the first person to decipher hieroglyphs.

---

* The unusual spelling is correct. Elizebeth was the last of nine children, and perhaps her mother guessed that her daughter was destined to be different. Though never as famous as her husband, Elizebeth Friedman became one of the most important codebreakers in American history. Jason Fagone tells her story in his fascinating *The Woman Who Smashed Codes*.

Young, too, displayed from childhood on an unwavering insistence on going his own way. (His Quaker upbringing, he speculated, had instilled in him a "complete contempt for public opinion.") At about age six, Young recalled in an autobiographical essay, he was sent to a "miserable boarding school." From the start, he insisted on his independence: "Even at this age, I began to be my own teacher." The highest praise he could offer one of his actual teachers was that he "had the good sense to leave his pupils some little discretion in the employment of their time." Young was a colt who would not be broken.

He never gave in. In his scientific work, and not only there, he proclaimed himself "convinced of the advantage of making every observation with as little assistance as possible."

Even if they are not geniuses like Young and Champollion, decipherers and codebreakers tend to be outsiders and oddballs. Talent can pop up anywhere. Bletchley Park recruited not only scientists and linguists but also the best crossword puzzle solvers in Britain (they were told only that they might be able to help in "a matter of national importance").*

In the world of deciphering, a flair for problem-solving is the only admission ticket; academic credentials are beside the point. "In our fantasies," writes the classicist Mary Beard, "we can all become code-breakers."

We can all do it, at least, so long as we are both brilliant and relentlessly hardworking. That is the true story of all *Eureka!* breakthroughs, and not only in the special field of deciphering. Even for Isaac Newton, Young's great predecessor and perhaps the most powerful intellect in Western history, genius was not enough. Stamina and stubbornness played as large a role. *How did you come up with the theory of gravitation?* Newton was asked in his old age, and his reply was straightforward. "By thinking on it continually."

Newton never joked—one close acquaintance could recall only

---

* The Nazis, also, used crossword puzzles to identify would-be cryptographers. Those who tested best were assigned to special training. By way of incentive, instructors informed the new recruits that those in the bottom 90 percent of the class would be sent to the Russian front.

a single time when he had seen the great man laugh (someone had asked what use it was to study Euclid)—and he meant it when he said that he concentrated without letup. "His peculiar gift was the power of holding continuously in his mind a purely mental problem until he had seen straight through it," wrote John Maynard Keynes, who took time from his work in economics to dive deep into Newton's biography. "I fancy his pre-eminence is due to his muscles of intuition being the strongest and most enduring with which a man has ever been gifted."

For ordinary mortals, focusing without letup is nearly impossible, like clenching your fist and never relaxing your grip. "I believe," Keynes wrote, "that Newton could hold a problem in his mind for hours and days and weeks until it surrendered to him its secret."

That sort of relentless concentration, which might give all the appearance of daydreaming, is in truth hard work. In the course of a chess competition, according to the Stanford neurologist Robert Sapolsky, a grandmaster can burn six thousand to seven thousand calories a day. The thinker sitting in a chair and pushing tiny pieces of wood consumes as much energy as a marathoner in full stride.

Historians of deciphering all make a point of emphasizing the physical aspect of the challenge. A passage describing Georg Grotefend, a pioneer in the deciphering of ancient Persian, sounds the characteristic note. Grotefend, a friend recalled, "possessed an extraordinary memory and excellent health, which allowed him to study from the earliest morning until late at night, without stint or relaxation."

As in chess and math and music, talent—or, at least, fascination—tends to show up early. Champollion had been consumed with hieroglyphs since about age thirteen; Michael Ventris with Linear B since fourteen; David Stuart, the youngest person ever to receive a Macarthur "genius" grant, with Mayan glyphs since age eight.

Often those early gifts take the shape of an instinct for navigating new languages. Ventris was perhaps the clearest example. Throughout his lifetime he retained the young child's gift of picking up languages quickly and without study. "For a charmed few," writes Margalit Fox, in her history of the decipherment of Linear B, "for neurological reasons that are not well understood, the critical period seems to continue un-diminished through adulthood. They can inhale foreign languages at twenty or thirty as readily as they did at six, with minimal effort. Michael Ventris was beyond doubt such a person."

A colleague who worked closely with Ventris on Linear B recalled seeing him read newspaper stories in Swedish. *Where did you learn to do that?* It turned out that Ventris had spent a few weeks in Sweden on an architectural project. (Architecture was his vocation; deciphering was a hobby.) That was all it took. For the rest of his life Ventris corre-sponded with Swedish scholars in their own language.

Perhaps because deciphering is a "game" that requires scarcely any equipment—it is like basketball or running in that regard, and unlike sailing or polo—talent tends to cut across class lines.

Ventris came from a wealthy family.* Young was well-off, Cham-pollion distinctly not, and nor was Alice Kober, another hero of the Linear B story. For years scholars disregarded Georg Grotefend—he was the scholar of ancient Persian with the relentless focus—because he was a high school teacher and not a university professor.

George Smith, whose story is as romantic as anything in the history of archaeology, never even attended high school. Smith had been ap-prenticed, in 1854, to a printer in London. He was fourteen, and this was the end of his formal education. He spent all his spare time in the British Museum staring at clay tablets from Nineveh and Babylon.

To outsiders, those tablets are utterly inscrutable. Cuneiform is made up of straight lines and wedges arranged in tidy formation;

---

* Ventris was handsome and charming, and from the outside he looked like one of nature's favored few. But his mother committed suicide when he was seventeen, and he himself died at thirty-four when his car ran into a parked truck. The death was of-ficially ruled an accident, although two weeks before the crash Ventris had written a letter declaring that he had come to "deeply doubt the value of both my vaunted intel-ligence and to a large extent that of life itself." But some friends and colleagues insist that the wreck was not a suicide, and no one knows with certainty.

it looks like what you might get if a flock of birds with obsessive-compulsive disorder took a walk across wet clay.*

In time George Smith would teach the world to read those mysterious inscriptions, and he would discover a version of the Flood story that predated the one in the Bible.

The high moment of Smith's life came in 1872, in the British Museum, when he managed to translate several lines from an ancient tablet from Nineveh. What he found was part of the *Epic of Gilgamesh*, perhaps the first story ever written down.

"I am the first man to read that after two thousand years of oblivion," Smith exclaimed, and, according to one eyewitness, he suddenly "jumped up and rushed about the room in a great state of excitement, and, to the astonishment of those present, began to undress himself."†

---

* The appearance of some scripts hints at their earliest days. Cuneiform is made up of wedges, for instance, because those are the easiest shapes to press into wet clay with a stylus. The Sri Lankan alphabet, in contrast, is made up almost entirely of beautiful, rounded shapes. Ancient scribes in what was then Ceylon wrote on dried palm leaves, which had straight but delicate veins. Any inscriptions formed from straight lines would have cracked open along the veins.

† The historian Stephen Greenblatt warns, in *The Rise and Fall of Adam and Eve*, that the eyewitness tale may be an exaggeration. "The undressing that so shocked Smith's colleague may, as the literary historian David Damrosch has observed, have been only a loosened collar. This was, after all, Victorian England. But almost any level of excitement could have been justified by the discovery."

The promise of such *Eureka!* moments lures decipherers on through all the dismal and confused nights. "The thrill of your life," the code-breaker Elizebeth Friedman called it. "The skeletons of words leap out, and make you jump."

# CHAPTER SIXTEEN

# Ancient Wisdom

By 1819 Thomas Young held the answer to the hieroglyphic mystery in his hand. He had shown that hieroglyphs could stand for sounds, just as letters in our alphabet stand for sounds ("*A* is for *apple*"). He even compiled a table, with the tentative heading "Sounds?," that linked a handful of hieroglyphs with sounds. A drawing of a lion was the sound *l*, a zigzag was *n*, a semicircle was *t*.

Then, brilliant and ambitious though he was, Young proceeded to reject his own brainchild. He had two reasons. One was narrow and one broad. Both were mistakes that sent him careening in the wrong direction.

The narrow mistake came first. Though hieroglyphs *could* stand for sounds, Young decided, that happened in only the most special of special cases—when you had a cartouche with the name of a non-Egyptian ruler. Only then. In all ordinary circumstances—whenever hieroglyphs occurred outside a cartouche and whenever they referred to anything other than a foreign king—they had nothing to do with sounds.

It was cartouches that led Young astray. He saw that cartouches were rare, and he saw that hieroglyphs inside cartouches corresponded to sounds. Taking those two facts together, he leapt to a conclusion—the vast majority of hieroglyphs, the ones outside cartouches, did *not* correspond to sounds.

That was wrong, but Young's mistake was not a matter of careless reasoning. A skilled mathematician, he would never have blundered into an error of logic. Instead, faced with incomplete evidence, he'd made a well-informed guess.

But he guessed wrong. What misled him was how rare cartouches were. He thought they were special, which was correct. Anyone glancing at a page of hieroglyphs might have wondered why some hieroglyphs had an oval drawn around them. And indeed, a cartouche was a signal, just as Young said. The problem was that he misread the signal. Young thought that a cartouche meant *the hieroglyphs inside this oval represent sounds, not ideas*. It didn't. A cartouche really meant *the hieroglyphs inside this oval spell out a royal name*. Cartouches were rare because kings were rare, not because sounds were rare.

Young never stopped to think he might have made a mistake. And why would he have second-guessed himself? His decoding of the Ptolemy cartouche was, after all, the greatest coup to that point in the history of Egyptian deciphering.

Almost inevitably, that very triumph seduced Young into staying put when he might have moved ahead. He was like an explorer who came to a clearing in the woods, probed it inch by inch, and finally found a stash of gold buried underground.

But then, as in a fable, came the twist. Dazzled by his discovery, our unfortunate explorer devoted all his efforts ever after to digging near the same spot, in hope of finding further treasure, while a far greater treasure sat ignored just around the corner.

Young's second mistake, the broad one, was the crucial one. Getting cartouches wrong was a misstep, but it was a technical, puzzle-solving mistake. Young's broader mistake was conceptual and therefore far more sweeping and far more dangerous. The error was misunderstanding the nature of hieroglyphs in a fundamental way.

Young had been pushed in the wrong direction. He had, in fact, been pushed by the accumulated weight of twenty centuries of conventional wisdom, and he had, unknowingly, given in to the pressure. "We are all tattooed in our cradles with the beliefs of our tribe," Oliver Wendell Holmes once observed. "The record may seem superficial, but it is indelible."

For generations of European scholars, the impact of those tribal beliefs was to imbue hieroglyphs with a mystique that made it nearly impossible to see them as simply a writing system. The name most closely linked with this mistaken doctrine was Horapollo, an Egyptian priest who lived around 400 AD. It was Horapollo who coined the word *hieroglyph*, which is Greek for *sacred engraving*. The choice of the word *engraving*—rather than *writing*—is key. Horapollo's point was that hieroglyphs were drawings and *not* the letters of some curious script.

Horapollo's life is shrouded in mystery; nearly every biographical "fact" we have is a guess. But until the era of the Rosetta Stone, he was regarded as the greatest authority on hieroglyphs.

Horapollo's fame derives from a thick book he wrote called *Hieroglyphics*. The book itself is nearly as mysterious as its author. Scholars believe that Horapollo wrote it, in Egyptian, around 400 AD, which was long after hieroglyphs had fallen into disuse.

*Hieroglyphics* was not discovered until 1419, a thousand years after Horapollo's death, when an Italian monk happened on a Greek translation. Where the book had been in the meantime and how it had come to be translated in the first place, no one knows. But as soon as it was unearthed, the work was hailed as *the* key to hieroglyphs, and it retained that status for four centuries. Throughout that time, one modern historian tells us, Horapollo's every pronouncement on Egyptian lore was regarded with "sacred awe."

Horapollo wrote with force and firmness. Questions or counterarguments were never considered, let alone rebutted. Like so many others, Young fell under his spell. In the two-hundred-some chapters of his opus, Horapollo hammered home his central theme—hieroglyphs were emblems and allegories, and they conveyed symbolic messages.

"When [Egyptians] wish to symbolize a god, or something sublime," he wrote, ". . . they draw a hawk." Why a hawk in particular? Because "other birds, when they wish to fly, proceed on a slant, it being impossible for them to rise directly. Only the hawk flies straight upwards."

In comparison with most of Horapollo's ventures into natural history, that account was straightforward. He explained that a hieroglyph of a vulture meant *mother*, for example, because it was well-known that all vultures are female. A goose meant *son* because geese are especially devoted to their offspring. A hare meant *open*, because hares never shut their eyes.

Other hieroglyphs relied less on knowledge of the natural world and more on a kind of symbolic decoding of the sort that art critics might bring to bear on the strange images in paintings by Hieronymus Bosch. "To indicate a man who has never traveled they paint a man with a donkey's head," Horapollo wrote. "For he never knows or listens to accounts of what happens abroad." To represent something that was impossible, "they draw men walking on water . . . or they draw a headless man walking about."

A typical hieroglyph had multiple meanings, according to Horapollo, few of them obvious. Often they spanned a broad range. A vulture meant not only *mother*, for instance, but also *vision* ("because it sees more keenly than all other creatures"), and *boundary* ("because, when a battle is to be fought, it points out the spot on which it will take place"), and *foreknowledge* ("because it looks towards that army which is about to have the greater number killed"), and *compassion* ("because, if it should be without food to give its young, it opens its own thigh and suffers its offspring to partake of the blood").

All these interpretations sound foolish, and most of them were. But there is one crucial catch. Some of Horapollo's outlandish explanations turned out to be correct. A vulture really did mean *mother*, for instance, though the true reason had nothing to do with Horapollo's account. A goose did mean *son* (or, at least, it *almost* did; actually it was *duck* that meant *son*), and a hare did mean *open*. But Horapollo's stories about dutiful parents and open eyes were completely beside the point.

Here were giant clues, if only someone could have seen them. Vultures *did* have something to do with mothers. But what?

This was different from the usual way that treasure was hidden. In Egypt wonders lay half-hidden by sand, like the Sphinx, or submerged by dirt and debris, like King Tut's tomb. Horapollo's insights—the true ones—were gems that sat in the open. The problem was that the gems sat amid heaps of costume-jewelry junk.

That led to giant trouble, in fact to two different kinds of trouble.

In the first place, scholars missed the gems and grabbed the gewgaws. They took all Horapollo's "translations" as true and exciting and then added dubious translations of their own. With serene confidence that hieroglyphs were symbols, just as Horapollo had taught, European thinkers happily marched off in the wrong direction. Centuries would pass before it dawned on them that they were lost.

But when disillusion finally set in, in the 1700s, scholars overreacted. This time they looked at the glittering heaps of gems, cringed at the tacky baubles, and contemptuously swept the whole pile aside. "Poor old Horapollo got discredited," the Egyptologist John Ray observes, "so the truth he was telling got thrown out with the mystical verbiage that he dressed it in."

Apparently Horapollo had learned about hieroglyphs from Egyptian priests or scholars who genuinely knew how the script worked. No one could have come up with the true observation that a vulture means *mother* without a hint. But then he went wrong—the great majority of his "translations" were utterly off base—and we can only guess why. Perhaps he misunderstood what he'd been told or mixed together solid information with tales from misinformed writers. Or perhaps he was a prisoner of his fixed beliefs and veered off course because he believed so deeply that hieroglyphs were symbols with hidden meanings.

Horapollo's message carried such clout in the first place because it echoed the accounts of other eminent figures. A Greek historian named Diodorus Siculus had visited Egypt in the first century BC and reported that Egyptian writing was different from all others; it was not based on letters or syllables but on pictures that carried metaphoric meaning. A crocodile stood for *evil*, for instance, and an eye for *justice*.

In around 120 AD Plutarch, a Greek historian far more prominent than Diodorus, had explained that a hieroglyph of a fish symbolized *hatred* because the sea, which teems with fish, devours the Nile, which provides life. A hippopotamus stood for *violence and immorality* because male hippos kill their fathers and mate with their mothers. These interpretations sound silly, but we still decode drawings in much the same way. A bald eagle on a poster stands for *bravery and patriotism* because eagles are swift and fierce and native to the United States. A skull and crossbones means *poison.*

Another much admired ancient writer, Clement of Alexandria, put a slightly different spin on what he called "the symbolic and occult teachings" of the Egyptians. Clement was a Greek-born theologian who taught in Egypt in around 200 AD. Just as proverbs conveyed profound truths in simple words, he wrote, hieroglyphs captured deep meanings in simple pictures. Only a fool would take proverbs at face value, as if they were how-to-do-it tips. *Do not poke a fire* meant *Do not provoke an angry man,* Clement explained. *Don't put food into a slop pail* meant *Don't waste clever arguments on a simpleton.*

In just the same way, Clement went on, hieroglyphs might look like pictures of everyday sights, but the true significance of these birds and plants and bowls was far grander and more mysterious. The deep meanings were hidden, it was true, but that was the point. The seeker who found his way to hard-earned truths would be well repaid. "All things that shine through a veil," Clement wrote, "show the truth grander and more imposing."

Of all those who drew deep, symbolic meanings from hieroglyphs, the most venturesome and the most prominent was a Jesuit priest named Athanasius Kircher, who rose to fame in the mid-1600s. Born in Germany, Kircher lived most of his life in Rome. There he churned out dozens of books and millions of words. (His magnum opus on Egypt ran to three volumes and two thousand pages.)

Kircher was a scholar of astonishing, almost ludicrous, range.* He was a mathematician, a theologian, an authority on Greek and Latin and Chinese and Hebrew and dragons and volcanoes and music and fossils and pineapples (they had the power to dissolve iron) and Noah's ark. Almost forgotten today, Kircher enjoyed international fame in his own time.

He came to the study of hieroglyphs by accident, when he chanced

---

* Kircher, outdoing Gottfried Leibniz and Thomas Young, is the subject of *two* biographies with man-who-knew-it-all titles. One is *The Man Who Knew Everything: The Strange Life of Athanasius Kircher,* the other *Athanasius Kircher: The Last Man Who Knew Everything.*

on a book with descriptions of Egyptian obelisks that had been brought to Rome as trophies of war fifteen centuries before. Kircher set out at once to decipher these "chronicles of ancient Egyptian Wisdom, inscribed from time immemorial."

The quest consumed decades, but Kircher emerged triumphant, at least in his own mind. "All the secrets of the Hieroglyphic Art, its rules and methods and principles, are," he wrote, "by the Influence and Grace of the Divine Spirit fully comprehended by me."

His "translations" were, in fact, mere guesswork and wildly off target. Kircher had read so widely over the course of his lifetime that every hieroglyph called up countless associations in his mind—*here was an image linked with the god Osiris and there an allusion to the goddess Isis*—but none of this had any connection with reality.

Egyptologists now know, for instance, that a string of hieroglyphs on one ancient obelisk spelled out the name and the titles of a pharaoh, Apries, who reigned around 600 BC. Just that and nothing more. But in those few hieroglyphs, Kircher saw a message about "virtues and gifts in the sidereal world" and "the fruitfulness of the Osirian bowl" and "power hidden in its two-faced self" and much else besides.

This was fantasy, although no one could have proved it until Young and Champollion came along a century and a half later. Kircher had unbounded faith in his own brilliance—he compared his achievement in deciphering hieroglyphs to the discovery of America or the invention of the printing press, and he began one of his books with an inscription, "Nothing is more beautiful than to know all." In modern times his highfalutin mistakes have made him a tempting target for mockery. Generations of scholars have yielded to temptation.

That's not quite fair. Misguided though he was, Kircher was indisputably learned, and his Egyptian writings did include some valuable contributions along with the fantasies. Kircher declared flat-out, for instance, that Coptic was "formerly the Pharaonic language." This was a controversial claim at the time, but it turned out to be absolutely correct. He went further. Kircher compiled a Coptic dictionary and wrote the first essay to lay out the basics of Coptic grammar. His successors, including Champollion, pored over those works.

Even in Kircher's writings on hieroglyphs, as one respectful but perplexed modern historian reports, there were "strange glimpses of genius" amid the seas of "nonsense." It was Kircher, notably, who was the first to correctly explain that a specific hieroglyph stood for a particular sound (it happened to be a drawing of a horizontal zigzag, like the letter *V* written upside down several times, and it was pronounced *n*).

Kircher gave only this single example, and he didn't follow it up (because he was interested in hieroglyphs' deep meanings and not in what he took to be their superficial sense). Still, in highlighting the link between pictures and sounds, he was the first to grasp the central truth of the whole hieroglyphic riddle.

Kircher's problem was that he had such faith in Horapollo's doctrine—*hieroglyphs are ideas, not letters or words*—that he could not think to question it, let alone consider an alternative. Had he been of a more practical mind, he might have argued that there were any number of everyday reasons that hieroglyphs were so difficult to decipher. Egyptians spoke a language that's dead to us, he might have noted, and they devised a script that looks odd and elaborate, and held beliefs we can only guess at, and lived in a world completely foreign to us.

He didn't. His notion (and the notion of classical and Renaissance writers generally) was that hieroglyphs had been made difficult on purpose. Egyptian scribes had invented them with the express goal, in one modern historian's summary, of hiding their meaning behind "veils of allegory and enigma."

This was a remarkable claim. *Many* symbols are difficult for outsiders to decipher. A musical score or a page torn from a calculus book might be hard to understand. But musical and mathematical symbols have clear meanings—clear, at least, to experts in those fields. They are obscure by necessity. They are languages, of a sort, and difficult for the same reasons that foreign languages are difficult.

Hieroglyphs were different. Like ciphers in wartime, the experts insisted, hieroglyphs were *designed* to be difficult. That belief, all but universal until the 1800s, sent would-be decipherers in the wrong direction. Rather than burrow into the ground in search of mundane meanings behind the cryptic symbols, they sailed aloft into ever more far-fetched realms of hot air and learned silliness.

With hindsight, it seems bewildering that deep thinkers insisted even into the Age of Science that hieroglyphs concealed mystic truths behind elaborate masks. The trouble began with misplaced faith. Plutarch and Horapollo and the others were names to reckon with, and the trappings of antiquity gave added weight to their pronouncements. Though they had lived long after the days of the pharaohs, they were still a thousand years closer to their Egyptian sources than the European scholars who echoed their words. Renaissance writers deferred to them much as theologians of their era deferred to the founders of the church.

Nonetheless, many present-day scholars find themselves shaking their heads in dismay when they try to explain the persistence of the symbol-decoding approach. "The tenacity with which the classical authors stuck to their erroneous interpretations, and, as it were, deliberately disregarded all evidence which could conflict with their preconceived allegorical ideas," the historian Erik Iversen scolds, "is indeed astonishing."

But perhaps it is not so astonishing. The impulse to find mystical meanings in mysterious symbols runs deep. We might wonder if modern scholars would do better than their counterparts of a few centuries ago, if they found themselves confronted with a similarly mysterious pictorial script. As it turns out, we don't have to wonder. We don't have to wonder, because we know.

It happened in the 1950s, when scholars were still wrestling futilely with Mayan glyphs. That New World picture-writing was finally deciphered in the 1970s, in one of the great linguistic and archaeological triumphs of modern times. The story is told thrillingly (by one of the participants) in Michael Coe's *Breaking the Maya Code*.

The story has uncanny echoes of the Egyptian tale, although there was no Mayan counterpart of the Rosetta Stone. But there was a counterpart of Athanasius Kircher, in the person of Sir Eric Thompson, *the* towering figure in the early years of Mayan scholarship. In 1950, after decades spent poring over Mayan hieroglyphs, he delivered an imperious verdict on how they should be interpreted.

Mayan glyphs, from Palenque, Mexico

At that point neither he nor anyone else could read the mysterious symbols. Still, Thompson declared, certain facts had been established beyond a reasonable doubt. Glyphs did not stand for ordinary things like sounds or syllables, despite what some scholars continued to insist; glyphs were symbols that represented ideas. The only question was, *which ideas?* "Without a full understanding of the text one cannot, for instance, tell whether the presence of a glyph of a dog refers to that animal's role as bringer of fire to mankind or to his duty of leading the dead to the underworld," Thompson wrote. "That such mystical meanings are imbedded in the glyphs is beyond doubt, but as yet we can only guess as to the association the Maya author had in mind. Clearly, our duty is to seek more of those mythological allusions."

Dutifully following the mythological path would crack the deciphering mystery. That was for starters. More important, Thompson continued, the symbol-decoding approach "leads us, key in hand, to the threshold of the inner keep of the Maya soul, and bids us enter."

It led, instead, to heartache and frustration. In the New World as in Egypt, the mysterious glyphs turned out not to be mystical symbols at all. Instead, they were symbols with the straightforward role of capturing the sounds of a language. The Mayan way of writing looked exotic, but it proved to be a writing system that worked more or less like any other.

The examples of Horapollo and Kircher might have served as red flags. They didn't. The impulse to find deep, symbolic meanings proved too strong.

# CHAPTER SEVENTEEN

# "A Cipher and a Secret Writing"

As the centuries passed, the awe surrounding hieroglyphs grew. But through the ages that awe changed form. Vague reverence—*hieroglyphs speak of deep and arcane truths*—shifted to hard-edged belief—*hieroglyphs express exact scientific insights*. Here was irony on a colossal scale. Ancient Egypt was a mighty culture built almost entirely on the most basic technology imaginable—muscle and sweat and little else, and nearly all of that muscle supplied by humans rather than oxen or horses or other animals. Science scarcely came into the picture at all.

Egyptian mathematics was rudimentary, Egyptian medicine a grab bag of folklore and false belief. (When preparing mummies, Egyptian embalmers venerated the heart but threw brains into the trash as worthless. The heart was special, they believed, because it was the seat of consciousness, the organ that we think with.) Ancient Egypt had no notion of scientific laws and viewed the world as ruled by witchcraft and magic.

And yet, in the great days of the Age of Science, around 1700, Europe looked to Egypt as the home and birthplace of scientific innovation. So here was still another reason that Renaissance decipherers went wrong. They presumed that everything that had to do with ancient Egypt was deep and difficult. Certainly this was true of hieroglyphs, which were among the most baffling mysteries of that baffling land.

"The Egyptians were clearly not as other men," writes the Egyptologist John Ray, summing up the European view. "Their thoughts were never mundane, and the many signs in the writing which they left behind them could never be like the workaday alphabets of Greek or Latin, Hebrew or Arabic."

These were the views of the deepest, boldest thinkers the world has ever known, not the fringe views of mad eccentrics or tenured mediocrities. Isaac Newton, who lived more than a thousand years after Horapollo, fervently believed that ancient Egyptians had grasped all the secrets of nature's cosmic choreography. The task of modern thinkers, Newton and his peers believed, was not to break new ground but to recover those ancient insights.

Newton was perhaps the most brilliant scientist who ever lived and certainly among the fiercest in claiming priority for his breakthroughs. Even so, he insisted that the ancient Egyptians had made all his most important discoveries thousands of years before him. They had known the law of gravitation and all the other secrets of the cosmos; the point of hieroglyphs was to hide that knowledge from the unworthy. "The Egyptians," Newton wrote, "concealed mysteries that were above the capacity of the common herd under the veil of religious rites and hieroglyphic symbols."

Young and Champollion came along a century after Newton, and they did not share his misplaced faith in Egyptian science. Like other progressive French thinkers of his day, Champollion disdained religion and the church, whether in Egypt or in France. Egyptian priests were not scientists, as Newton had believed, but spokesmen for backwardness. Young was even more contemptuous. Egyptian religion was mumbo-jumbo. But, even so, both men swam in the same intellectual sea as Newton and the other advocates of ancient wisdom. They all took for granted that every hieroglyph stood for an idea. Their only disagreement was that Young and Champollion believed those ideas were misguided, and Newton thought they were beacons of truth.

The view that thinkers who lived thousands of years ago knew more than we do, even about scientific matters, upends everything that we believe today. But in the 1600s and 1700s, it was common sense. The doctrine was called "the wisdom of the ancients." In ancient days thinkers had been privy to nature's secrets, scholars proclaimed, but then corrupt and sinning humankind had fumbled away those divine gifts. As the world decayed intellectually and morally, countless truths vanished. "The past was always better than the present," in the summary of the historian Frances Yates, and "the earliest thinkers walked more closely with the gods than the busy rationalists, their successors."

Some ancient cultures, and Egypt first of all, had embodied that lost learning. "Egypt was the original home of all knowledge," Yates writes. "The great Greek philosophers had visited it and conversed with Egyptian priests," and there they had imbibed "the religious magic which they were thought to perform in the subterranean chambers of their temples."

So when scientists like Newton made discoveries, they did not think they had found anything new. (They had all the more respect for ancient Egypt because, in that pre-Darwinian era, nearly everyone believed that the world was six thousand years old. Egypt had thrived not merely long ago, but very nearly at the beginning of time itself.) The vocabulary we still use today reflects their belief in a long-ago golden age. "To 'dis-cover' was to pull away the covering cloth, disclosing what may have been hidden, overlooked, or lost, but that was in any case already there," explains the historian Darrin McMahon.

The same was true of inventions. "To 'invent,'" writes McMahon, "was to access that *inventory* of knowledge long ago assembled and put in place." There were no new ideas; there was only unveiling.

For us today, the words *new* and *improved* seem to belong together. But for our predecessors, *new* had no such good associations. *New* meant "untested" and "dubious"; in contrast, *old* conjured up "time-honored" and "reliable." The writer John Aubrey, who lived in the 1600s, thought he could pinpoint the shift. "Until about the year 1649," he wrote, "it was held a strange presumption for a man to attempt an innovation in learning; and not to be good manners to be more knowing than his neighbours and forefathers."

And it was Egypt, the birthplace of civilization, that inspired the most elaborate fantasies about learned forefathers and lost knowledge and buried secrets. Partly this was because distance breeds mystery, and Egypt was about as far away as it was possible to get, whether you measured in years or in miles. But the more important reason that Egypt spurred thoughts of secrets and secret knowledge was that it was almost impossible to come to terms with the grandeur of Egypt at its height.

The result was that every traveler's dazzled descriptions served to reinforce the message that Egypt, in general, was a wondrous riddle, and that hieroglyphs, in particular, should be approached with deference and wonder and a mind alert to hidden meanings.

We should go easy on the scholars and decipherers who lost their bearings. To this day Egypt's antiquities have the power to stun even the jaded. No one can see the famous sights without marveling at their sheer implausibility.

For starters, the scale is disorienting. The Great Pyramid was the tallest structure in the world until the Middle Ages, and it is vast as well as tall. (St. Peter's Basilica, in Rome, could nestle comfortably inside the Great Pyramid, like a cake in a cardboard box. St. Paul's, in London, would rattle around.)

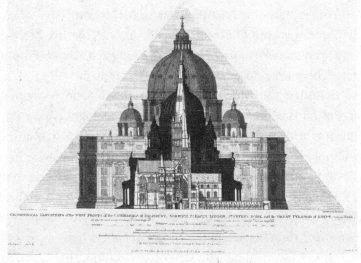

This etching, made in 1831 and drawn to scale,
shows the Great Pyramid and, inside it, St. Peter's Basilica,
St. Paul's, and two smaller cathedrals.

The pyramids were brutal boasts, in one historian's words "the grandest symbols of authoritarian rule ever built," but they were not simply monuments to unchecked power. They were machines whose purpose was to transport the pharaohs to the afterlife. The machinery was astonishingly inefficient—the shriveled mummy at the core of the Great Pyramid weighed less than fifty pounds, and the man-made mountain that encased him weighed five million pounds. But who would quibble over numbers when the prize was immortality?

Egypt's grand sights could inspire as well as intimidate. When Napoleon's soldiers first gazed at the temples of Karnak, in modern-day Luxor, "the whole army, suddenly and with one accord, stood in amazement at the sight of its scattered ruins," according to the savant Denon, "and clapped their hands with delight."

The ruins that left the French army slack-jawed still awe visitors today. The temple complex at Karnak is the biggest in the world; the tallest of its elegant stone columns rises 70 feet in the air, and there is a forest of them, 134 in all. Each is immense. If half a dozen adults took hold of one another's hands, they could not encircle a single column. ("I shall never forget my first impression of the temple at Karnak," Flaubert wrote in 1850. "It looked like a house where giants live, a place where they used to serve up men roasted whole, à la brochette, on gold plates, like larks.")

The construction of those columns, like that of the pyramids, testifies to what an endless supply of labor could accomplish. Each column was built in sections, one thick slab at a time. First a short, squat cylinder of stone was set in place. Then a ramp of sand and dirt was built, a new slab was set atop the old, the ramp was raised (by adding more sand and dirt), and the process was repeated.

Over and over and over again, until finally the last cylindrical slabs were set atop the towering stone columns and roof beams were laid across them. At this point the ramps reached seventy feet in the air (and there were dozens and dozens of them), and the columns filled an immense hall. Then came the next order. *Remove the sand!*

A temple at Karnak. Note the tiny humans at the center of the picture.

So it makes sense that Egypt was viewed with astonishment from the days of Greece and Rome through the Middle Ages and the Renaissance. Then, as we have noted, a curious thing happened. In the Age of Science, an era that might have been expected to scorn a culture based on dogma and reverence for authority, Egypt instead soared to new levels of prestige.

Crucially for our story, it was hieroglyphs above all else that intrigued the great thinkers of the Scientific Revolution. That fascination stemmed from their belief that *they* lived surrounded by hieroglyphs. Newton and his contemporaries took for granted that the world was a cosmic code, a riddle designed by God. Their mission, in the words of one prominent writer of the day, was to decipher that "strange Cryptography."

God had fashioned each object in the world with his own hand, these scientific thinkers believed, and each object contained some secret essence hidden from the ordinary run of mortals but visible to those who had learned to read God's mind. A French diplomat put it succinctly. "All nature is merely a cipher and a secret writing."

Scientists flipped that message around, too. When they unearthed one of nature's secrets, they disguised *their own* discovery in code. (This let them stamp their name on their findings, in case of priority disputes, and it kept others from making use of insights they had not earned.) As a result, no one saw anything odd in the notion that obscure messages concealed hidden meanings.*

Early in the year 1610, for instance, Galileo sent a note to his fellow astronomer Johannes Kepler. Galileo had built a telescope and found, to his astonishment, infinite depths and unsuspected wonders in the night sky. "The mother of love emulates the figures of Cynthia," he wrote. By "the mother of love," it turned out, Galileo meant the planet Venus. "Cynthia" was a name associated in mythology with the moon.

The cryptic language concealed a bold claim. Venus had phases like the moon, Galileo was saying, which meant that Venus orbited the sun. That was big. If Galileo was right, the church was wrong; the sun was the center of the universe, and the Earth was just a nondescript dot in the cosmos.

To early scientists, the implication seemed plain. Nearly every mystery in the world called for a kind of deciphering. That was true of nature's hieroglyphs, and it was all the more true of Egypt's hieroglyphs. The riddles posed by the sun and the moon were, in a sense, hieroglyphs at second hand. Egypt's hieroglyphs were the thing itself.

As the decades passed, the presumption that Egyptian hieroglyphs concealed secrets grew ever stronger. A much admired Scottish academic named Hugh Blair, a friend of David Hume and Adam Smith, explained this thinking in 1783, a century and more after the era of Galileo and Newton.

Hieroglyphs, wrote Blair, were a higher, more refined form of painting. Ordinary paintings depicted everyday objects, whereas "hieroglyphics painted invisible objects" using "analogies taken from the external world." An eye, for instance, meant *knowledge*, and a circle, because it has neither beginning nor end, stood for *eternity*.

---

* This sort of intellectual sleight of hand, where we take our own tastes and assign them to nature, has a long history. "God does not play dice with the universe," Einstein declared, because *he* had no use for dice and randomness. Montesquieu pointed out this impulse centuries ago. "If triangles had a god," he wrote, "he would have three sides."

At the time of the discovery of the Rosetta Stone only a few years later, in 1799, such were the blinders that nearly all scholars wore. When Young and Champollion came along, they wore them, too, and their first great challenge was to realize the need to tear them off.

## CHAPTER EIGHTEEN

# The Exile

Thomas Young's deciphering of the hieroglyphs that spelled *Ptolemy* was a great advance, but it stood alone. It might have been a breakthrough, it might have been a fluke. And Champollion, by all accounts, had not even made it that far. If Young and Champollion were to move ahead, they needed a *method* of reading hieroglyphs that could be employed in case after case. They needed new names, new cartouches—in short, new test materials. Where would they find them?

And then, just when they were flailing about, the next piece of the puzzle *did* turn up, and it *did* prove crucial. The story of how that came to be could scarcely be stranger, or sadder.

In England, in the early 1800s, no one was as handsome, as dashing, as charming as William Bankes. His family was rich beyond measure—Bankes's father had inherited an estate that sprawled across sixty thousand acres, an area four times the size of Manhattan—and Bankes took advantage of his wealth to become one of the great travelers of his era.

Life in England was "very dull, very meddling, very silly and very false," he told his friend Lord Byron, especially in comparison with the "free and vagrant life" of a traveler. When Bankes was between ventures abroad, no dinner party in London was complete without him. One delighted hostess reported that she had "laughed for two hours" as Bankes spun tales about his travels.

But Bankes was far more than an ideal dinner guest. From his twenties on, he was a serious and intrepid traveler. (He had come into his fortune unexpectedly, at twenty, when his older brother died in a shipwreck. William, the second son, suddenly had unlimited opportunity to indulge his wanderlust.) He became the first European to make drawings of the "lost" city of Petra, in Jordan,* and he ventured across Egypt making dangerous excursions into tombs and temples that the Western world had forgotten or barely known.

Bankes could not read the hieroglyphs he encountered—in 1815, when he first traveled in Egypt, no one could—but he spent hours meticulously recording them in his notebooks. Bankes was no dilettante, despite his wealth, and he was as careful as he was curious. His drawings, in particular, emphasized floor plans and careful measurements rather than grand vistas and moonlit melodrama.

Temples and ruins intrigued Bankes, but so did street scenes of every sort. Almost nothing was too mundane to investigate. (Byron called his chum "the father of all mischiefs.") When a local man presented him with a batch of live locusts, Bankes asked what they were for. Lunch, it turned out. Bankes found them crispy and delicious when fried in butter, "not wholly unlike a shrimp."

A dash of risk improved any excursion. At Luxor, in 1815, Bankes and a group of companions met a snake charmer who claimed he had mixed a magic powder that rendered snakebites harmless. Bankes volunteered to give it a try. The conjuror anointed Bankes with a chalky white powder, recited an incantation, and draped him with snakes. Their bites drew blood, but Bankes reported cheerily that he felt perfectly fine. Most likely, he decided later, the snakes had been drained of their venom ahead of time.

On several occasions Bankes's curiosity paid off in important ways. In 1818, he found an inscription on a temple wall in the city of Abydos, near Luxor. Cartouche after cartouche—seventy-six in all—stretched into the distance in long rows. Bankes guessed, correctly, that he had discovered a chronological list of pharaohs. (Young had provided the crucial hint, in a letter imploring Bankes to copy as many hieroglyphs

---

* A few decades after Bankes's visit, in 1845, the poet John Burgon would famously describe Petra as "a rose-red city half as old as time." Burgon was an English clergyman who meant his description literally; like many of his peers in that pre-Darwinian era, Burgon believed that God had created the world six thousand years before.

as he could and to look especially for the names of kings, which could be recognized "universally by an oval ring which surrounds them.") He set immediately to work making a copy of this vital list of names.[*]

In the same year, 1818, Bankes made another major discovery. It, too, involved cartouches, but this time only two of them. In a temple on the island of Philae, near modern-day Aswan, Bankes found an immense obelisk that had toppled to the ground. (The temple, so beautiful that early explorers dubbed it "the Pearl of the Nile," would have drowned under Lake Nasser when the Aswan High Dam was built. It was moved, stone by stone, to a nearby island in the 1960s. Today it enthralls visitors who wander through its sixty-foot-tall entrance gates and into its vast, colonnaded courtyards.)

The obelisk that drew Bankes's eye in 1818 was a single, massive piece of pink granite. Adorned with hieroglyphs, it measured twenty-two feet long and weighed six tons. Even so, Bankes immediately thought of transporting it home and installing it on the grounds of his country house, Kingston Lacy.

The obelisk had once stood on a granite pedestal, which at some point had been lost. Bankes managed to find it, not far from the obelisk but submerged in mud. He would not know until years later that his finds would point the way to the heart of Egypt's labyrinth.

Retrieving the obelisk and moving it home took three years and involved a series of fiascos that might have been orchestrated by Laurel and Hardy. Bankes's crew chief was an ex–circus strongman turned archaeologist named Giovanni Belzoni. He ordered his men to build a pier that extended far into the Nile. The plan was to set the obelisk on top of some scavenged sticks and poles that would serve as rollers, drag it onto the pier (which the men had built by piling up stones ran-

---

[*] Bankes left the inscriptions in place. A decade later the French consul general cut the writing off the wall and brought it to France. The British Museum purchased the King-List, as it is now called, in 1837. It remains in the museum to this day.

sacked from a temple), and then wrestle it onto the boat. "All hands were at work," one eyewitness recalled, "and five minutes more would have sufficed to set it afloat."

But the makeshift jetty collapsed under the weight of the obelisk. "Alas!" recalled Belzoni, "the pier, with the obelisk, and some of the men, took a slow movement, and majestically descended into the river."

Bankes took it fairly well, managing to keep quiet, if not calm. Belzoni was not merely quiet but nearly comatose. "For some minutes, I must confess," he wrote later, "I remained as stiff as a post."

A tiny bit of the obelisk poked up above the water's surface. For the most part, though, the only signs of its resting place were the eddies swirling around it in the chest-deep water near the river's edge.

Belzoni was larger than life, in every sense, and we will meet him again. Now he had a problem on his hands. First, he ordered a team of laborers into the river to heap stones near the obelisk. The idea was to wedge levers under the obelisk, using the stones as a pivot point; then the obelisk could be lifted up, seesaw-fashion, by pulling down on the levers' high end.

The men assigned to the levers found they could not budge them. Belzoni issued a new order: Quit pulling and climb to the end of the levers instead. Then balance out there, so that your weight forces the levers down.*

Other workmen grabbed ropes, looped them around the sunken obelisk, and wrapped the free ends around date trees on the riverbank. They yanked the ropes with all their might, trying desperately to coax the obelisk back to shore. As the obelisk lurched its way along, still other workers raced into the river to shove more stones under it and steady it in its new position.

Eventually they managed to tumble the obelisk back onto land. Belzoni fashioned a makeshift gangplank out of palm trees and ordered his men to drag the stone onto the boat. This time it worked.

---

* Almost frantic with frustration, Belzoni lambasted his laborers, whose "utmost sagacity reaches only to pulling a rope or sitting on the extremity of a lever as a counterpoise."

So long as the water was calm, the boat managed to wallow its way along under its heavy load. But, then, a faint rumble that quickly grew to a thunderous roar! These were the famed Nile cataracts. Just ahead was a gauntlet stretching some three hundred yards. Lined with boulders, churning with waves and whirlpools, the rapids terrified both crew and captain. (Most of the boulders that once clogged the Nile, and the rapids they formed, have since drowned under Lake Nasser.)

"If the boat touched the stones in the smallest degree," Belzoni wrote later, "with such a weight on board, and in such a rapid stream, it could not escape being dashed to pieces."

The strongman did his best to prepare his clumsy, overburdened boat, but his precautions did not inspire confidence. A cable with plenty of slack ran from the boat and around a tree on shore, where men stood at the ready in the hope that they could pull like mad and avert a crash. Naked men perched atop rocks on both sides of the river, clutching ropes tied to the boat's gunwales, so that they could try to tug the boat this way or that. A crew of five stood ready at the oars.

All was chaos, one of Bankes's companions recalled, "the great boat wheeling and swinging round and half filling with water while naked figures were crowding upon all the rocks or wading or swimming between them, some shouting and some pulling at the guide ropes, and the boat-owner throwing himself on the ground, scattering dust upon his head, and hiding his face."

But everyone survived, and several years and several boats and ships later, Bankes's obelisk arrived safely in England. (The pedestal, which had proved so troublesome that at one point it had been abandoned on a Nile sandbank, also eventually reached England.)

The obelisk still stands proudly on the grounds of Kingston Lacy, although two centuries in rainy England have done more damage to its hieroglyphs than did two millennia in sun-baked Egypt. Bankes carefully sited it for maximum effect, with the help of his friend the Duke of Wellington. (When it came to the overall look of his house and grounds, Bankes once told Wellington, his aim was to "combine much comfort with a sufficiency of splendour.")

Bankes thought that perhaps his obelisk would look even more striking with additional adornment. He drew two versions here, one topped with a fleur-de-lis, but decided to let the idea drop.

When the obelisk's base finally reached England, Bankes had it carefully cleaned. Twenty lines of Greek, faintly inscribed, took shape. As it turned out, obelisk and base were *not* another Rosetta Stone, because their messages did not match. But this Greek-Egyptian pairing proved crucial even so.

William Bankes, and then Thomas Young, and finally Jean-François Champollion would pore over these inscriptions. Bankes had first crack. He began with the Greek on the base, where the text made reference to a king and queen, Ptolemy VIII and Cleopatra III. (This was not the Ptolemy of the Rosetta Stone nor the Cleopatra of Roman times. With royal names, as with stone blocks, Egypt went in for intensive recycling.) Two royal names, then, written in Greek.

Then Bankes turned his attention to the obelisk. It was inscribed exclusively with hieroglyphs, not Greek. Among the mysterious symbols, Bankes spotted two cartouches. Precisely two. Better still, the hieroglyphs in one of those cartouches matched the hieroglyphs in the Rosetta Stone's cartouches. That made perfect sense, if both cartouches spelled the same name, *Ptolemy*.

That left Bankes contemplating the second cartouche. He had prints made showing all his inscriptions, both Greek and Egyptian. In the margin next to the second cartouche, he jotted down a single word in pencil: *Cleopatra*.

If that guess was right, this was big. Bankes hadn't *read* the name. He'd just taken a new name and a new cartouche and guessed that they belonged together.

But Young and Champollion could presumably go further. *Cleopatra* was not just another name; it was a foreign name, which meant that the hieroglyphs that spelled it out should correspond to the sounds that made up the name. Better still, several of the letters in *Cleopatra* also turned up in *Ptolemy*. And that meant that, at last, there was a way to check if the *Ptolemy* cartouche on the Rosetta Stone really did say *Ptolemy*.

Bankes sent copies of the inscriptions to a large number of scholars, including Thomas Young and Vivant Denon, the French artist who had been one of the most prominent savants. The inscriptions found their way from Denon to Champollion, with momentous consequences.

In 1821, the year Bankes shared his inscriptions, all was right in his cozy world. With prominent friends, an imposing home, and a thick wallet, he seemed a man profoundly to be envied. Then his life fell apart.

Bankes's downfall took place well after his days in Egypt, but his contribution to the deciphering saga was so essential—and his story so poignant—that we should take a moment to tell his tale. The troubles began in 1833. Bankes was forty-seven years old and a member of Parliament. He was arrested for "attempting to commit an unnatural offence" with a soldier in a public toilet near Westminster Abbey. Police hauled the two men away. An angry, howling crowd of two thousand people surrounded the police station, shouting abuse at the sinners inside.

For homosexual men, these early decades of the 1800s were terrible times. A conviction for "sodomy," as it was called, meant the pillory and then death by hanging. This was far from a paper threat. In England in the year 1806—when Bankes was a twenty-year-old student at Cambridge—"there were," the present-day historian A. D. Harvey tells us, "more executions for sodomy than for murder." Between 1800 and 1835 England executed more than fifty men for sodomy.

England would finally change the law in 1861, when the penalty for sodomy was reduced from death to life in prison.* (In practice, the typical sentence was ten years, and the last hanging for sodomy took place in 1835.) The death penalty for sodomy remained on the books after it had been abolished for piracy, slave trading, and rape.

Europe, in the meantime, was far less hostile to gay men. No laws called for punishing homosexuals, and certainly not for putting them to death. In Italy, Byron observed in 1820, "they laugh instead of burning—and the women talk of it as a pity in a man of talent."

William Bankes, at about the time of his trial

Bankes was put on trial in 1833. A host of eminent witnesses testified on his behalf. The Duke of Wellington, perhaps the best character witness imaginable in the England of his day, declared flatly that his

---

* English laws posed far less of a threat to lesbians. In one notorious case in 1811, though, two women were charged with "indecent and criminal practices" for having sex. The women sued their accuser for slander. Eventually the case reached the House of Lords. The accused women won their case, and Lord Gillies declared, "I do believe that the crime here alleged has no existence." This notion of "the physical impossibility of the thing charged," as another judge put it, was central to the case. How could anyone take seriously an accusation that was plainly ludicrous? "It is," Lord Justice Clerk Charles Hope insisted, "as if I were told that a person heard thunder playing the tune of 'God Save the King.'"

friend Bankes was "utterly incapable of such an offense as he is now charged with." Bankes was acquitted.

But in 1841 he was arrested again. Caught with a soldier in Green Park, in London, he was condemned as "a person of wicked, lewd, filthy and unnatural mind and disposition." So lost in depravity was Bankes, the state went on, that he had "endeavoured to persuade a person unknown to commit and perpetrate that detestable and abominable crime (among Christians not to be named) called Buggery."

With the death penalty still in effect, Bankes's lawyer advised him to flee abroad before he could be put on trial. Bankes signed over his grand house and all his other property to his brothers, to safeguard it from confiscation, and sailed to France. He would never return home.

The government threatened and blustered, but it never pursued Bankes. After a short time in France, he moved to Italy, and he would pass most of the rest of his life in Venice.

In exile, Bankes's obsession with the grand house that he would never see again grew ever stronger. He sought out the best craftsmen in marble, gold, wood, and leather and shipped home an endless stream of statues, carved railings, ornate doors, and candelabras. Old Masters filled the walls, and even, in one room, the ceiling.

All of this called for a myriad of design choices, and Bankes took minute care with every decision. "By around 1850 he was writing daily instructions about the exact shade of a wood stain or the smooth functioning of door hinges," writes Bankes's biographer Anne Sebba. "'Let me know at once how it looks,' he asks, or 'I recommend starting this immediately.'"

There is a good chance, Sebba believes, that once before he died Bankes managed a secret visit to his home. In the spring or summer of 1854, she suggests, he arranged a rendezvous at a spot once favored by smugglers, at a secluded beach on the Dorset coast.

The evidence is tantalizing but perhaps not quite conclusive. What is certain is that William Bankes died the following year, in Venice. He left instructions directing that his body be sent home. In the summer of 1855, he was buried in a family vault, home at last.

# CHAPTER NINETEEN

# Here Comes Champollion

Champollion, who had long been on the sidelines, now leapt into the game. He left no record of precisely how Bankes's inscriptions opened his eyes, but suddenly he was sprinting at full speed.

The key bit of good fortune was that *Ptolemy* and *Cleopatra* contained several letters in common, namely *P*, *T*, *O*, and *L*. Young had guessed years before that the Rosetta cartouches spelled out *Ptolemy* (actually the Greek form of the name, *Ptolemaios*) in hieroglyphs.

Now Champollion did the same. He looked at this cartouche from the Rosetta Stone:

and deduced that $P =$ , $T=$ , $O =$ , $L =$ , $M =$ , $E =$ , and $S =$ .

That was exactly what Young had done, years before. Perhaps Champollion figured it out for himself; perhaps he had read Young's account in his 1819 *Encyclopedia Britannica* essay. (Champollion's brother wrote to tell him about Young's essay soon after it was published. Champollion sneered—"the Englishman knows no more Egyptian than he does Malay or Manchu"—but he asked his brother to send him a copy at once.)

For two centuries now, partisans of both men have hurled insults at one another. We're likely never to know if Champollion made his way independently of Young—as he always insisted—or whether Young's ideas set his mind afire. In years to come Champollion would skip over any discussion of how his thinking had evolved; he simply described his conclusions while scarcely referring to Young at all. Young, the unlikeliest man in the world to turn up in a street brawl, seldom ventured beyond mild complaint: "I did certainly expect to find the chronology of my own researches a little more distinctly stated."

The *Ptolemy* cartouche was a first step. In 1822, soon after he received his copy of Bankes's inscriptions, Champollion moved on to *Cleopatra*. Back in 1810, he had remarked that foreign names could provide a way into an ancient script. Now here was *Cleopatra*, which was Greek, not Egyptian, and which overlapped with *Ptolemy* besides.

Champollion examined Bankes's cartouche. Was this *Cleopatra*?

Champollion had just assigned hieroglyphs to *P*, *T*, *O*, and *L*, based on the Rosetta Stone's *Ptolemy* cartouche. Now he looked to see if those hieroglyphs turned up in the right place in the new cartouche. Would they fit properly in the name *Cleopatra*?

Substituting the letters from *Ptolemy*, this new cartouche read: _ L E O P __ __ __ __

Better still, a new symbol—Champollion called it a "sparrow hawk"—turned up in two places in the new cartouche, immediately after the P and again after two intervening symbols. This was *Wheel of Fortune* without Vanna White but with a prize of eternal fame.

If ![hawk] = *A*, Champollion saw immediately, then the new cartouche would read: _ L E O P A __ __ A.

One mismatch stood out. Both *Ptolemy* and *Cleopatra* contained the letter *T*, but according to Champollion's deciphering, the *T* in

*Ptolemy* was a semicircle, and the *T* in *Cleopatra* was a hand. How could that be?

Champollion's hope was that Egyptian simply had more than one way to write the same sound. If he was right, the *Ptolemy/Cleopatra* mismatch would be a curiosity rather than a crisis, as if one historian's list of English monarchs included a *Catherine* and another's listed a *Katherine*.

But that was a hope rather than an argument. Inconsistencies like ⌒ versus ⊂──⊐ were a major reason that cracking the hieroglyphic code was so difficult. (Codebreakers had it far easier, at least in the early days of spycraft and codemaking, because codes stuck to the rules.)

It would be years, in fact, before Champollion managed to prove that he had been right all along. The proof involved scanning reams of text and finding many examples that showed that ⌒ and ⊂──⊐ were more or less interchangeable.

The best way to understand the strategy is to think of *Catherine* and *Katherine* again. Champollion's goal was, in essence, to find pairs where the letter *C* could be substituted for *K*, or vice versa. In time he came up with Egyptian names and words akin to *Carl* and *Karl*, and *Chris* and *Kris*, and *curb* and *kerb* (as it's spelled in England). A find like *Krispy Kreme* doughnuts would have clinched his argument in one swoop.

With a stack of examples in hand, Champollion could look back at his decision to overlook the *Ptolemy/Cleopatra* mismatch with pride and relief. He had not turned a blind eye to unwelcome evidence; he had read a message in tiny clues that few others would even have noticed.

Champollion raced ahead. Filling in the blanks in the name *Cleopatra* gave him several new hieroglyphs—the ones corresponding to the sounds *c*, *r*, and *a*—to add to his collection. Then he looked at other inscriptions and other bits of papyrus, searching for more cartouches.

The strategy was straightforward but laborious—when you found a cartouche, you guessed that it contained a ruler's name. Then you sounded out the hieroglyphs you had already identified and hoped that those choppy fragments called to mind a name you had encountered somewhere before. If they did, you filled in the blanks with new

hieroglyphs and turned, with growing confidence, to still more cartouches. Each success would unlock another door.

That was the plan. And it worked, although with countless misfires
along the way. With the *Ptolemy* and *Cleopatra* cartouches, Champoll-
lion had benefited from an enormous head start—he'd known, from
the Greek inscriptions, the names he was looking for. Now he'd run out
of bilingual inscriptions. From here on, he'd be working blind.

Champollion began sifting through his hieroglyphic haystack.
Nearly always he found nothing but frustration. In the great majority of cases a cartouche simply didn't have enough familiar hieroglyphs to be of any use. In the rare but fortunate cases where you
knew enough hieroglyphs to venture a guess at a name, you were
unlikely to turn up anything valuable. Most such guesses were gibberish, hodgepodges that certainly did not correspond to anything
Egyptian.

Sometimes a hit might sound plausible but not match up with any
known ruler. That could happen in a host of ways. You might simply have guessed wrong. You might have happened on a pharaoh who
was lost to history (as Tut almost was). You might have stumbled on
a name that had been recorded in some ancient list but in so mangled or misunderstood a fashion that you missed it. (One of Egypt's
mightiest pharaohs was best known by the Greek name Ozymandias.
"My name is Ozymandias, King of Kings," Shelley wrote in his famous
poem about the ruler whose statue was found, broken and forgotten, in
the desert. But Egyptian texts knew him as User-ma'at-re.)

Champollion forged ahead regardless of all such hazards. His first
success after *Cleopatra* came with this cartouche:

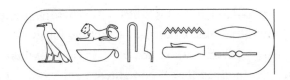

Champollion immediately recognized the first hieroglyph. This
was the "sparrow hawk" that he had seen in *Cleopatra*. He had decided

that it stood for *A*. Next was a lion. He'd seen that before, too, in both *Ptolemy* and *Cleopatra*. A lion was *L*.

Then "a shallow teacup" that Champollion didn't recognize; after that "a curved line" that he had identified as *S* in *Ptolemaios*; next, "a feather," which was *E* in *Ptolemaios*; an unidentified zigzag; an "open hand," which was *T* in *Cleopatra*; an "open mouth," *R* in *Cleopatra*; and, finally, a mysterious horizontal line with a doodad in the middle, which looked to Champollion like "two horizontal inward-facing scepters."

Putting it all together, Champollion had: A L _ S E _ T R _. It took only an instant for him to fill in the blanks. This was *Alksentrs*, or, with a tiny bit of massaging, *Alexandros*, Greek for *Alexander*.

This was a coup, and not just because Champollion had found a new and important name. Just as important, he had found it by using a method that he could apply again and again to other cartouches. He had, also, *not* found something, and in this case that was a good sign, too.

From the get-go, Champollion had been thrilled to see hieroglyphs turn up where they should (like the little square that stood for *P* in both *Ptolemy* and *Cleopatra*). Now he saw with glee that others didn't turn up where they *didn't* belong. The "sparrow hawk" that Champollion had decided stood for *A* in *Cleopatra* shouldn't have appeared in *Ptolemy*, for instance, and it didn't. The same was true of the oval shape—Champollion called it "a front view of a mouth"—that stood for *R* and turned up in *Cleopatra* but not in *Ptolemy*.

Champollion raced on. Soon he had deciphered the hieroglyphs that spelled out *Berenice*, and *Caesar*, and *Autokrator* (Greek for *Emperor* and related to our word *autocrat*).

Champollion had sped past Young. Several years before, as we have seen, Young had almost but not quite read *Berenice* for himself. He'd had the considerable advantage of knowing what to look for, because a nearby inscription had written the name in Greek. Even so, he'd fallen short. (In an essay setting out his discoveries, Champollion would later devote a long footnote to rehashing the amusing blunders of "this English scholar.")

The *Cleopatra* cartouche had helped speed Champollion on his way. For Young, the same cartouche represented an enormous missed chance. Bankes had sent him his obelisk inscriptions, too, and Young had immediately spotted something odd. He knew, from the Greek inscription, that Bankes's second cartouche likely spelled out *Cleopatra*. (The first cartouche spelled out *Ptolemy*, which Young recognized from the Rosetta Stone.) But the copyist who had recorded the hieroglyphs had made a mistake—the first symbol in Cleopatra's name should have been a hieroglyph that stood for the sound *k*, but instead the copyist had written the hieroglyph for *t*.

Young had frowned and put the inscriptions aside. "As I had not leisure at the time to enter into a very minute comparison of the name with other authorities, I suffered myself to be discouraged with respect to the application of my alphabet to its analysis." Young had tripped over a typo.

This was a terrible break. Had Young examined the *Cleopatra* cartouche for a moment, he could have matched up its hieroglyphs with the *P, T, O*, and *L* hieroglyphs in the *Ptolemy* cartouche, exactly as Champollion had, and then moved on to tackle other names. Instead, he had turned away. In a cops-and-robbers movie, this would have been the moment when an impatient detective glanced at video footage from a security camera but missed the bad guy, even though he was right there, because he was distracted by the suspect's "disguise" of a baseball cap and a three-day beard.

The question of how to deal with a finding that seems to shoot down a theory is tricky. As textbooks tell it, there should be no problem. Thomas Huxley famously described "the great tragedy of science" as "the slaying of a beautiful hypothesis by an ugly fact." But quite often, theories live on contentedly even after running into hideously ugly facts. "Ninety Percent of the Universe Found 'Missing' by Astronomer," the *New York Times* once shouted in alarm, in a page 1 headline, but the astronomer in question noted calmly that he "hoped the missing matter in the universe can be found."

This is often the way. *Something will turn up.* (In the astronomers' case, the search for the universe's missing mass led to some of the most crucial breakthroughs in the recent history of science.) But in the Cleopatra case, Young lost heart at a typo and moved on to other things.

CHAPTER TWENTY

# "A Veritable Chaos"

It's hard to look past Young's near-miss, because the stakes were so high. But even geniuses make mistakes. Their rare blunders serve those of us on the sidelines as something akin to a figure skater's pratfalls—they remind us that, easy as the pros make it look, their path is fraught with danger.

For Young, Champollion, and their fellow decipherers, copyists' errors ranked high on the list of hazards. In the days before photography, they were a constant headache for decipherers and also for translators. (Champollion and Young first made contact, we saw earlier, when Champollion complained to Young that his copies of the Rosetta Stone were inaccurate.) A little mistake could cause enormous problems.

One of the most famous—and most puzzling—passages in the Bible, for instance, may turn on a copying error. "I say unto you," Jesus told his disciples, "it is easier for a camel to go through the eye of a needle, than for a rich man to enter into the kingdom of God." Since the early days of Christianity, scholars have wondered about that odd image. *A camel?* One theory, first suggested by Cyril of Alexandria in the fifth century AD and endorsed by a variety of modern writers, proposes a down-to-earth explanation. In ancient Greek, Cyril pointed out, the words for *camel* and *rope* were almost identical; *camel* was *kamilos*, and *rope* was *kamêlos*. What happened, perhaps, is that somewhere along the way a tired copyist wrote *camel* for *rope*—thereby transforming a straightforward image into a bizarre one—and then generations of biblical scholars perpetuated the error.

In nature's codes, too, the hardest-to-spot typos can have vast consequences. The DNA in each of our cells consists of thousands upon thousands of genes, each of them a long string of the letters A, T, G, and C in a myriad of combinations. In effect, DNA is a four-letter Morse code, and the cost of a slipup can be lifelong. Take retinitis pigmentosa, which is a form of blindness. It can be caused by a mistake of a single letter. The difference between sharp vision and none at all can be as small as a single G where there should have been a T in a sequence that begins AGTTTCTTTCGC and continues on for another ten thousand letters.

In ancient times, copying was difficult and agonizingly slow. With no tools to speed up the process, "Make me a copy of this" was a command that presaged not pressing a button but endless hours of drudgery. The fearsome Assyrian ruler Ashurbanipal—notorious for countless cruelties, including such innovations as putting a rope through the jaw of a conquered king and then tying him inside a dog kennel—declared his intent to stock the royal library with a copy of every book in the world. (This was in about 650 BC, and nearly all the "books" Ashurbanipal had in mind were clay tablets inscribed in wedge-shaped cuneiforms.) He commanded scribes in conquered lands to copy the texts in their own libraries and send them to him.

"Day and night we shall strain and toil to execute the instructions of our lord the king!" the message came back, and the scribes, having no choice, set to work at once. Some of these copyists served in a kind of white-collar chain gang; prisoners of war or political hostages, they had no collars but they did literally work in chains.

Ashurbanipal's library did indeed become one of the treasures of the ancient world, though its hundreds of thousands of clay tablets were lost for two thousand years. These were the very tablets we encountered earlier, in chapter 15, in which the self-taught genius George Smith deciphered the story of Gilgamesh and the pre-biblical tale of a flood that drowned the world. Strangely, the tablets survived because the libraries that housed them were destroyed.

It was fire, the destroyer of libraries ever since Alexandria, that saved the texts from the earliest libraries, which were written not on paper or papyrus but on clay. "When in wars and invasions the great Mesopotamian cities were burned down," writes the historian Stephen Greenblatt, "the sun-dried tablets in the libraries and royal archives were in effect baked into durable form. In their death agonies, the palace and the temples had become kilns."

When it came to hieroglyphs, all the generic difficulties that came with copying grew even worse. Copying a manuscript in a known language and a familiar script was challenging, even in the quiet of a library. But making perfect copies of great swaths of unfamiliar symbols on a temple wall, in Egypt's heat and commotion, was next to impossible.

(Another hazard made for still more problems—sometimes there were errors in the *originals*, because the craftsmen who carved hieroglyphs into stone or painted them on walls and monuments were seldom literate; they worked from texts written by scribes, but they could not read what they were copying. In contrast, texts on papyrus were written by the scribes themselves and therefore far less likely to contain mistakes.)

One early traveler left a vivid account of the hazards facing a copyist. Carsten Niebuhr, a Danish explorer and scholar, visited Egypt in the 1760s. Niebuhr was a meticulous observer who carried with him a host of scientific tools, including a telescope, an astrolabe, a compass, and a thermometer. When he was not measuring the precise dimensions of the pyramids or recording the temperature (he took measurements at three specific times each day), he carefully copied down long hieroglyphic inscriptions that he could not read. While he worked, surly crowds swarmed around, trying to sort out what he was up to. Police demanded payoffs and threatened to beat him up.

Niebuhr did well, against the odds, and so did Napoleon's savants, who had to deal with rifle fire as well as hostile locals. But the decipherers back in Europe were in a race, and good manners were an early casualty. As Champollion hunted for hieroglyphs in the savants' *Description of Egypt*, he fumed and snapped about careless mistakes and slovenly scribes.

This was a harsh judgment, but "for scholarly purposes," one modern Egyptologist concedes, "the drawings were a mishmash." Inevitably, some hieroglyphs had been miscopied or passed over altogether, or lines were skipped or transposed. *Was a bird facing right the same symbol as a bird facing left? Was the snake with a pair of little horns different from the snake with a bend in its middle?*

To put yourself in the copyists' shoes, imagine trying to copy even a single sentence in an unfamiliar script like, say, Thai. (Like Egyptian, Thai does not place spaces between words.) Here's "I'm pleased to meet you": ฉันยินดีที่ได้พบคุณ.

Champollion was far less likely than Young to be undone by a typo, because his focus on Egypt was so relentless. Young always had a dozen pressing projects on his mind. "He long retained the habits of a schoolboy in mixing his studies," he wrote about himself (in the third-person voice he favored), "so as to devote an hour or two only at a time to each." At the time the *Cleopatra* cartouche turned up, he had just taken on a major assignment that involved revising and reassessing a vast trove of nautical and astronomical data for a publication called *The Nautical Almanac.*

His all-things-considered approach had its risks, Young acknowledged. Perhaps he could have accomplished more by "confining his talents within narrower limits." But no sooner had he raised this possibility than he rejected it. On second thought, he decided, the habit of hopping from subject to subject had granted him "a versatility of powers."*

More important, Young went on, life confined to "narrow limits" bore a strong resemblance to life stuck in a rut. He sympathized, he wrote, with workmen who resisted the call to break a job into tiny tasks for the sake of efficiency. For a thinker as for a manual worker, special-

---

* This notion is now in vogue. In his impressive book *Range*, David Epstein quotes the Nobel laureate Santiago Ramón y Cajal, who believes that the most successful scientists tend to be those with the broadest range of interests. "To him who observes them from afar," writes Ramón y Cajal, "it appears as though they are scattering and dissipating their energies, while in reality they are channeling and strengthening them."

ization was a formula for "reducing his dignity in the scale of existence from a reasoning being to a mere machine."

Champollion presumably saw the Cleopatra typo that had thrown Young off his game. He proceeded ahead nevertheless, too hopeful to blanch at a trifle. He quickly found new confirmation for his deciphering strategy.

Once again a foreign ruler's name provided the key. Xerxes was the formidable Persian king who had invaded Greece in 480 BC. His was a name familiar to scholars. The ancient world had cowered before Xerxes—he rode at the head of a two-million-man army (according to Herodotus), the largest military force that anyone had ever assembled.

Champollion suggested to another French linguist, an expert on cuneiform, that the two of them look at a particular vase in a private collection. The lure was plain—the vase was ancient, and it carried inscriptions in two different scripts, Persian cuneiform and Egyptian hieroglyphs. Scholars had already learned a bit about deciphering cuneiform. They could read the first Persian word on the vase—*Xerxes*. Now to the Egyptian, which began with a cartouche. Champollion recognized its hieroglyphs from other names and sounded them out: *Xerxes!*

That was a breakthrough, but Champollion still had not seen what it might mean (and certainly Young had not). *Yes, certain hieroglyphs stood for sounds and could be used to spell out names. You could even assemble them into a sort of alphabet. But then what?* "It is abundantly clear . . . ," writes the classics scholar Maurice Pope, "that he never suspected that his alphabet would have any application beyond the sphere of proper names and foreign words, or that it was going to prove the long-looked-for key to the hieroglyphs."

Having advanced so far only to find himself still lost, Champollion sputtered in frustration. "The look of a hieroglyphic inscription is a veritable chaos. Nothing is in its place. There is no relation to sense. The most contradictory objects are put right next to each other, producing monstrous alliances."

Certainly hieroglyphs were a script and not some bizarre form of wall decoration. But how could a system of writing place so much emphasis on pictures? Any script based on decoding pictures, Champollion lamented, would lead to an endless and futile guessing game. "Inevitably [it would be] very obscure, being compelled to express its ideas by a string of metaphors, comparisons, and hardly soluble riddles."

*What could the Egyptians have been thinking?*

# CHAPTER TWENTY-ONE

# The Birth of Writing

Think about Champollion's question for a moment—how *could* you capture an entire language in pictures?—and you quickly come to understand his bafflement.

Words like *dog* and *hat* would be easy enough to draw, and so would phrases like *falling rock zone*. But the world is full of things that are nearly impossible to capture in pictures. What of *hope* or *tomorrow* or *why* or *unlikely*? Hieroglyphs would quickly grow inscrutable, exactly as Champollion had suggested. The notion that a drawing of a hawk might mean *god* or *sublime* comes to seem almost plausible.

By way of example, look at this drawing from 2007, which was meant to carry a mortal warning to people thousands of years from now.

Nuclear waste will still be deadly in ten thousand years. Our descendants will need to know to keep away from the sites where it lies buried, although it is almost certain that English will have changed unrecognizably after so many millennia. In the year 12007, will this warning from the International Atomic Energy Association convey the intended message: "Danger! Something Here Will Kill You! Go Away!"?

But it is not just abstractions that create problems. The board game *Pictionary* was popular precisely because it was so hard to convey even ordinary words in pictures—*jazz, surprise, enemy*. And images that are easy to recognize can still be hard to interpret. "A hard-hat symbol means 'wear hardhats (and if you don't have one, get one),'" writes the historian John Man, "but a wheelchair symbol does not mean 'sit in a wheelchair (and if you don't have one, get one).'"

Move from words or phrases to entire sentences, and the challenges grow far worse. You might manage to draw pictures that convey *She drinks coffee*, but what about *She's trying to cut down on coffee*? Or, worse still, *She always stops for coffee unless she's running late*?

Most scholars believe that the earliest forms of writing *did* begin with pictures—ancient counterparts of the *Caution: Wet Floor* drawing of a tumbling man or the stylized gas pumps and coffee cups on highway signs—but quickly ran up against their limits.

Then, at roughly the same time, several cultures around the world came up with the answer. In Mesopotamia and Egypt sometime around 3100 BC, in India in 2500 BC, in China in 1200 BC, scripts arose that could capture any words whatever in a handful of lines and curves.

As archaeologists view history, that two-thousand-year span was the blink of an eye. (Archaeologists are slow blinkers.)* But why did it happen *then* and not tens of thousands of years earlier, when our forebears had already grown sophisticated? Take cave paintings. The artists who adorned cave walls with charging bulls and galloping horses drew with surpassing skill. Their paintings date from twenty thousand years ago; the earliest writing is only five thousand years old. Those early artists drew, but they did not write. *Could* they have chosen to add captions to their paintings?

---

* Over the course of *hundreds of thousands of years*, scholars tell us, culture stood still and our ancestors' lives changed not in the slightest bit. They "sat for 0.3-million years in the drafty, smoky caves of [northern China]," for instance, one distinguished linguist writes, "cooking bats over smoldering embers and waiting for the caves to fill up with their own garbage."

Presumably not, but why not? It wasn't for lack of tools. Paints, inks, and carving tools have been used from art's earliest days, and surely they would have worked just as well for writing. Nor was the problem lack of brains. No brutes could have conjured up the images that adorn Lascaux.

So what took so long? The standard guess is that, oddly, the birth of writing had to do with the rise of cities. More specifically, with the rise of trade and commerce. At some point about five thousand years ago, cities grew so large and trade grew so complex that no one relying on memory alone could keep track of who owed how much to whom. The rise of trade brought a need for records, and records meant writing— *this belongs to me, that belongs to you; this is a receipt for five bushels of grain; that's an IOU for three wicker baskets.*

The push for a way to keep records came straight from the top. The more powerful the king, the more compelling his desire to have a finger in every pie (and an accurate count of the number of pies in the kingdom). As cities grew, there were armies to raise, harvests to tally, fields to survey, canals to dredge. Most important, there were taxes to collect. All such projects made heavy use of what later generations would call "paperwork."*

By most accounts the development of writing was a saga that played out over the course of thousands of years. The story is still far from settled, but the Middle Eastern portion of the tale is the best-documented. The first clues that offered a peek at writing's earliest days turned up about a century ago in the ruins of several ancient cities in what is now Iraq. There archaeologists found large numbers of clay lumps shaped into ovals, or spheres, or discs, or cylinders, or cones. These tokens, as they came to be called, seem to have been used from about 8000 BC to 3500 BC. Scholars had no idea what to make of them (and archaeologists often tossed them aside as junk). A German researcher

---

* The Incas were the exception to the rule—the only known example of an empire that made no use of a writing system. The knotted cords the Incas called *quipu* did provide a sophisticated way of recording numbers (but apparently not words).

named Julius Jordan *almost* solved the riddle. The clay lumps, he wrote in his journal in 1929, looked "like the commodities of daily life—jars, loaves, and animals."

At some point around 3500 BC, thousands of years into the story, the plot thickened. Now ancient Sumerians took to enclosing the tokens inside hollowed-out clay "envelopes." On the outside of the envelopes were small indentations, apparently made by pressing the tokens into the clay's surface before sealing them inside.

In the 1970s, a French Sherlock Holmes came along and sorted out what this was all about. Denise Schmandt-Besserat, a young archaeologist, explained that these cones and spheres were not lumps but symbols. A cone represented a fixed amount of grain, for instance, an oval a jar of oil. A middleman hired to transport two jars of oil might carry two clay ovals as a sort of receipt.

As time passed, Schmandt-Besserat went on, the system grew more involved. Someone had the bright idea that, to prevent any hanky-panky, the tokens could be sealed inside clay envelopes where they couldn't be tampered with. But, with the tokens sealed away, how could you know an envelope's contents without going to all the trouble of cracking it open?

To the young Frenchwoman the answer practically shouted itself out. *By making marks on the* outside *of the envelope that told what was* inside *it*. At first, in Schmandt-Besserat's telling, those "labels" were exact imprints of the tokens, produced by pushing the tokens into the surface of the envelope.

In time it dawned on someone that drawing a picture of the token on the envelope would be easier and would do just as well. In a great deal more time, someone saw that a rough-and-ready symbol on the envelope would work as well as a careful drawing. And, later still, yet another innovator figured out that the token-and-envelope business could be done away with altogether, in favor of a clay tablet that captured all the same information in symbols, in a few meaningful lines and scratches. The inscribed symbols *represented* the clay tokens; there was no need for the actual tokens. Behold, the birth of writing!

The key that unlocked the whole story, Schmandt-Besserat recalled, was one particularly fortunate find. At one site in northern Iraq, archaeologists found two cuneiform inscriptions that recorded a single transaction. One was a clay tablet that read, "21 ewes, 8 full-grown male sheep, 6 she-goats," and so on. The second inscription was a clay envelope that listed, on the outside, the identical "21 ewes, 8 full-grown male sheep, 6 she-goats" array. The list totaled 49 animals. Researchers broke open the envelope. Out spilled 49 tokens. Twenty-one were of one shape, eight of another, and so on. "That hollow tablet," wrote Schmandt-Besserat, "proved to be the Rosetta Stone of the inscription system."

That long sequence of ever-increasing abstraction—from clay tokens to impressions pressed in clay to drawings in clay to symbols written on clay tablets—played out with excruciating slowness. Still to come was yet more abstraction, as writing advanced from symbols that depicted tangible objects like sheep and goats to symbols that stood for the fleeting sounds and tiny bursts of air that make up spoken language.

How could it have been so hard to grasp? It seems like no trick at all to see that symbols can have meanings even though they don't look like anything in particular. Paul Revere used lanterns—"One if by land, two if by sea"—to convey the enemy's plans, and no one had any trouble understanding him. Theseus used sails. He told his father that he would have his men put up a black sail on his ship if the Minotaur had killed him, and a white sail to signal that he was returning home in triumph. (In the hubbub of events, as it turned out, Theseus forgot to change sails. His father saw the black sail that signaled his son's death and leapt into the sea to drown himself.)

We know, though, that the step from recognizable pictures to arbitrary symbols proved immensely difficult. In the evolution of human culture, abstraction is always the great hurdle.

Every generation patronizes its predecessors for having been so dim, forgetting that soon enough it will be our turn to stand in the corner and feel foolish. "It behooves us always to remember that in physics it has taken great men to discover simple things," wrote the scientist (and classics scholar) D'Arcy Thompson. "They are very great names indeed which we couple with the explanation of the path of a stone, the droop of a chain, the tints of a bubble, the shadows of a cup."

The story is the same no matter the field and no matter how simple the "simple thing" might be. In the case of writing, Plato said, the "simple" invention was in fact so difficult that only "some god or some divine man" could have managed it. No mere human could have found a way to capture on a page "the unlimited variety of sound."

Not everyone buys the token story. But the skeptics' doubts turn on *how* writing came to be. On the question of *why* writing was invented, there is widespread consensus. It was not to record deep thoughts. Whether in China or the ancient Middle East or Egypt or India or the New World, the spur was always business. Everywhere in the world, the earliest writing was less in the vein of "she walks in beauty like the night" and more on the lines of "Received: two pottery mugs, one with a chipped handle."

After a time, literature came along. After a *long* time. Like the development of writing itself, the transition from writing as commerce to writing as art played out in slow motion. (Through that long span, songs and *spoken* stories were presumably common.) In Egypt, by one scholar's reckoning, it took a *thousand years* for writing to move from tax records to stories and fables.

But one crucial new role for writing came along much earlier than storytelling and never faded away. This was writing as propaganda. Rulers seized on the new tool early on, taking every opportunity to proclaim their might and celebrate their divine mission. Carved in stone, a king's boasts would last forever.

All through Egyptian history in particular, pharaohs indulged in wildly over-the-top bragging and verbal swagger. One typical Egyptian inscription, on a stone stela from around 1400 BC, described what happened when the pharaoh Amenhotep spied enemy troops venturing near him, in chariots: "His Majesty burst after them like the flight of a divine falcon." Amenhotep was alone—"not a single one was with His Majesty, except for himself with his valiant arm"—but no matter. "They quailed when they saw His Majesty. Then His Majesty felled their commander himself with his battle-axe." Amenhotep quickly followed up that victory with yet another conquest. "Now the Ruler was raging like a divine falcon, his horses flying like a star of heaven."*

Modesty was not a virtue in ancient Egypt, and you did not have to be a pharaoh to thump your chest. One provincial ruler, who held office around 2100 BC, recorded his good deeds on the walls of his tomb. A long recitation worked up to a rousing finale. "I was the beginning and the end of mankind, since nobody like myself existed before nor will he exist. Nobody like myself was ever born nor will he be born. I surpassed the feats of the ancestors, and coming generations will not be able to equal me in any of my feats for millions of years." The inscription concluded, "I am the hero without equal."

The history of invention is dotted with examples of bright ideas that turned out to have uses no one ever foresaw. Elevators were originally designed to lift materials at building sites; soon they carried passengers rather than lumber, and city skylines soared upward. Lenses were first meant for spectacles that would let old men read small print; they found their way into telescopes that revealed stars beyond counting and into microscopes that unveiled miniature worlds—whose existence had never even been suspected—that teemed with living creatures.

The brain itself is an even more striking example, though in this case it was nature that played the role of inventor. Here was a living machine built to convey thoughts like, "Run! It's a lion!" But that same machine inspired poets to write love sonnets and spurred men and women everywhere to look beyond today and shudder at the prospect of their death.

Writing, though, is perhaps the ultimate example of an invention with unintended consequences. With the brain, the simplest responses

---

* Compared with examples of royal boasting from other ancient empires, this was almost benign. In Assyria, for instance, thousands upon thousands of inscriptions and carvings depict tortures and massacres in careful detail. This royal reminiscence, from a king named Sennacherib who ruled around 700 BC, is typical: "I cut their throats like lambs . . . With the bodies of their warriors, I filled the plain, like grass. Their testicles I cut off, and tore out their privates like the seeds of cucumbers."

and the deepest insights sit at different points along the same straight line—to spot danger in the quivering of a bush is perhaps not so different, after all, from seeing mortality in the trembling of a hand.

Not so with writing, where the story veers so sharply that no one could have guessed the outcome from hearing the opening lines. Who could have foreseen that a tool that was built for counting goats would give us literature and history and memory?

*Napoleon Crossing the Alps* by Jacques-Louis David. Napoleon instructed David to paint him atop a "fiery horse," although he actually made the crossing on a mule.

The two rivals who raced to decipher the Rosetta Stone. Young (at left) was English and renowned for the breadth of his intellectual interests. Champollion (at right) was French and consumed entirely with Egypt. Both were geniuses but they were utterly different in almost every way.

4                                                                                    5

Hieroglyphs were everywhere in Egypt, but no one in the modern world knew how to decipher them. Egypt was an open book that no one could read. "There is hardly the space of an awl or needle-hole," a traveler from Baghdad wrote in the year 1183, "which did not have an image or engraving or some script which is not understood."

6

In ancient Egypt scribes were highly regarded because they were among the few who could read or write. Here a scribe reads a papyrus text while the god of writing, Toth, looks on. Toth was sometimes depicted as an ibis-headed human and sometimes as a baboon, as here.

7

Hieroglyphs were not only mysterious but alluring; they were so elaborate and carefully drawn that it seemed they must carry deep and mystical meanings. The ovals in the center spell out the name of the pharaoh Horemheb and an honorary title. Horemheb ruled shortly after Tutankhamun. One reason that King Tut was so little known to history was that Horemheb chiseled away his name wherever it appeared on statues or monuments.

Ramesses II reigned sixty-six years and outlived a dozen crown princes. His towering statues served, in the words of one Egyptologist, as "a giant *Beware of Pharaoh* sign."

8

9

All four of these colossal statues depict Ramesses II, Egypt's mightiest pharaoh. Each figure is as tall as a six-story building. (The statue just to the left of the temple entrance lost its head and torso long ago. They toppled to the ground at the statue's feet, where they can still be seen.) Today, the stone-carved temples at Abu Simbel are one of the world's most famous sights.

Giovanni Belzoni. In the 1800s the line between archaeology and looting was fuzzy. Belzoni was a larger-than-life figure who began his career as a circus strongman and went on to explore Egypt (and to plunder it). He unearthed inscriptions that played a key role in the deciphering saga.

William Bankes. When his older brother died in a shipwreck, Bankes inherited an enormous fortune. He took up a life of travel and exploration. Fascinated with Egypt, he found hieroglyphs that served as crucial puzzle pieces for Champollion and Young.

Bankes and Belzoni shipped this obelisk to Bankes's country house in England, where it stands to this day. Hieroglyphs on one side spelled out the name Cleopatra and provided a crucial clue to decipherers.

Bankes fled England after he was charged with committing "unnatural" acts with a man in Green Park, in London. The maximum penalty was death and Bankes escaped to Europe, never to return. Throughout his exile Bankes collected furniture and paintings for the home he would never see again. This was the most ornate room of all, and even the ceiling was lined with Old Masters.

14

Napoleon brought artists and scientists with him to Egypt. When they returned home in the early 1800s, their accounts of the wonders they had seen triggered a craze for all things Egyptian. The frenzy, called Egyptomania, lasted for decades and extended to America as well as Europe. (That is why the Washington Monument is an obelisk.) In 1912 one of America's most renowned architects submitted this design for the Lincoln Memorial. Lincoln's body would have been housed inside the pyramid.

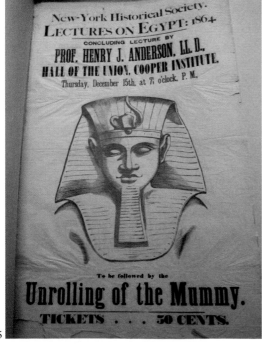

15

16

Everything to do with Egypt packed a thrill. Lecturers tempted the public with invitations to see mummies unwrapped from their linen, and artists made use of a paint made of ground-up mummies.

Egypt is so hot and dry that it can serve as an inadvertent time capsule. The colors in these wall paintings—from the tomb of Nefertari, the favorite wife of Egypt's mightiest pharaoh, Ramesses II—are as vibrant today as when the tomb was sealed shut three thousand years ago. The hieroglyphs below the large figures are from the Book of the Dead.

18  The wall paintings in this tomb show Osiris, the god of the underworld (with green skin and a pharaoh's garb). The pink shape at the left represents the Mountains of the West. The tomb was rediscovered in 1834.

This statue depicts Hatshepsut, "the lost pharaoh." Hatshepsut was a female pharaoh—in Egyptian history, such a thing was almost unheard of—and she reigned for twenty years. By one scholar's reckoning, she was "the first great woman in history of whom we are informed."

Hatshepsut's successors tried to erase her from history because, many scholars believe, they could not bear the thought of a female ruler. They chiseled her name out of inscriptions and smashed her statues with sledgehammers. It nearly worked.

Decipherers raised an alarm when they found a few overlooked inscriptions with strange words (on the order of *kingette*), but the full story emerged only in the 1920s, when archaeologists found a pit full to the brim with broken bits of statue. They pieced together several statues (including this one) and the story.

# CHAPTER TWENTY-TWO

# The Paduan Giant

Despite all the progress he had made, Champollion was still frustrated and confused. By now—it was 1821, and he had been consumed by Egypt and hieroglyphs for more than a decade—he had managed to decipher dozens of names in cartouches, but he knew that he had not yet seen the big picture. Nor had Young, nor anyone else.

They were nearly there, though they couldn't have known it. In one famous passage in *The Sun Also Rises*, one character asks another how he went bankrupt. "Two ways," comes the answer. "Gradually and then suddenly."

So it was with the breakthroughs in the deciphering story, and now the "gradual" steps were coming in such close succession that the "sudden" moment was all but inevitable.

Champollion never offered any hints about just how he had come to make his discoveries, or just when. Rather than retrace his steps, he preferred to jolt his audiences with a series of rabbit-out-of-the-hat revelations.

This was partly a matter of style—Champollion was a man of flash and dash as well as solid genius. But showmanship was only part of the story. Champollion was surrounded by skeptics, and he knew that a tidy presentation would be more compelling than a messy one that included wrong guesses and false trails. In addition, he was racing for a great prize and presumably saw no gain in presenting his rivals with hints and half-finished theories.

Even a decade into his quest, Champollion believed that hieroglyphs were "not in any way alphabetical." Instead, he wrote in a learned essay, they were "signs of things and not sounds." Egyptian writing, in other words, was an elaborate concoction whose elements could be understood but not sounded out (except for a handful of special hieroglyphs reserved for writing foreign names).

Then, sometime between 1821 and 1823, two things happened. Neither was startling in itself. Each pushed Champollion toward an insight that would stand all his previous thinking on its head. (Young, overcommitted as usual and preoccupied by his *Nautical Almanac* chores, remained on the sidelines.)

At some point, probably in 1822, Champollion had the bright idea of counting the words and hieroglyphs on the Rosetta Stone. That seems bewilderingly late in the game for such an elementary step, but Champollion himself told the story, and he had no reason to downplay his own perceptiveness.

He counted 1,419 hieroglyphs and 486 words in Greek. (Many of the hieroglyphs occurred several times each; there were 166 different hieroglyphs). That was strange.

Why? Because there were both too many hieroglyphs and too few. (We saw earlier that Georg Zoëga, a Danish linguist, had made a closely related observation back in 1798.) Too many, because it didn't make sense that there were three times as many hieroglyphs as words in Greek. If each hieroglyph stood for a word or an idea, as everyone believed, then the number of hieroglyphs and the number of Greek words should match, more or less.

The mismatch was even worse than it first appeared. The hieroglyphs on the Rosetta Stone were at the top, and it was sections from the top that had been lost and never seen again. So the 1,419 figure was surely an undercount.

But looked at a different way, there were too *few* hieroglyphs. If one hieroglyph stood for one word or one idea, then capturing an entire language would require countless images. The total number of hieroglyphs would surely be thousands upon thousands, and nothing like a mere 166.

That was puzzle number one. Puzzle number two seemed, at first, to have nothing at all to do with Egypt or hieroglyphs. It involved the work of an obsessive young Frenchman named Jean-Pierre Abel-Rémusat, a scholar who had made a self-guided journey deep into the mysteries of the Chinese language. Rémusat had endured a miserable childhood—an accident had blinded him in one eye and confined him to bed for several years. Then his father died, leaving Jean-Pierre and his mother scrambling to get by. The young man went on to study medicine, half-heartedly, for the income it would provide. What roused him was an accidental encounter with a Chinese book on herbal medicine. The herbs and potions weren't the draw; it was the mysterious, enticing script on every page that seduced Rémusat.

Fascinated, he threw himself into the study of Chinese "without a teacher, without a textbook, without a dictionary." He was eighteen years old. Five years later, in 1811, he emerged with his first publication, *Essay on Chinese Language and Literature*. That brought Rémusat to the attention of Champollion's old mentor Silvestre de Sacy, and thereby to Champollion.

By 1822 Rémusat was France's reigning authority on Chinese, "the first," in Champollion's words, "to clear the study of Chinese from the darkness, one might say the mystical darkness, in which his predecessors had enveloped it." When Rémusat published a new work called *Elements of Chinese Grammar*, in 1822, Champollion dove in.

One point in particular caught his eye. Chinese script made use of thousands of characters, by Rémusat's count, which was far more than the hieroglyph count Champollion had come up with. But even with so many characters to work with—this, specifically, was puzzle number two—Chinese made use of a special category of characters called *hing-ching*, which Rémusat translated as *representing the sound*.

Not only did these characters stand for sounds, Champollion noted, but "they constituted a good half of normal written Chinese."

The key was the word "normal." Rémusat wasn't talking about how Chinese writers dealt with foreign names; he was talking about how the Chinese wrote plain, everyday words.

Here was a shift with huge significance. A decade earlier Champollion had explained that if you were writing foreign names in a nonalphabetic script, you would have no choice but to use characters that stood for sounds. But here was Rémusat asserting that "sound characters" turned up in ordinary words, not just in foreign names, and in lots of them.

Champollion began to ponder an idea that had never dawned on him or anyone else. *Perhaps the Egyptians used "sound characters" for run-of-the-mill Egyptian words and not just for names imported from far-off lands?*

In hindsight, it sounds obvious. At the time it was astonishing, so far from what anyone had ever proposed that in more than a decade's hard work, the idea had never popped to the surface of Champollion's mind.

While Champollion perused Chinese grammars in France, and Young compiled nautical tables in England, the ex–circus strongman Giovanni Belzoni hunted for hieroglyphs in Egypt. What he found there would soon leave Champollion literally faint with surprise.

In the early decades of the 1800s, Egypt was a vast, unmapped treasure house swarming with scavengers racing to dig up—and sell—ancient relics. For tourists no souvenir was as exciting as a mummy. "Discovering" your own mummy was most exciting of all. Dealers would sneak into tombs and stash mummies for their clients to find. Eager tourists wrenched off a hand or an arm—it was difficult to fit an entire body into a traveler's luggage—for later display at home.

Archaeologists behaved nearly as badly. Most were hard to distinguish from looters, and Belzoni in particular was a skilled and diligent looter. He was, as well, a showman's showman.

Six-foot-six, handsome, and as sturdy as an Alp (in his performing days he had devised an apparatus that let eleven men at a time perch atop him), Belzoni came late to Egypt but quickly racked up a string of coups. It was the Italian strongman, for instance, who discovered the broken statue of Ramesses the Great that inspired Shelley's poem "Ozymandias," about the mighty ruler with a "sneer of cold command." (Today the statue is one of the treasures of the British Museum.)* And

---

* Shelley never set foot in Egypt and never saw the colossal statue of Ozymandias even after it reached the British Museum. But he had read about it, and he dashed off his poem in ten minutes. He published it two weeks later, almost without revision, shortly before the statue arrived in England.

as we have seen, it was Belzoni who managed—eventually—to haul Bankes's obelisk off the island of Philae and send it on its long journey to England.

In the end it would be Belzoni's tomb-raiding prowess that unearthed the clues that set decipherers back in Europe quivering with excitement.

Giovanni Belzoni, archaeologist/plunderer, in the Arab-style garb he favored (*left*). Belzoni began life as a circus strongman. A highlight of his act involved holding several men at a time off the ground. In time he devised a way to support eleven men at once.

Belzoni described his Egyptian adventures in a rip-roaring volume of memoirs. He recalled one early foray in particular detail. He had crawled deep underground into a series of ancient tombs across the Nile from Luxor. After wriggling hundreds of yards through choking dust, he had finally emerged into a room high enough to sit upright in. "But what a place of rest!" Belzoni shuddered, "surrounded by bodies, by heaps of mummies in all directions." The only light came from torches held aloft by Belzoni's Arab workmen, who were "naked and covered with dust, themselves resembling living mummies."

By good fortune, Belzoni happened to have lost his sense of smell long before, but even so, he gagged on the taste of mummy dust in his mouth and throat. "Nearly overcome," he wrote, "I sought a resting place, found one and contrived to sit; but when my weight bore on the body of an Egyptian, it crushed it like a bandbox."

Belzoni crashed to the ground. For fifteen minutes he lay helpless, struggling to catch his breath. Eventually he managed to crawl down a passage about twenty feet long and just wide enough to wriggle through. "It was choked with mummies, and I could not pass without putting my face in contact with that of some decayed Egyptian," Belzoni wrote, "but as the passage inclined downwards, my own weight helped me on.

"However I could not avoid being covered with bones, legs, arms, and heads rolling from above. Thus I proceeded from one cave to another, all full of mummies piled up in various ways, some standing, some lying, and some on their heads."

Why volunteer for that ordeal? "The purpose of my researches," Belzoni continued matter-of-factly, "was to rob the Egyptians of their papyri; of which I found a few hidden in their breasts, under their arms, in the space above the knees, or on the legs, and covered by the numerous folds of cloth that envelop the mummy."

In ancient times, looters hadn't bothered themselves with papyrus scraps. Not when there were golden bracelets to snatch, and necklaces and drinking cups and sculptures. But after "a thousand generations of tomb robbers," by one Egyptologist's reckoning, many of the conspicuous treasures had vanished.

With European collectors and museums in an Egyptomania-induced frenzy, papyrus sheets—or any other items adorned with hieroglyphs—were guaranteed to draw buyers waving money and clamoring for more. But, for several years, Belzoni had been eyeing an even bigger prize. So far it had eluded him.

# Abu Simbel

I t was the lure of treasure that had drawn Belzoni to Egypt. But he made perhaps his greatest find—and certainly his most spectacu-lar—only after he crossed paths with another European traveler who was motivated almost solely by curiosity and wanderlust.

That find would lead to the next breakthrough in the deciphering race. Once again, it would involve a collaboration between Belzoni and William Bankes, this one close on the heels of their obelisk ad-venture.

In the years from about 1810 to 1820, Belzoni and Bankes were among a handful of Europeans dashing back and forth across Egypt in a kind of high-stakes scavenger hunt. The lives of both men changed, and the whole deciphering story veered onto a new track, when they met a tall, bearded, half-starved figure who spun tales of his travels that might have come from *The Thousand and One Nights*.

Jean Louis Burckhardt was a traveler almost without peer. Swiss-born, he had left Europe in 1809, at age twenty-five. He would never return. He spent his first few years abroad in Syria, where he im-mersed himself in the study of Arabic. Soon Burckhardt spoke so well that, with the help of a thick beard and a turban and robe, he could pass as a local. As Sheikh Ibrahim ibn Abdullah, he set off to explore the Middle East and Africa, unarmed, unaccompanied, and endlessly curious.

He would become one of the first Westerners to visit Mecca and the first to see Petra, in Jordan. (As we have seen, Bankes was the first to capture Petra in drawings.) The year 1813 found him deep in the Nubian desert, some seven hundred miles south of Cairo. This was harsh, lawless territory, more than a hundred miles beyond the most remote spot that any of Napoleon's savants had reached.

Burckhardt was chasing down rumors of an ancient, neglected temple on the banks of the Nile. He found it.

Carved into a cliffside in the forbidding land then called Nubia stood six enormous statues, three on each side of an entranceway that vanished into the rock. (The site is about 170 miles south of present-day Aswan.) For anyone approaching overland, the temple complex was hard to spot until the last moment, but from the river it was impossible to miss. Inside, Burckhardt saw more carvings, painted figures, and countless hieroglyphs.

He explored a bit and then turned to leave. As he clambered back up the cliffs from the river, he happened to glance toward the south. Suddenly he saw four immense statues, far bigger than the colossal statues he had already found. These, too, were carved from the sandstone cliffs, but sand now buried them almost completely.

Burckhardt had nearly missed what would prove to be one of Egypt's grandest "lost" temples; what he had found first was a kind of secondary, companion temple.

He ran closer. The head and chest of one statue stood above the sand. The next statue in line was almost completely hidden. "Of the other two," Burckhardt wrote, "the bonnets only appear."

Those "bonnets," it would turn out, were crowns; the statues depicted pharaohs—more accurately, *one* pharaoh four times. Burckhardt climbed his way up to the one statue whose head lay exposed. Here was "a most expressive, youthful countenance, appearing nearer to the Grecian model of beauty" than any other statue in Egypt.

Burckhardt measured the distance from shoulder to shoulder—seven yards. He measured an ear from top to bottom—one yard, four inches. There was no way to tell if the statues showed standing figures or seated ones. If they were standing, Burckhardt guessed, they were sixty-five or seventy feet tall. *What was this place?*

If only the sand could be cleared away, Burckhardt suggested, "a vast temple would be discovered, to the entrance of which the above colossal figures probably serve as ornaments."

Burckhardt had found the site now known as Abu Simbel. No Westerner had seen it for perhaps two thousand years.[*] Today it is a World Heritage Site and a place of pilgrimage for tourists from around the world.

The smaller temple that Burckhardt had encountered first, it would turn out, was dedicated to a queen named Nefertari. (A photo of Nefertari's tomb, its colors still gleaming bright, is included in the art insert.) The second, larger temple honored Nefertari's husband, one of the most famous pharaohs of them all, Ramesses II.

In 1813 no one would have recognized the name Ramesses (or Rameses or Ramses, as it is sometimes written). They might have found it on an ancient list of pharaohs' names, among scores of others, had they known to look.

Later, after scholars had learned to read hieroglyphs, an astonishing story emerged. Ramesses took the throne at about age twenty, in 1279 BC, and ruled for sixty-six years, building monuments to himself all the while. By the time of his death vast swaths of Egypt groaned under the burden of colossal stone statues depicting Ramesses as serene, aloof, unchallengeable, and eternal.

Everything about his life and reign was exaggerated, as if written in boldface. Ramesses ruled so long that he outlived a dozen crown princes. (There was no danger of running out. Ramesses claimed to have fathered one hundred sons and sixty daughters.) By some accounts Ramesses was "Pharaoh" in the Bible, which would make him not only *a* pharaoh but *the* pharaoh.

So say movies like *The Ten Commandments* and a slew of popu-

---

[*] Abu Simbel is still in the middle of nowhere, but now it is served by an airport that brings in endless streams of day-trippers. The whole complex was moved a few hundred yards in 1968, so that it would not vanish underwater with the construction of the Aswan High Dam.

lar books. There is no real evidence for that view. The most we can say is that the biblical Pharaoh was a creature with a monstrously bloated ego, and so was the historical Ramesses. In the Book of Exodus, Pharaoh thunders, "Who is the Lord, that I should obey His voice to let Israel go?" The tone, at least, is authentic. Everything to do with Ramesses conveys the same sense of unlimited power and unchecked ego. Inscriptions hail his prowess as a warrior and wall carvings depict him with spear raised, poised to stab one enemy while he tramples another underfoot.

He built himself a new and lavish capital city, and named it the House of Ramesses, Great and Victorious.* More statues and temples honor him than any other pharaoh, in part because he appropriated whatever caught his eye. When Ramesses could not be troubled to order new monuments, he took over old ones and carved his name in place of the names of his predecessors, or tore down existing temples and used the same stones to rebuild in his name.

Ramesses was everywhere in Egypt. In his new capital city, near the Mediterranean, a statue of him towered ninety-two feet high. Today, all that remains is a forlorn foot, broken in half. So outsized is it that a grown man extending his hand to its full width could not reach across the top of the titan's big toe.

The magnificent "Ozymandias" statue in the British Museum depicts Ramesses, as we noted earlier.† It was found at Luxor, about five hundred miles south of the new capital. (Ramesses's mummy was discovered nearby, in the Valley of the Kings, in 1881. The statue portrays a gorgeous ruler; the mummified king bears a striking resemblance to Mr. Burns, Homer Simpson's boss. But even in death, Ramesses continued to earn special treatment. In 1976, when the mummy began to

---

* Modern-day tyrants have continued the tradition of naming cities in their own honor, but they have had to make do with plainer names—Saddam City, Stalingrad— and with renaming existing cities rather than creating new ones.

† Each pharaoh had several names, including a birth name and a throne name chosen when the king's reign began. *Ozymandias* was a Greek version of Ramesses's throne name.

show signs of deterioration, Egyptologists shipped it to Paris for examination. Ramesses traveled on a French military plane with an official passport—it listed his occupation as "King (deceased)"—and officials at Le Bourget Airport greeted his arrival with the full military honors due a living king.)

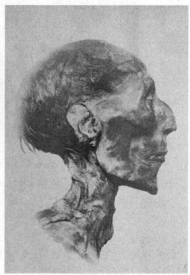

This statue of Ramesses II, which inspired Shelley's poem
"Ozymandias," is one of the treasures of the British Museum.
(The French drilled the hole near the right shoulder, apparently
in the hope that they could find a way to transport the immense statue.
Historians believe they planned either to attach a cable or to insert
gunpowder to blast the head from the torso.) Ramesses's mummy
was discovered in 1881.

Of all the tributes that Ramesses ordered for himself, Abu Simbel, at Egypt's southernmost border, was perhaps the most imposing. Each of its four gigantic statues depicted Ramesses. This display of extravagant homage also served as a message proclaiming Egypt's power to any enemies who might have contemplated a move north. The whole complex served, in the words of the Egyptologist Peter Brand, as "a giant *Beware of Pharaoh* sign."

Four immense statues, each one as tall as a six-story building and each one
depicting Ramesses. The head and chest of one statue (to the left of the
temple door) toppled to the ground long ago, and there they remain.

The size of those statues was a brash, unmissable boast, a mega-
lomaniac's shout through a supersized bullhorn. In sculpture and in
architecture, there was never any mistaking Egyptian taste. Bigger
was better, and colossal was better still. The Ozymandias statue of
Ramesses weighed more than twenty tons when it was intact,[*] and
the head and shoulders alone weigh seven tons. (Michelangelo's *David*
weighs six tons.) At Abu Simbel, each statue of Ramesses seated on his
throne is sixty-seven feet from head to toe. In the Lincoln Memorial,
the seated figure of the president extends nineteen feet.

Burckhardt found Abu Simbel in 1813. Two years later, in the winter of
1815, in Cairo, he and two new acquaintances spent many an evening
chattering away excitedly about the fabulous, inaccessible temple that
Burckhardt had seen.

* The partial statue in the British Museum, which is eight feet tall, is only the top
one-third of the original.

They made a conspicuous trio, not least because at the time Europeans in Cairo were rare. The tall, golden-haired man was William Bankes, the wealthy English collector who had found the obelisk at Philae. His huge companion was Belzoni, the strongman-turned-archaeologist who had helped Bankes ship the obelisk home. Both men tended to defer to Burckhardt, the most experienced traveler of the group. Burckhardt spun tales of disguises and beatings and robberies and narrow escapes. But his listeners clamored especially for tales of Abu Simbel. *What riches might lie under the sand?*

For archaeologists in Egypt, sand was always the problem. (When the savants first saw the Sphinx, it lay buried in sand to its chin, like a dad at the beach indulging toddlers with buckets and shovels.) At Abu Simbel the sand had been accumulating for thousands of years, as judged by graffiti inscribed high on one statue by two Greek soldiers around 600 BC.*

Belzoni had seen in his own explorations how sand heaps formed. On many days the wind blew with such force that it lifted a cloud of sand into the air. "The whole is like a chaos," Belzoni wrote. "Often a quantity of sand and small stones ascends to a great height, and forms a column sixty or seventy feet in diameter, and so thick, that were it steady on one spot, it would appear a solid mass."

Those rock cyclones spun along the ground sometimes for half an hour at a time, Belzoni noted, and then finally dumped a pile of sand and stones to the ground. "God help the poor traveller who is caught under it!"

Once sand had begun to form a hill, more sand was likely to fall in the same place. Flinders Petrie, a renowned Victorian archaeologist, had seen it happen. Sandstorms "tear over the ground," he wrote, "as opaque as a London fog, bearing just as much sand as their whirling will support; and as soon as any obstacle checks their velocity the surplus of sand is dropped."

Petrie was a towering figure in the history of archaeology and a dil-

---

* They scratched the ancient Greek equivalent of *Kilroy was here* into Ramesses's leg—*Written by Archon son of Amoibichos and Hatchet son of Nobody.*

igent scholar rather than a treasure hunter. He was, moreover, a wild eccentric whose nonchalance in the face of a stone storm was characteristic. Indifferent to hardship, or perhaps even fond of it, Petrie labored away under the desert sun in a pink onesie or sometimes in the nude. The harshest conditions did not faze him. As intrepid a visitor as T. E. Lawrence, later better known as Lawrence of Arabia, found himself cringing at the state of Petrie's camp. "A Petrie dig is a thing with a flavour of its own," Lawrence wrote to a friend. "Tinned kidneys mingle with mummy-corpses and amulets in the soup." Throughout his visit Lawrence slept with his feet on the bread box, to keep rats from the provisions.

Everyone who ventured into Petrie's camp took special note of the food. "He served a table so excruciatingly bad that only persons of iron constitution could survive it," one dismayed visitor reported. The food was canned, and much of it dated from digs in previous seasons. Petrie and the other archaeologists "tested for freshness by throwing the cans at a stone wall," one historian writes. "If a can did not explode, the contents were deemed fit to eat." Two young researchers in camp, who went on to distinguished careers in archaeology, fell in love while recuperating together from ptomaine poisoning.

Sand that had piled up in great heaps was nearly impossible to clear away. Belzoni, who had Burckhardt's tales of sand-covered temples dancing in his head, determined he would try even so. He made his first attempt to dig his way inside Abu Simbel in 1816.

When he arrived he saw a carving of a hawk's head high on the cliffside and more or less centrally located. He made a double guess. *If* the hawk was about twenty feet in full (as the size of the head seemed to indicate), and *if* it marked the temple's main entrance, then the top of the entranceway lay under about thirty-five feet of sand.

Shoveling through that dune would be "like making a hole in the water," Belzoni conceded, but he set to work. Soon he ran out of money to pay his laborers and gave up.

He returned the next year. This time he found a way to divert the sand away as his crew dug. Tons of sand later, the entranceway lay clear.

On August 1, 1817, candle in hand, Belzoni stepped inside Ramesses's temple. Casting his eye around rooms that had not seen a visitor for hundreds of years, or thousands, he scanned for treasure.

He didn't find any. He did find painted walls and hieroglyphs and eight more statues of Ramesses, though these stood a mere thirty feet tall. Three days later, Belzoni sailed off, disappointed. (Burckhardt died in Cairo two months later, of food poisoning. He was thirty-two. He never saw Abu Simbel without its sand.)

William Bankes followed not long behind Belzoni. In January 1819, he set a crew to work. Clearing the sand from just one of the temple's huge statues took three weeks, but it was the temple's interior, with its paintings and its hieroglyphs, that truly tempted Bankes.

The working conditions could hardly have been more oppressive. Bankes and a handful of colleagues clambered up flimsy ladders made of wood scraps tied together with rope (because trees were scarce) to copy inscriptions written high on temple walls. Even in the near darkness inside the temple, the temperature seldom fell below 110 degrees. The only light came from flickering candles, dozens of them, fastened to palm branches with wax and held aloft on poles. Bats darted through the gloom, and Bankes and the other copyists flinched when they swooped close. Then they turned to their work once more, squinting to make out the details of hieroglyphs.

One local official stopped by and stared, perplexed, at the sweating foreigners working away in an empty room. "What treasure have they found?" he asked repeatedly.

On September 14, 1822, Champollion would happily have answered the visitor's question.

# CHAPTER TWENTY-FOUR

# Eureka!

B ankes spent a month at Abu Simbel copying inscriptions with painstaking care. Of the men who worked alongside him, one stood out. An architect by training, Jean-Nicolas Huyot had an artist's eye (he had studied with Jacques-Louis David, whose portrait of Napoleon on horseback is included in the art insert) and a deep knowledge of architectural history. The ancient world fascinated him, and he had spent years traveling and studying ruins and monuments in Rome, Greece, and Egypt. (In time he would work on the design of the Arc de Triomphe.) By good fortune, he was a friend of Champollion.

On the morning of September 14, 1822, Champollion received an unexpected package in the mail. He carried it up to the garret he used as a study—Champollion, now age thirty-one, lived in his brother's house, with his brother's family—and tore it open.

Here were hieroglyphs from Abu Simbel, as meticulously recorded by Huyot. This was a particularly fortunate gift, because Bankes himself would not have shared his work with Champollion. He had tried that before, when he had passed along the *Cleopatra* inscription from his obelisk. Champollion never acknowledged him, and Bankes had vowed to have no more to do with that "dirty scoundrel."

Few things are more humdrum than the arrival of the mail. But September 14 was destined to be the greatest day in Champollion's life.

Once again, it was a cartouche that would prove crucial. Champollion focused on one he had never seen before. In its simplest form—there seemed to be several closely related versions—it contained just three hieroglyphs:

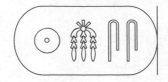

The last symbol was familiar. It occurred in *Ptolemaios* and represented the sound *s*. Here the symbol was repeated **twice**—*SS*. That looked odd, but Champollion guessed—correctly, as it turned out—that in Egyptian, as in Hebrew and Arabic, vowels could be omitted.

The middle symbol, which looked a bit like three vines tied together, was new and unknown. The first symbol, a circle with a dot in the middle, looked, perhaps, like the sun. Champollion drew on his study of Coptic: The word for *sun* in Coptic was *ra* or *re*. Moreover, Ra was the name of the sun god himself. Ra was special, the god of gods, not only the creator of Earth and heaven but the creator of all the other gods as well.

Putting the pieces together, the name in the cartouche was RA __ SS. Did that evoke any name from Egyptian history? Yes, it did, at least

if you made a guess about the mysterious symbol in the middle, . Champollion guessed it might be *M*.

Why? (Not because it looks like an *M*; Champollion knew that had to be coincidence.) Because he had carefully studied the scraps that were all that remained of a history of Egypt written in the second century BC. The author was an Egyptian priest named Manetho, who had written in Greek for Egypt's new rulers. Manetho had compiled a list of pharaohs through the ages. As soon as Champollion looked at RA __SS, a name from Manetho's list leapt to his mind: *Ramesses*.

This was a true *Eureka!* moment, in fact a three-insights-in-one breakthrough. First, Champollion had managed to decipher a purely Egyptian name, not a latter-day Greek import for which Egyptian symbols might have been employed in some makeshift way. Manetho had listed several kings named Ramesses, and all had flourished five hundred years and more before the Greeks arrived in Egypt. Champollion had pulled a curtain aside, peered back three thousand years into an age still untouched by Western visitors, and read a message he had found there.

Second, he had reason to expect that he had found not just an answer to a single riddle but a method that would work more generally. If he was right that Coptic had shown him the way to *Ramesses*, then presumably countless Coptic words besides *sun* would turn up in other hieroglyphs. The bet Champollion had made as a teenager, that a knowledge of Coptic would lead him to the language of ancient Egypt, had begun paying off.

Third, Champollion had fought his way to a clear glimpse of the complicated intellectual machinery that was Egyptian writing. The Egyptians plainly had not used a simple alphabet but a complex hybrid system. Some hieroglyphs, it was already clear, stood for sounds (like *s*). Some stood for words (like *ra*). Some no doubt concealed still deeper-buried secrets.

On this same day, September 14, 1822, Champollion turned to another cartouche that had turned up in Huyot's hieroglyphs. It bore a striking resemblance to the *Ramesses* cartouche.

Here was *Ramesses*:

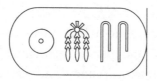

Here was the new cartouche:

So—a drawing of a sacred ibis followed by two hieroglyphs that Champollion had just deciphered as *MS*. And a sacred ibis, for anyone steeped in Egyptian lore, was as recognizable a symbol as a bald eagle is to Americans.

The ibis had always been associated with the god Toth,* one of the towering figures in the Egyptian pantheon. Champollion knew about him because the Greeks knew about him. In a passage in one of Plato's dialogues, for instance, Socrates recounts a story about the birth of writing. He begins by bringing his main character onstage, almost with a drumroll—"one of the ancient gods of Egypt, the one whose sacred bird is called the ibis, and the name of the god himself was Toth."

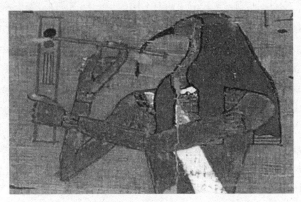

The ibis-headed god who invented writing, Toth.
He is shown here with stylus in hand.

The Greeks absorbed Toth into their own stable of gods (he reemerged as Hermes), and they assigned him a dazzling constellation of talents. He had invented astronomy and mathematics and medicine. Above all, the Greeks believed, he had invented writing. "He invented figures, and the letters of the alphabet, and the arts of reading, writing, and oratory in all its branches," one modern-day historian writes, "and he was the author of every work on every branch of knowledge, both human and divine."

Champollion stared at this new cartouche. *Ibis M S.* The answer

---

* There is no convention about how to write Egyptian names in English. *Toth* is sometimes spelled *Thoth* or *Thot* or *Theuth* or *Thoout*.

practically jumped out. *Tothmes!* Was there a pharaoh with a name like that?

Once again, Champollion turned to Manetho's list of pharaohs. Once again, he struck gold.

Just as there had been a series of pharaohs named Ramesses, so Manetho had listed a series of pharaohs named Tuthmosis. That Greek name was almost exactly how Manetho would have translated the Egyptian *Tothmes*.

Better yet, Tuthmosis I had reigned around 1500 BC, which put him even farther back in time than Ramesses. Here was more proof that, long before the Greeks ever came along, Egyptians had used hieroglyphs to write Egyptian names.

At that point Tuthmosis's name and every fact surrounding him had been lost for millennia. In time—with the ibis cartouche as the first building block in a large structure—Egyptologists would manage to reconstruct his strange story. Tuthmosis had no royal blood. He was a military leader who had been singled out by a pharaoh named Amenhotep and installed as his successor.

In ancient days, the question of who would inherit the throne was always crucial. Amenhotep and his queen were childless. That infertility is no surprise. Amenhotep's wife, the queen, was also his sister; the royal couple were themselves the children of a brother-sister marriage; and *their* parents were the children of a brother-sister marriage.[*]

To avoid a battle over who would reign after him, Amenhotep finagled Tuthmosis onto the throne. It would prove a good choice, for Tuthmosis was a shrewd leader as well as an ambitious, bloodthirsty one. Unlike Ramesses, who was a dud on the battlefield but a master of propaganda, Tuthmosis excelled at both fighting and boasting. He specialized in a kind of gruesome theatrics. After one victorious cam-

---

[*] Ordinary Egyptians didn't marry their siblings. But, at least in certain eras, royalty did see marriages between brothers and sisters as a good way to keep the family business in trusted hands. The family trees of some royal dynasties feature loops and U-turns; they look less like a tree than like the flight path of a bumblebee. In comparison, the family trees of Europe's royal families in the years around World War I, despite all the marriages between cousins, were trim and orderly.

paign, he sailed home at the head of a triumphal procession. Hanging upside down from the prow of his ship, like a macabre figurehead, was the lifeless body of the defeated leader who had dared oppose him.

Perhaps, with two names newly added to our collection, we should pause for a moment to acknowledge the deciphering hazard that Champollion had managed to overcome. Two hazards, really. The first was easier. Egyptian was written with very few vowels, or none at all. This was true of ordinary words and of names as well. *Ra-mss.* *Toth-ms.* That left Champollion forced to guess the missing vowels; in effect, he had to look for a match on Manetho's list without knowing if he should be searching for *Disney* or for *Edison*.

The second, trickier hazard had to do with how Manetho had set those names down in the first place. He had begun with Egyptian names and done his best to transliterate them into Greek. Just what sort of records Manetho had to work with, no one knows. But even in the best of conditions, names often suffer when they travel far from home.

The problem is that every language divvies up the world's sounds in its own way. We speak with an accent when we venture into a foreign language precisely because the pigeonholes of our old language don't suit the sounds and melody and rhythm of the new language. Speakers of a given language may find themselves unable to produce some sounds (or even *hear* some sounds) that turn up all the time in other languages. Thus, English speakers mangle the French *u* (as in *tu*), and the French struggle with the English *th* (as in *this* or *Thursday*).

Occasionally these difficulties have been a matter of life and death. In World War II, the Dutch identified German spies in Holland by demanding that they pronounce the name of the town *Scheveningen*. American GIs in the Pacific theater challenged soldiers they could not see to shout out *lollapalooza.**

---

* This dark history has ancient roots. The word *shibboleth*, which today refers to in-group beliefs, originated as a way to tell friend from foe. In the Bible, we read in Judges of a confrontation between two armies: "Then said they unto him, Say now *Shibboleth*: and he said *Sibboleth*: for he could not frame to pronounce it right. Then they took him, and slew him at the passages of Jordan: and there fell at that time of the Ephraimites forty and two thousand."

When names are transliterated into a new language—which was the job confronting Manetho—they can be twisted almost beyond recognition. In Japanese, for instance, *Johannes Brahms* is *Yohanesu Buraamusu*. *Babe Ruth* is *Beibu Rusu*. In Chinese *Lyndon Johnson* is *Lindeng Yuehanxun*. (The passage *into* English is just as precarious. The American pronunciation of *Van Gogh*, for instance—*van go*—is a long way from the guttural Dutch original.) And we have seen already that the Egyptian *User-maʾat-re* ended up transmogrified into the Greek *Ozymandias*.

So Champollion's task, as he searched through Manetho's list of pharaohs, required not only persistence but also imagination.

For Champollion, in his garret on rue Mazarine on September 14, the day's work had only begun. He had guessed *Ramesses*, first of all, and that had been a giant breakthrough. But *Tuthmosis* zoomed him even further ahead. For starters, it confirmed that he had been right to say

that stood for *M*. (To be precise, he had been *almost* right. As we

will see, would turn out to be *MS*.) Which meant that he could be confident that his decipherment of *Ramesses* stood on solid ground.

That was the least of it. Now, as Champollion stared at the hieroglyphs that spelled out *Ramesses* and *Tothmes*—or, more likely, as he read the names aloud—the fog that had engulfed him for years suddenly cleared. As a teenager Champollion had boasted, "I give myself up entirely to Coptic," and "I dream in Coptic." By 1822 he had been steeping in Coptic for more than a decade. Now, it seems likely, Champollion rolled the pharaohs' names across his tongue, drawing out the syllables. *Ra-mes-ses. Toth-mes.*

And he thought of the Coptic word *mise* (pronounced *me-say*), which meant *birth*. So *Ramesses* and *Tothmes* were not merely names, but names with meanings. *Born of Ra, the Sun God. Born of Toth, the God of Writing.*

That might have been coincidence, but think of the odds. It would be as if—far in the future, after the knowledge of how to read English had died out—archaeologists found a manuscript in an English castle. Picture them hovering above the text, sounding out a name letter by letter. Imagine how their hearts would race when they recognized that their halting efforts had yielded not gibberish but a name they recognized from a list of bygone kings. *Richard*. And then imagine their astonishment, as they continued to pore over the manuscript, when it dawned on them that the name was not just *Richard* but *Richard the Lionheart*!

To Manetho, who was Egyptian, the *Born of Ra* and *Born of Toth* meanings would have been perfectly plain, just as it would have been plain to an English-speaking historian that *Richard the Lionheart* was a name with meaning and not simply a string of sounds. This observation would have been so unremarkable to Manetho that he would not have bothered to comment on it, any more than an English historian would have written, "*Richard* was just a name, but *Lionheart* was a word that referred to lions and hearts." But what went without saying for Manetho was destined to stay a dark mystery for twenty centuries after his death.

Thrilled by his *mise means birth* breakthrough, Champollion made a wild surmise. Just as hieroglyphs *inside* cartouches could spell out words (like *birth*), those same hieroglyphs could spell out words *wherever* they appeared, whether inside cartouches or not.

That was giant, if it was true. Cartouches were rare, so although knowing how to read them was progress, it brought you only a small way toward the real goal of knowing how to read hieroglyphs generally. But now Champollion had found a way to burst out of the confines of his cartouches and tackle the language in all its vast expanse.

Or so he hoped. Now came a test. Champollion grabbed his copy of the Rosetta Stone. At this stage every advance pointed the way to others, in much the way that filling in a single square in a sudoku puzzle compels a series of further moves. The fun and the frustration of sudoku is that the rules of the game force your hand. Now Champollion faced a similar opportunity, and a similar risk.

The rules of sudoku decree that each three-by-three mini-grid must contain digits 1 through 9. If a mini-grid has only one empty square and you have yet to use a 7, then you're in business—you know where the 7 belongs. But the rules declare, as well, that each row must include all nine digits and so must each column, so filling in that 7 leads to more decisions, which have consequences of their own, and so on.

Champollion scanned the Rosetta Stone's hieroglyphs. Was there a place *outside* a cartouche where and appeared together? That pairing meant *birth* inside the Ramesses and Tuthmosis cartouches. Did *birth* turn up anywhere in the Rosetta Stone?

He found it. Amid the ovals and birds and snakes, Champollion spotted his prey. It came deep into the hieroglyphic section, eight lines from the bottom, almost at the left-hand edge: .

Now for the test—had he really found the word *birth*?

Champollion turned to the Greek text. He had read it countless times, but if he was right, he could skip close to the end. There he would find his prize, or learn that somehow he had lost his way. He ran his eyes over the text, scanning and searching. *Birth, birth . . .*

And there it was, immediately after a stretch of boilerplate about "King Ptolemy, the ever-living." So vast and daunting were the pharaoh's accomplishments, the stone declared, that the priests had resolved "to increase greatly the existing honors of King Ptolemy." New statues would be built, new shrines dedicated, new festivals celebrated. And what dates would be most suitable for these tributes? No single day would do, for the ceremonies would inevitably continue longer than that. But surely they must include one especially momentous day, that very day "on which the birthday of the king is celebrated." *Birthday!*

It was not yet noon on September 14, 1822. Champollion snatched up an armful of manuscripts, clomped down the steps, and ran into the streets bursting to tell the news. *Where was his brother?* At work, in the Academy of Inscriptions and Literature. That was only a few blocks away, not even five minutes by foot. Champollion raced into the grand building and ran to his brother's office.

He burst through the doors, flung his manuscripts on his brother's desk, and shouted, *"Je tiens mon affaire!"* (*"I've got it!"*) Then he fainted dead away.

CHAPTER TWENTY-FIVE

# The Unveiling

Champollion's collapse was the most dramatic moment of his life. It fit perfectly with his own temperament—Champollion was fully as romantic and over-the-top as an operatic tenor in full swoon—and it fit perfectly with the era, as well. This was the age of Byron and Shelley and Beethoven and Napoleon, the era of illicit romance and crashing chords and "history on horseback."

Perhaps the fit was a bit *too* perfect. The fainting story was family lore, passed along by Champollion's nephew Aimé, one of the sons of his beloved brother. Do we entirely buy it? The argument could run either way. On the one hand, Aimé was only ten years old on the day Champollion shouted, "I've got it!" On the other, he grew up to become a specialist in ancient manuscripts and his father's assistant at the Bibliothèque Nationale, France's national library. This was not a gossipy hanger-on prattling about matters he only dimly understood.

Aimé told the story in his joint biography of his famous uncle and his father, written when he was seventy-seven. He held Champollion in the highest regard—he hailed him as the Oedipus who had solved the riddle of the Sphinx—but his account of Champollion's collapse was fairly subdued. Champollion bursts into the room and faints in less than a page, and we move on after a few businesslike sentences.

Two decades after Aimé's book, in 1906, a German writer named Hermine Hartleben produced the first full-scale Champollion biography. The new work was immense, filling two fat volumes and thirteen hundred pages. In Hartleben's telling, Champollion took on almost mythic proportions, and the fainting story grew a bit, too. As Hartleben told it, Champollion's brother stood "paralyzed with fear" over the younger man's body, convinced that he had dropped dead. In a moment he realized his mistake and carried Champollion off to bed, where he lay helpless and unresponsive for "five full days."

Champollion fainted on September 14, 1822. Two weeks later, on September 27, he presented a talk on his work to a rapt audience at the Academy of Inscriptions in Paris. It was a gloomy, rainy morning, but for days Paris had been buzzing with rumors that Champollion had marvels to reveal, and the room was packed.

Champollion's old mentor de Sacy was there. So was a jealous rival named Edme-François Jomard, the editor of the savants' *Description of Egypt*. Alexander von Humboldt, the renowned German explorer and geographer, was in the audience. François Arago, an eminent physicist, had come to listen, as well.

And, by absurd coincidence—any screenwriter would have blushed to write such a scene—Thomas Young had shown up, too. Champollion and Young had never met.

Young had arrived in Paris shortly before, on a pleasure trip that also gave him a chance to hear a brilliant young Frenchman named Augustin-Jean Fresnel deliver a lecture on physics. Fresnel's topic was the wave theory of light, the very subject where Young had made his greatest contribution to science. Young had never received due credit for that work (partly out of resentment that he had contradicted Isaac Newton). Now, with Fresnel's help, Young finally received the notice he had earned.

Young could not have been more pleased with Fresnel's talk. His young colleague had "acknowledged with the most scrupulous justice and the most liberal candour, the indisputable priority of my investigations."

Now, in the same week in the same city, Young had the opportunity to hear another scholar speak on another subject where Young felt he had "indisputable priority." Champollion began to read his paper to the roomful of scholars. Young was in the seat next to him.

In keeping with tradition, Champollion's essay bore a formal title— *Letter to Monsieur Dacier* (Dacier was the secretary of the Academy of

Inscriptions)—but few letters have ever carried news like this. Ancient Egyptians had devised a hieroglyphic alphabet to write the names of Greek and Roman rulers, Champollion told his listeners, and he presented example after example of his decoding work.

Much of this work had been published before, but Champollion's presentation was dramatic and compelling. Nor did he bog down his story with history or references to other researchers. Instead, he promised that he would show his audience "step by step and very briefly" just what he had found.

Champollion's focus was on names, not words in general, but he had more than names to offer. Having proposed his alphabet, he went on to explain "why the Egyptians decided to use a particular hieroglyph to represent a particular sound." The key was Coptic. A *lion* hieroglyph stood for the letter *L* because that was the first sound in the Coptic word for *lion*. Similarly, a *mouth* hieroglyph stood for the letter *R* because that's how the Coptic word began. The same principle held for the hieroglyphs for *hand* and *water* and *hawk* and *feather*.

Nor was that all. Champollion went on to argue that the hieroglyphic alphabet had traveled and transformed itself as it moved from Egypt to the Middle East and on to Greece and the rest of Europe. Look closely at the modern alphabet that we employ every day, Champollion insisted, and you will see that it descends directly from Egyptian hieroglyphs. As modern creatures are to ancient fossils, so are our letters to hieroglyphs.

Armed with the techniques he had honed, Champollion concluded, "We can finally read the ancient monuments." The audience rushed to congratulate him. The physicist Arago interrupted the hubbub for a moment to make a formal introduction. *Jean-François Champollion, Thomas Young.*

Champollion knew that his talk had been a "great success," and he basked in the acclaim. "I have received praise higher than the towers of Notre Dame," he wrote his oldest friend, an ally and sounding board dating back to high school days. He followed up that note a few days later with another one to the same friend, just as exuberant. After years of struggle, fortune had finally begun to turn his way. From here on life would be different. "Now anything is possible."

Young called on Champollion at his home the morning after his talk. The two men visited back and forth over the next few days, with their mutual friend Arago playing the role of middleman. These first en-counters were cordial, perhaps because in these early days both rivals assumed there was enough glory to go around. Young and Champol-lion pored over papyrus texts when they were together and then kept up a chatty correspondence over the following several months.

Champollion sent Young two copies of his *Letter to Monsieur Dacier* lecture, fresh from the publisher, and Young wrote to a friend that he had "many things that I should like to show Champollion in England."

Or perhaps the explanation of this peaceful lull was that at first neither man quite took the other seriously. Champollion had scarcely mentioned Young (or anyone else) in his *Dacier* lecture. In Champol-lion's view, Young was a scientific dabbler who had wandered too far from his home territory. In Young's view, Champollion was a bright young assistant who had filled in the details in a picture that Young had sketched, "a junior coadjutor in my researches." Champollion dis-missed Young with a sneer, and Young patronized Champollion with an indulgent smile.

But Young was capable of generosity, too. Two days after hear-ing Champollion's talk, he wrote a long letter about it to a prominent friend, the diplomat William Hamilton, stationed in Naples. (Hamil-ton was a dealmaker and an admirer of ancient art and sculpture. He played a key role in acquiring, for England, two of the greatest treas-ures in the British Museum—the Rosetta Stone and the Elgin Marbles, from the Parthenon.) Champollion had done "*gigantic*" things, Young told Hamilton, and both the unabashed praise and the excited tone were unusual for him.

Perhaps Champollion had taken too much credit for himself, Young went on, "but if he did borrow an English key, the lock was so dreadfully rusty that no common arm would have had strength enough to turn it."

That was generous, but Young reconsidered a moment later. The proverb says that "it is the first step that takes all the effort," he reminded Hamilton, so perhaps Champollion had done him wrong after all.

But then Young backtracked once more. Maybe the proverb didn't apply to this case; maybe Champollion *had* done more than follow Young's lead. "In a path so beset with thorns, and so encumbered with rubbish, not the first step only, but every step, is painfully laborious." All in all, Young conceded, Champollion had done remarkable work.

One reason for Young's wavering was that Champollion had played it coy in his *Dacier* talk. He had delivered his lecture two weeks *after* his breakthrough about *Ramesses* and *Tuthmosis*, but he'd left out that part of his story entirely.

The moral of those discoveries was that hieroglyphs had been used to spell out *Egyptian* names, not just names imported a thousand years later from Greece and Rome. And, as we saw, the *mise*, or *birth*, story carried the even more startling message that hieroglyphs could be used to spell out words as well as names. Those were the revelations that had sent Champollion falling to the floor in a joyous, astonished faint. But he skipped that news.

Only the most attentive listeners to the *Dacier* talk would have guessed that he had any such ideas in mind. Champollion's title offered no hints. Instead, he announced (long-winded titles were characteristic of the era) that he would discuss "the Alphabet of Phonetic Hieroglyphs Used by the Egyptians to Inscribe on their Monuments the Titles, Names, and Sobriquets of Greek and Roman Rulers."

He *did* want to talk about how hieroglyphs could be used to convey sounds, in other words, but he claimed to have in mind only the most narrow and specialized circumstances. That was deeply misleading. Champollion waited until almost the end of his talk to offer a peek at his true ambition. "I am confident that the same phonetic hieroglyphic symbols used to represent the sounds of Greek and Roman names," he explained, had also been used in "pure hieroglyphic writing."

That cryptic reference to "pure" writing hinted at a bold claim. Egyptians had used hieroglyphs to convey sounds, Champollion meant, and they had done so at least a thousand years before the Greeks or Romans or any other Europeans had appeared on the scene. *That* was a claim that would have roused the drowsiest listener, if Champollion had spelled it out. He didn't. This was not the time, he murmured instead, for "getting into long drawn-out details."

Champollion was never one for diplomacy or understatement. Why had he passed up a chance to dazzle his eager audience with a fireworks display?

Probably because the stakes were so high. Champollion's ideas were revolutionary but they were also brand-new. Better to polish his argument than to present it in its raw, untested form. And, besides, this was a race. Some of the contestants had stepped into the open. (Three of them—de Sacy, Jomard, and Young—were in the room at the Academy of Inscriptions.) Perhaps there were others laboring away in secret. Champollion had already put in ten years' work on hieroglyphs. Why offer hints to a rival?

But Champollion was moving fast now, and soon he would burst into the open. Oddly, the next breakthrough that would propel him on his way had nothing to do with subtle points in linguistics or relics from an ancient tomb. It was something far more childish than that.

# CHAPTER TWENTY-SIX

# A Duck May Be
# Somebody's Mother

For fifteen hundred years, scholars had been baffled by a handful of passages written by Horapollo, the Egyptian priest who compiled an all-but-worshipped book on hieroglyphs. His magnum opus seems to date from around 400 AD. Two claims stood out as especially strange. According to Horapollo, as we saw earlier, a drawing of a vulture meant *mother*, and a goose meant *son*.

*Why in the world?* Horapollo provided only the lamest explanations. (A goose meant *son* because, as everyone knows, geese are notably devoted to their young.) Horapollo claimed to be passing along ancient knowledge—he seems to have obtained some of his information about hieroglyphs from vocabulary lists that priests had put together many centuries before his own era—but by his day, no one truly understood what hieroglyphs were all about. Certainly Horapollo did not know.

Then, in 1822 or 1823, Champollion figured it out. The secret behind Horapollo's ancient riddles turned out to be hiding in plain sight, in the children's puzzles called rebuses. Today the appeal of those little drawings doesn't extend much beyond fourth graders. You find them, along with connect-the-dots puzzles, on placemats in restaurants that cater to families with children.

C U

I can see you!

In the hands of Champollion, a notion that occurs to every ten-year-old—that she can write words by using pictures as puns—proved to be one of the great breakthroughs in humankind's intellectual history. Champollion's insight was straightforward. The idea that ancient Egyptians had hit on, back near the dawn of writing, was that you could convey a hard-to-draw word by substituting an easy-to-draw one that happened to be pronounced the same. In effect, you could convey *son* by drawing *sun*.

In Egyptian, Champollion explained, the word that sounded like *son* was *duck*. (He knew from his study of Coptic that both words were pronounced *sa*.) The duck wasn't the point, or at least the *picture* of the duck wasn't the point. The *sound* of the word *duck* was the point.

The duck itself was, in a manner of speaking, a red herring, and it had led would-be decipherers astray for two thousand years. Horapollo had come close to the truth, except for confusing *duck* and *goose*, but he hadn't understood.

Just as the word for *duck* sounded like the word for *son*, the Egyptian word for *vulture* sounded like the word for *mother*. The words were homonyms—utterly different words that were pronounced the same, like *night* and *knight*.

To Champollion's delight, Young blundered badly at precisely this point, although he came very, very close to getting things right. He had seen that in many inscriptions you found two cartouches next to each other and in between them what he took to be a hieroglyph of a goose followed by a hieroglyph of an egg.

As it turned out, the first cartouche listed a pharaoh's official title and the second his name. (If the names of English kings followed similar rules, the first cartouche might read "Defender of the Faith" and the second "Henry VIII.") Young figured that, as usual, each cartouche contained the name of a pharaoh. *But why would the names of two pharaohs occur one after the other?*

Young had already stumbled, and now he fell headlong on the ground. He had guessed, incorrectly, that two cartouches meant two pharaohs. Building on that mistake, he made a second, natural error. This time he focused on the two hieroglyphs between the cartouches.

"I had long suspected that a goose with an egg above it meant *son*," he wrote, "this emblem being interposed in many different inscriptions between two proper names."

As Young put the pieces together, the first cartouche contained the name of a pharaoh; then came a goose and an egg, meaning *son*; and then came the second cartouche with the name of a second pharaoh. What could be easier to decode? These pairs of cartouches, Young explained, spelled out phrases on the lines of *Amenhotep, son of Ahmose.*

The system was so tidy, Young exulted, that "it is possible that we may at some future time obtain a complete genealogical series of the kings of Egypt."

This was almost right and a mile wrong. In reality, the goose and egg were a duck and the sun. Together they meant *son of the sun*, which was a suitably grand way of proclaiming the pharaoh's divine status.

Young had nearly guessed that *duck* meant *son* (although he had called the duck a goose), but the reasoning that had led him close to the truth was all wrong. Champollion happily corrected the record.

His simplest argument was based on cartouches that contained the names of Roman emperors. Champollion had deciphered *Caligula* and *Nero*, as well as several others. Each name was preceded by the duck and sun hieroglyphs. According to Young, that meant *son of Caligula* or *son of Nero*. But Caligula and Nero had no sons.

• • •

It might seem odd that puns once played a respected role in the history of writing, as if court jesters had once occupied honored seats at royal tables. But, historically speaking, our disdain for puns and wordplay is new. One of the best-known passages in world literature is built around a pun. Everyone knows that Eve offered Adam an apple and that all the trouble started there. But the apple was a late addition to the story. The Bible never specifies just what kind of fruit grew on the Tree of Knowledge of Good and Evil. Genesis refers only to a generic fruit.

The apple didn't come along until around 400 AD, when Saint Jerome produced a new Latin translation of the Bible. Because the Latin word *malum* happens to mean both *apple* and *evil*, Jerome had the bright idea of placing a pun at the heart of one of the Western world's founding myths.

Rebus-style puns, too, were once more than childish entertainments. They featured often, for instance, in the coats of arms favored by distinguished families in England. Queen Elizabeth II's mother was Elizabeth Bowes-Lyon, to cite one famous example. Her coat of arms shows bows (as used by archers) and lions.

The Chinese are wary of the number 4, to cite another such instance of the role of wordplay, much as Westerners are skittish about

13. (Chinese skyscrapers skip not just the fourth floor but also the fourteenth and twenty-fourth and so on.) The reason is that the Chinese word for *four* sounds like the word for *die*. (And a clock makes a bad wedding gift for a Chinese couple, because the word for *clock* sounds like the word for *end*.)

In the history of writing generally, and not just in special cases to do with coats of arms and superstitions, rebuses and puns served as crucial stepping-stones. For scripts that made use of pictures, these little diversions helped bring every word and every idea within reach. Abstractions no longer posed problems. If English went in for such things, the word *nightmare* might show a knight in armor next to a horse. *Belief*, a bee and a leaf. *Melancholy*, a melon and a collie.

Those examples are contrived, but Egyptian hieroglyphs were genuinely full of rebuses, which were ideally suited to a form of writing that consisted entirely of pictures. *Vulture* and *mother* and the other examples we have cited were only the beginning.

One of a scribe's main tasks, for instance, was recording business transactions. That required setting down large numbers. But no one would want to write, say, *1,000 cattle* by drawing an ox's head one thousand times, or even by drawing one ox with one thousand scratches next to it.

Instead, scribes took advantage of puns. In Egyptian, the word for *thousand* sounded like the word for *lotus*, and so a lotus flower meant *thousand*. In similar fashion, the word for *ten thousand* sounded like the word for *finger*, and the way to write *ten thousand* was to draw a picture of a finger. In ancient texts you see such entries as an ox head followed by three fingers and two lotuses. Voilà, thirty-two thousand cattle.

Once you had begun to use rebuses, you were poised to take a bigger and more important step. Rebuses pointed the way to a solution to the whole riddle of capturing a language in symbols. The crucial idea, so clear in hindsight, was simply put: *if pictures could stand for sounds when they were part of a rebus, they could also stand for sounds when they stood on their own, with no rebus at all.*

Precisely what that sound was could be sorted out later. The key point was that pictures conjured up sounds. A drawing of a dog, for instance, might stand for the sound *dog*, or it might stand for just the first sound of the word, *d*. And the second choice—*dog* means *d*—offered vastly more possibilities. You could use the dog's picture (in a string of other pictures) to spell out the word *sadness* or *ditch* or *candy*, and you'd never have to bother dreaming up a suitable rebus.

That was exactly parallel to the situation with cartouches. In both cases ancient scribes had seen—and, thousands of years later, Champollion had seen—that hieroglyphs could spell out words when they were inside cartouches or in rebuses, *and also when they weren't*.

That was the significance of the *mise* insight. For Champollion, the discovery that he could read hieroglyphs *wherever* they occurred was his Helen Keller hand-in-the-water moment. In a single luminous instant, Helen Keller wrote later, "The mystery of language was revealed to me." Champollion, too, could pinpoint the exact moment when the world split into before and after.

The revelation about sounds came so late partly because hieroglyphs were so visually compelling. The first thing anyone would say about them was that they were pictures, and that made it terribly difficult to see that they were not *just* pictures.

Champollion had seen how important rebuses were, but he had yet to sort out all their tricks. Maddeningly, it turned out that a given hieroglyph could change roles without warning. A duck might mean *son* in one context; in another setting it might mean an ordinary, quacking duck, such as you might see on any pond; and still elsewhere it could mean the sound *sa*, the sound of the Egyptian word for *duck*.

There were rules and hints to guide the reader along—Champollion's next task would be to search them out—but none of this was straightforward. In science, you can often propose laws that work each and every time—*drop a rock, and it will fall*. With language, matters are seldom so tidy. Every rule—I *before* E *except after* C; *in French the symbol* ^ *above a letter stands for a missing* S—has a host of exceptions.

What is the moral of exceptions to the rules, like *vein* and *weird*, or *mûr* and *âge*? For the linguist, the challenge is to decide if you have found a genuine (but imperfect) rule or if the time has come to reject a pet theory and start over.

Learning the rules that governed Egyptian was maddeningly hard because Egyptian, like every language, had grown and evolved without the help of a central planner. That made for a difference in complexity akin to that between a tidy architectural blueprint and the haphazard branching pattern of a living tree.

Puns and rebuses did offer clues, but often the clues were all but impossible to unravel. Even in ancient times many hieroglyphs were "dead metaphors," in the words of the Egyptologist Richard Parkinson, with their original associations long forgotten.

In English, too, words and phrases that once conjured up pictures quickly become mere labels. It happens all the time with names—*Sawyer, Carpenter*—but it is a feature of language generally. *Toe the line* is nowadays merely a string of words (hence its frequent misspelling as *tow the line*); we hear *ride roughshod over* and think of football teams winning a game, not of horses with nail heads protruding from their shoes (for traction and for doing extra damage to enemies trampled underfoot). No one recalls that once upon a time it was axe blades that *flew off the handle* and not bad-tempered men.

The consequence for Egyptologists is that there is typically no guessing what a string of hieroglyphs means, just as there is no way of guessing from the appearance of the letters what *apple* means. The hieroglyphs for *suffer*, to choose a word almost at random, look like a birthday cake, a zigzag, and a sparrow.

Sometimes you *can* guess. The hieroglyphs for *husband* include a drawing of a penis that could have come straight from a men's room stall. But most often an outsider would never catch on. Who would look at two snakes and two half-moons (which, as it turns out, are meant to be loaves of bread) and guess *leap*?

In a few respects, English and hieroglyphs work in similar ways. Rather than restrict ourselves to the letters of the alphabet, for instance, we also use symbols like *&* and % that stand for words, not sounds. Sometimes we throw together a whole string of symbols—*Could you please* *keep down the #@%@\*%# noise!*—that convey meaning but not sounds. Or we use letters—*XOXO* at the end of a note—that, in some special cases, aren't sounded out.

We use pictures, too, and more every day. Smiley faces have been around for decades, and the skull-and-crossbones warning symbol for longer than that, and every birthday greeting and text and tweet includes a swarm of emojis.

kingjames ● Highest in the Room 🙌
🎤 🤴 🚀 #ThekidfromAKRON 👑
#TheManintheArena 🏟 #KingMe👑
#WashedKing👑

But those are minor features of our script. If English truly worked in the same way as Egyptian, it would make vastly more use of rebuses and pictures than it does. Books would be thick with messages like 👁 ♡ U. But 👁 would sometimes stand for the word *I* and sometimes for the letter *I* (as in *ink*) and sometimes for an actual eye. The drawing of a heart could play all the same tricks, and so could the letter *U.*

A great many words would still be written just as they are now, but *Winston Churchill*, for instance, might be written not in letters but with a drawing of a pack of cigarettes followed by stylized pictures of a church and a hill. (And making matters trickier still, the symbols might endure long after the cigarette brand had gone out of business, when nobody could recall what *Winston* had once brought instantly to mind.)

Champollion tackled the whole complicated setup, and his tone reflected both his pride in all he had managed to deduce and his surprise at just how elaborate and jury-rigged the structure had proved to be. "Hieroglyphic writing is a complex system," he wrote in 1824, "a script at the same time figurative, symbolic and phonetic, in one and the same text, in one and the same sentence, and, if I may put it, in one and the same word."

# Straining to Hear

Champollion now had the field to himself. By this time he and Young had moved on from polite wariness to barely concealed disdain. The *Letter to Monsieur Dacier* lecture marked a turning point in their relationship. Young had listened politely as the talk was delivered, but he grew grumpier when it was polished and published. With a chance to examine Champollion's words closely, Young bristled. Where was the acknowledgment that he had opened a door for Champollion to stroll through? He could not help observing, Young sniffed, "something like a want of liberality" in his rival's conduct.

That formality was characteristic. Even in the midst of an argument, Young's preferred tone was one of pained disappointment rather than overt anger. *It troubles one to suggest. One might almost wonder.* "I fully and sincerely acquit Mr. Champollion of any intentions actually dishonourable," Young wrote, while reminding his readers that he, and not Champollion, had been first to publish an essay on deciphering hieroglyphs. "It may not be strictly just to say that a man has no right to claim any discovery as his own till he has printed and published it, but the rule is at least a very useful one."

Those remarks appeared in a book that Young published in 1823, as a counter to Champollion's *Dacier* lecture, which had appeared in print the year before. Young's book carried a long title, as Champollion's had, but there was a sting in the tail. *An Account of Some Recent Discoveries in Hieroglyphical Literature and Egyptian Antiquities*, the title began, blandly enough. Then came the put-down, though in ever-so-polite guise. *Including the Author's Original Alphabet, as Extended by Mr. Champollion.*

• • •

If Young's dueling style was to jab and flick with an épée, Champollion's preference was to knock his enemies over the head with a club. Since his earliest ventures into deciphering, he had sneered at every would-be rival. Åkerblad, the Swedish savant, "couldn't look at an Egyptian inscription and read three words in a row." A German scholar's supposed "discoveries" were in fact fantasies. Zoëga, the learned and conscientious Dane, had gathered enough material to build a monument but "hadn't even managed to put one stone on top of another."

Young came in for special scorn. The learned doctor was an Englishman, first of all, and in Champollion's view that was a hard burden to overcome. More to the point, he was a pompous old fool prone to "ridiculous boasting" about matters he scarcely understood. Champollion, on the other hand, had known all his life that it was his destiny to solve the riddle of the hieroglyphs.

That was how Champollion spoke to his brother, at any rate. In public he toned things down. Still, he couldn't always resist temptation. In his *Dacier* essay, he offered up a bit of polite praise—"Dr. Young did some work in England on the inscriptions of ancient Egyptian monuments similar to that which occupied me for so many years"—and he even remarked that Young had obtained "very important results." Then he went on the attack.

Though Young had managed to decipher *Ptolemy* and a few other names, Champollion wrote, he had then veered off course. Rather than stick with the correct observation that certain hieroglyphs functioned like an alphabet and stood for sounds, "this English scholar thought that the hieroglyphs that form proper names could express whole syllables, and they could act as some form of puzzle or rebus."

This was a low blow, because Champollion knew that hieroglyphs *could* "express whole syllables" (like *Ra* in *Ra-mes-ses*), and he knew that they *did* sometimes play the role of "some sort of puzzle or rebus" (as the *sun* hieroglyph does in the name *Ramesses*).

He knew all that, but he hadn't yet told the world. And it wasn't just that he knew it. These were the very insights that had sent him toppling to the floor in a faint.

•  •  •

Champollion shouldn't have disowned rebuses, in any case, because they had been so good to him. And they had still another gift to bestow.

Wordplay only works in the language it was made for; puns don't translate. Any English speaker who looked at a rebus of a *pan* and a *tree* would immediately see *pantry*. A German or a Spaniard would have no way of guessing.

So Champollion's success with *duck/son* and other rebuses provided still more proof that his big gamble had paid off—Coptic was indeed the key to ancient Egyptian.

With so much pinned down, Champollion could now give himself a well-defined assignment. He had compiled a kind of hieroglyphic alphabet, from all the names he had deciphered. □ was *P*, for instance; ⌂ was *T*; 🦁 was *L*.

In addition, he had devoted years to the study of Coptic. The next step was to combine the two, hieroglyphs and Coptic, into a single, targeted investigation. Champollion's task was to find every hieroglyphic text he could lay his hands on and read it aloud while listening intently for words that sounded like Coptic.

This was simple in principle but daunting in practice. Emptying the ocean with a teaspoon is simple in principle. If Champollion had troubled to list the obstacles in his path, he might have pulled the blankets over his head in despair.

The first obstacle was that ancient Egyptian was written largely without vowels, which means that no one in modern times can truly know what that language sounded like. A lack of vowels might sound like a minor hazard. *If you cn rd ths, you cn gt a gd jb.*

The problem turns out to be a serious one. It cropped up in dramatic fashion in the 1960s, when archaeologists clashed angrily over the meaning of an inscription found in Egypt on a broken piece of pottery. Thousands of years before, someone had scratched a message in Aramaic, a language related to Hebrew and Arabic. (All three languages skimp on vowels.) "Behold, I have seen a dream," the inscription began, according to one group of scholars. But rival linguists translated the same passage as, "Behold, I have seen a vegetable."

Depending on which experts you believed, the text went on to describe either a ghostly apparition that proclaimed the word "peace" or a warning that "there are no cucumbers left."

How could such a dispute arise? Partly because of the difficulty of reading cramped and twisted letters that had been written so many centuries ago. Some letters were hard to make out. Others appeared midway between two lines of text and might conceivably have belonged to either one. Some were missing and had to be guessed at.

But the main problem was the lack of vowels, which meant that even complete and perfectly legible words could be ambiguous. This was the source of the dream/vegetable mystery. Roughly speaking, it was as if English were written with consonants only and scholars had to decide whether *crt* meant *carrot* or *create*.

For Champollion, the lack of vowels brought an unexpected difficulty in its wake. In ancient Egypt, the notion of "homonym" was broader than it is for us—so long as the consonants in two words matched, that would do. You could draw a picture of one to stand for the other.

The words might have sounded the same, but they might not have. A scribe might have drawn a *pear* to mean *pair*, but a *pear* could equally well have meant any of a host of words with the consonants *pr*—it might have meant *pier* or *peer* or *poor* or *pour* or *pore* or *pry* or even *pyre*. (That slack in the system makes Champollion's identification of *duck/son* and *vulture/mother* all the more impressive.)

A bigger problem loomed. Two intertwined problems, in fact. First, Coptic was not the language spoken in ancient Egypt but a descendant of that dead language, as Italian is a descendant of Latin. Champollion's only hope was that he could sound out words in Egyptian and then recognize their distant relatives in Coptic.

Making matters worse, Coptic was nearly dead itself. *Think of the odds*, one nineteenth-century scholar marveled. Champollion and the other early codebreakers had only a single tool in their arsenal, their knowledge of Coptic, and that lone weapon was "the mutilated and imperfect fragment of an extinct language."

By way of grasping how difficult it would be to decipher an unknown language by ear, think how often we mishear our *own* language. Students mangle the Pledge of Allegiance—*I led the pigeons to the flag*—and young churchgoers raise their voices and sing, *Gladly, the cross-eyed bear.*

Adults are as prone to such mistakes as children. In the nineties so many people insisted they heard creepy subliminal messages in the movie *Aladdin* that Disney felt obliged to respond. Worried parents warned one another that Aladdin whispered, *Good teenagers, take off your clothes.* The actual line, Disney reported, was, *Scat, good tiger, take off and go.*

Understanding speech, it turns out, is a matter of filling in blanks on the fly. We miss a good many words, no matter how sharp our hearing, but we seldom notice because we're perpetually, and automatically, guessing at possibilities. Context is key, and we choose from a range of possible meanings without ever realizing we're doing it. Primed by thoughts of tangerine trees and marmalade skies, we hear *a girl with kaleidoscope eyes* and not *a girl with colitis goes by.*

But this guessing-on-the-go turns out to be quite a trick. For decades, scientists have labored to make machines that can transcribe speech. After all this time the machines still take pratfalls. The phrase *to recognize speech* emerges as *to wreck a nice beach.* A *relationship* becomes a *real Asian ship.*

Which means that Champollion faced an absurdly difficult challenge. He had to breathe life into a dead language, by way of a nearly dead language, *and* he had to hear sounds in silent symbols written on a page.

He did have clues to work with. Coptic used vowels, for instance, though Egyptian did not. So if an Egyptian word had lived on into Coptic, Champollion would have had a good idea of its pronunciation. Similarly, if an Egyptian word had a close relative in a language whose pronunciation was known, Champollion could guess that the two words sounded nearly alike.

Still, it is dismayingly easy to go wrong when you guess at the sounds of an unfamiliar language. If French were a dead language, no English speaker would ever guess the pronunciation of even as simple a word as *oui.*

Mistakes crop up even if you stick with one language but travel a

century or two back in time. Characters in old novels were always wandering into pubs with names like *Ye Fox and Hounds*. In past eras, *ye*
was pronounced *the*. The use of *Y* for *Th* was just a typographical convention (like *f* for *s* in *we hold these truths to be felf-evident*).

Novices can make far bigger blunders than stumbling over a word
or two. You might not know about tones, for instance, and in many
languages they play a crucial role. A well-known Chinese tale, about
a poet who ate a lion, consists entirely of the same sound repeated
ninety-two times, in different tones. Written in Classical Chinese, the
story looks perfectly ordinary. Read aloud, it sounds to Western ears
like *shi* (pronounced roughly like *sure*) repeated dozens of times.

Intonation doesn't play a major role in English, although it does
sometimes come up. I knew a writer who labored over the dedication
to a book. He had focused on his book, and almost nothing else, for
years. At last he finished, and he wanted to pay his wife a proper tribute. But how to summarize all he owed her? Finally he had it. *For Rose*,
he wrote, *who knows why*. He brought Rose the manuscript so she
could savor the dedication. *For Rose*, she read aloud. *Who knows why?*

Many languages present opportunities for similar blunders in
nearly every sentence. In one language spoken in a tiny region of the
Amazon rain forest, the words *friend* and *enemy* are identical except
for a change in tone in one syllable.

The English linguist John Carrington noted his misadventures in
trying to learn a Bantu language called Kele, spoken in what is now the
Democratic Republic of Congo. Changes in pitch made all the difference. To his mortification, Carrington could not hear them. He could
not tell when *Alambaka boili* meant *He watched the riverbank* and
when it meant *He boiled his mother-in-law*.

So the sounds of ancient languages will always remain out of reach. No
matter how many hieroglyphs scholars decipher, we will never know
exactly the sound of a pharaoh proclaiming his magnificence or an
Egyptian mother cooing a lullaby to her baby.

It is not only the sounds of ancient Egypt, of course, that we will
never hear. Until well after the year 1850, the sound of *every* human's

voice vanished forever with that person's death. The earliest recording was long thought to date from 1877, when Thomas Edison recorded himself reciting "Mary Had a Little Lamb." Edison was not sure
how his invention would be put to use, though he made some sugges-
tions—*perhaps clocks could announce that it was time for dinner?*—but
he thrilled at the thought that he had found a way to preserve sounds
for eternity.

"This tongueless, toothless instrument," he wrote, "without larynx
or pharynx . . . mimics your tones, speaks with your voice, utters your
words, and centuries after you have crumbled into dust will repeat
again and again, to a generation that would never know you, every idle
thought, every fond fancy, every vain word that you chose to whisper
against this iron diaphragm."

But it turns out that Edison was *not* the first to capture a whisper
with an iron diaphragm. In 1860 an unknown woman sang a line of the
French folk song "Au Clair de la Lune," and we have that recording. It is
only ten seconds long, but we can hear it to this day.

The French inventor who made it, a typesetter and tinkerer named
Édouard-Léon Scott de Martinville, did not know that he had captured
the *sound* of a woman's voice, and recording sound was not even his
intent. His goal had been to build a machine that could convert sounds
into patterns inscribed on a page.

He succeeded in his quest, and for more than a century the squiggles that he preserved sat silently on a sooty page in a forgotten archive.
The tracings were not rediscovered until the twenty-first century.*
Soon after, a team of American scientists found a way to convert the
transcribed peaks and valleys into sounds floating through the air. A
voice that had been silent for one hundred fifty years then sang once
again, tentatively but unmistakably.

· · ·

---

* The filmmaker Peter Jackson recently embarked on a different sort of venture
aimed at giving new life to long-vanished spoken words. Jackson enlisted the help of
lip readers who painstakingly examined archival footage of soldiers in World War I.
They were able to recapture words (but not voices) that had drifted away more than a
century ago. Jackson's documentary, *They Shall Not Grow Old*, appeared in 2018.

Champollion had no such tools to draw on, nothing but brainpower and his own sharp ears, as he labored to re-create the sound of ancient voices. He had no choice but to rely on Coptic, which was a frayed and tattered lifeline. That was his first problem. His second was just as daunting. Every language changes over its lifetime, and in the case of Egyptian that lifetime had reached an extraordinary length. So Champollion's challenge was not just that he had to grapple with a dead language. He had to grapple with a dead language that had shifted and changed over the course of more than *thirty* centuries.

Think of how English has transformed itself over a vastly shorter span. Here is a famous passage as it appeared in Old English, around the year 1000 AD. *Fader urer, ðu bist in heofnum, sie gehalgad noma ðín.* It would take a keen ear to recognize *Our Father, who art in heaven, hallowed be thy name.*

*Beowulf* was written in Old English, too, and also in about 1000 AD. That was ten centuries ago. On an Egyptian timescale, that would make *Beowulf* a near neighbor of ours. *Beowulf* should be nearly as accessible as *The Da Vinci Code.* But the great epic is just about incomprehensible today. The first line is, *Hweat we gardena in gear dagum,* which means, *Hark! The Spear-Danes, in earlier days.*

A closer look reveals that Old English is not *entirely* murk and mystery. Some words are a kind of compressed poetry. The Old English for *body* is *banhus,* for instance, for *bone house.* The sea is a *hronrad,* not a vast and empty expanse but a *whale road.* A library is a *book hoard.* Without a guide, though, we are lost and helpless. "We joyously recite the nursery rhyme 'Hickory, Dickory, Dock,'" writes the linguist John McWhorter, "with no idea that those are the numbers eight, nine, and ten in the Celtic speech spoken by the indigenous people of Britain that the Angles, Saxons, and Jutes encountered."

Champollion's task was to ferret out such deeply buried clues. Day after day he sat at his desk reciting snippets of ancient Egyptian, perhaps not always joyously, while straining to detect faint, familiar echoes.

# CHAPTER TWENTY-EIGHT

# Strength in Numbers

I n the early days of his quest, Champollion had been able to draw on the Greek section of the Rosetta Stone for guidance. That approach had yielded glistening trophies—dramatic words like *king* and *god* and *decree* and *priests.*

His decipherment of one of Ptolemy's royal titles shows how he worked. Several of the cartouches on the Rosetta Stone included Ptolemy's name followed by several more hieroglyphs. *How to read those extra signs?*

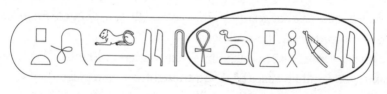

A cartouche that began with Ptolemy's name and then included
several more signs. Champollion set out to decipher those
extra hieroglyphs, indicated in this drawing by an oval.

Well, the Greek text of the stone referred to Ptolemy as "ever-living, beloved of Ptah," so that seemed the natural place to start. (Ptah was the most important god of the city of Memphis.) Then it was simply a matter of filling in the blanks and making educated guesses.

The Coptic word for *life* or *living* was *ankh,* for instance, and that presumably corresponded with the first of the "extra" hieroglyphs. (To this day no one knows the origin of the *ankh* symbol.) The *ankh* turns up in *Tutankhamun,* too; the name means *the living image of the god Amun.*

Next in the Ptolemy cartouche came several hieroglyphs—a snake, a semicircle, and a skinny rectangle—that should have corresponded with *ever* or *forever* or *eternity*, which was *djet* in Coptic. And since Champollion already knew that the semicircle hieroglyph corresponded to *T*, he could deduce that the snake was pronounced *dj* (more or less like the *J* in *jail*).

Similarly, he already knew that the next two hieroglyphs—the square and the semicircle—stood for *P* and *T*, and he knew the Greek word *Ptah*. That made it easy to guess that the next hieroglyph in line, 𝆑, corresponded to *H*.

Champollion played that game for all it was worth, until he had pried free nearly all the Rosetta Stone's glittering gems. Then he shifted focus and began looking to other texts and, just as important, to other sorts of clues.

"You need big, important words in order to get a hypothesis about what letters might be what," says the linguist Amir Zeldes. "But it's only a hypothesis. A big word isn't good for cracking the entire thing. It's good for making a suggestion. What you really care about is *frequency*. You want something that's all over the place."

If you were trying to decipher a text written in English, Zeldes explains, you would be excited if you thought you had picked out words like *liberty* and *president*. Those are words with heft, and they might point the way to other weighty words. Once you had identified *liberty*, say, you might have been able to find other words that also had the letter *T*. You would have taken a step on the way to recognizing words like *truth* and *battle*. But those are rare words.

"Great, you have a theory about three words," Zeldes says sarcastically. "Either you're right or you're wrong. That's not really what you want, because where do you go with it? You want strength in numbers. You want to see super-frequent things, when everything suddenly makes sense and you can say, 'Oh! Got it!'"

Zeldes is young, slender, fast-talking, and an authority on Coptic. More important, he has a rare knack for traveling back and forth from ground-level investigation of tiny details to high-in-the-sky scans of the big picture. He is alternately ant and eagle.

To find a word like *liberty* or *truth* is a thrill and a surprise, he says, like finding a waterfall on a walk in the woods. But learning to spot far less imposing sights, akin to blue squares of paint on trees along a hiking trail, might prove even more important, because those humble markers show the way to further prizes.

What you want are words that pop up over and over again, like *the* or *a* or *of.* Where you have *the,* for instance, the next word is quite likely a noun. And even a rough notion of what you're looking for makes the guessing game far easier.

As a result, the most learned decipherer poring over an ancient text sets to work in precisely the same way as the rawest amateur whiling away a long commute with a newspaper acrostic. The challenge with an acrostic is to identify a quotation. You're given a series of clues and a string of blank spaces, one for each letter of the quotation. The trick is to start with the shortest words. If you find a blank on its own, it must be *I* or *A.* A string of three blanks that starts with a *T* is most likely *the,* an especially valuable word.

Amir Zeldes explains how it works for actual decipherers. "Ask anybody who's taken five lessons of Coptic what the most frequent letter in Coptic is, and they'll tell you it's an *N.* Everything is *N.* It can be a verb, it can be a preposition, it can be a pronoun, there's lot of *N*'s. But the most common meaning is *of.*

"And if you look at Egyptian script," Zeldes goes on, "what's the most common sign? It's this." Zeldes points at a zigzag hieroglyph that looks like a stylized depiction of moving water.

〰〰〰

"Anybody who's looked at a temple wall in Egypt will recognize the water sign, right? Guess what? It's an *N.*"

Zeldes is excited now, and impatient. "That's it! Bang! Do you see?"

Well, not quite, actually. But Champollion did.

•   •   •

Champollion had, in fact, seen two marvelous things at once. First was the match between the most common Coptic letter and the most common hieroglyph. That was good news, because it fit with Champollion's operating principle that Coptic was a descendant of Egyptian.

That was for starters. But the key insight came from Coptic itself. *N* wasn't just a letter. It was also a word. (In roughly similar fashion, the letter *A* in English represents a sound and also the word *a*, as in *a book*.) One meaning of *n* was *of*, which turned up all the time.

So Champollion knew how you wrote *of* in hieroglyphs—you wrote it by drawing a picture of water. Rather than searching blindly through countless hieroglyphic inscriptions, he had a good notion of where he might find nouns waiting to be unearthed. *Ruler of the land. Master of the house. Sounds of the night.*

And Champollion's knowledge of Coptic led him to another, closely related discovery. In Coptic, *P* was a letter, and *P* was also a word. It was, in fact, the supremely useful word *the*. Which meant—this was the real news—that the hieroglyph with the sound *p* could stand for *the*. (It could also stand for the sound *p*, as Champollion had learned at the very beginning of his quest, when he'd deciphered *Ptolemy*.) So off he sped.

Or off he hurried, more accurately, for, just as Young had said, the work was more like a plunge into a thicket of brambles than a sprint across an open field. Champollion's strategy was simplicity itself. With the basic rules of reading more or less mastered, he proceeded as if he were the world's brightest third grader confronted with a stack of books grabbed at random from a library shelf.

Pause for a moment to think how hard this would be. Every text would consist of line after line like *xxxxofxxxxthekingxxxxxxxxthexxx*. So vocabulary was the first hurdle. For Champollion, who no longer had Greek to lean on, every sentence was dotted with strange new words. Here were bills of sale and tax receipts, presumably, but also myths and tales of adventure. How could you move from words like *king* and *priest* to words like *dungeon* and *sorcerer* and *shipwreck*?

You did it by guessing, from context and by drawing on other languages. "Maybe it says, 'They went for a walk and then *something* chased them,'" Zeldes explains. "You don't know if it's a bear or what it was, just some sort of bad animal. And then it says, 'They killed it and ate it.' So that rules out, I don't know, *wolf.* You're not going to eat a wolf."

Some words are impossible to guess, no matter how diligently you look. Those dead-end words turn up often enough that linguists employ a hideous bit of jargon—*hapax legomenon*—to denote a word that has only ever been seen once. Confronted with such elusive beasts, dictionaries of ancient Egyptian concede defeat. An entry might read: "Unknown. Presumably a religious object."

Such one-of-a-kind words can create exasperating problems, and not only for Egyptologists. One of the most familiar verses in the Bible—*Give us this day our daily bread*—contains a word that has tormented writers and translators since ancient times. The Greek word *epiousios*, which is customarily translated as *daily*, occurs in the Lord's Prayer and nowhere else in the Bible or in Greek literature. (The original language of the New Testament was Greek.) No one knows for sure what it meant, and Greek had a perfectly ordinary word for *daily*.

Looked at afresh, the standard translation is hard to embrace. Why would the word *daily* immediately follow the phrase *this day*? And why a mundane phrase like *daily bread* rather than something more uplifting, especially considering another passage that also comes from the Sermon on the Mount, only a few lines after the Lord's Prayer, "Take no thought for your life, what ye shall eat, or what ye shall drink"?

Scholars have been wrestling with those questions for seventeen centuries. A cautious reading of one of the most famous of all biblical passages would be the deeply unsatisfying *Give us this day our [unknown] bread.*[*]

Shakespearean scholars face similar challenges. Shakespeare in-

---

[*] The Bible has other troublesome one-of-a-kind words. In a famous passage in Leviticus, God tells the Jews which animals they may eat and which are forbidden. But one of the "abominations" on God's list is a problem. No one knows what *anakah* meant. The Hebrew word in the Old Testament is traditionally translated as *hedgehog*, because it looks like *hedgehog* in Arabic, but that is only a guess. Some scholars believe that God actually meant to denounce moles or geckos or beavers or mice.

vented thousands of words, including many that are now familiar, such as *horrid*, *vast*, and *lonely*. But some words occur only once, and in phrases where context does not come to the rescue. In one of the history plays, for instance, Shakespeare refers to soldiers killed in battle and says they were "balk'd in their own blood." No one knows what he meant. One theory is that *balk'd* was a typo for *baked*.

If you somehow managed to figure out a fair number of words, you would next have to cope with all the complexities of grammar. The building blocks that form sentences, for instance, may turn up in nearly any order. Mark Twain complained that, by putting verbs at the end of sentences, German makes every sentence into a mystery story, where you only learn the solution at the last moment. (A reformer could improve matters, he suggested, if he would "the verb so far to the front pull that one it without a telescope discover can.")

Champollion and his fellow decipherers had Coptic to help them, but the long transformation of Egyptian into Coptic created countless opportunities for trouble. The most common was to mistake words that looked alike for words that truly were alike. Students and tourists all know the risk. *Pies* in Spanish is *feet*, not *pastries*. *Blessé* in French is *wounded*, not *blessed*. *Pain* is not *hurt and suffering* but *bread*.

In deciphering (and in translating as well), even little words can cause big problems. The word *the* is notorious. In Coptic, for instance, *king* is *ouro*, and the reason has to do with a misunderstanding built around *the*. The Coptic word for *the*, as we have seen, is *p*. Also, it is a feature of Coptic that articles and nouns form a single word—*thehouse* rather than *the house*. The result is that Coptic speakers heard the ancient Egyptian word *pharaoh* (pronounced something like *pouro*), knew that it referred to the king, and mistakenly assumed that it was made up of two words, *the* plus *king*, or *p* plus *ouro*.

Similar mistakes built around *the* dot modern languages, too. The word *alligator* came to English by way of Spanish, after people misunderstood *el lagarto*, meaning *the lizard*. English speakers did not know they had swallowed up a *the* and squeezed two words into one. Arabic speakers made the same mistake, in reverse, with *Alexander the Great*.

The name *Alexander* sounded as if it began with *the*, like many names in Arabic, and the conqueror's name sometimes became *al-Exander*. (By way of returning the favor, English speakers to this day refer to the Moorish palace as *the Alhambra*, which means *the the Hambra*.)

So Champollion struggled on, reading as best he could but bedeviled by unfamiliar and rare words. Then he made a discovery that rocketed him ahead. This was, in the judgment of the Egyptologist John Ray, Champollion's single greatest accomplishment.

# CHAPTER TWENTY-NINE

# A Pair of Walking Legs

Champollion's newest insight was simply put—certain hieroglyphs that looked ordinary in fact played a special role. He named these special signs "determinatives," because they helped determine the meaning of a string of hieroglyphs.

Determinatives were hints to the reader—*these hieroglyphs refer to a town* or *this is a royal name* or *this is a verb*—but they were not pronounced. One type of hint was especially useful. Egyptian, because it omits vowels, is thick with words that look alike but have totally different meanings. (*Threat* and *throat* would be indistinguishable if English dropped its vowels.) The hieroglyphs that spell out the Egyptian words for *tax* and *horse* and *twin* share the same consonants and therefore look exactly the same. *Beautiful woman* is *nfrt*, and so is *cow*.

The Egyptian solution was to add a determinative after an ambiguous word. *Old* and *praise* look identical, but the hieroglyphs for *old* are followed by a hieroglyph of a bent man tottering along on a walking stick; *praise* is followed by a man with his hands lifted in homage. Similarly there are determinatives to distinguish *stairs* and *foot*, which share the same consonants, and *brother* and *arrowhead*, and countless others.

There are hundreds of determinatives in all, and you can't get far without them. Students taking their first classes in Egyptian begin by memorizing two dozen common hieroglyphs that correspond to sounds and then immediately move on to learning several dozen determinatives.

Some are easy to guess. A drawing of a hippopotamus means *hippopotamus*, and a stick figure standing on his head means *upside down*. A typical determinative, like a hieroglyph of a sail, suggests a whole category—*breeze* and *wind* and *breath* and *storm*—rather than a single word.

A few determinatives are charming. The determinative for *cat* shows a cat sitting on its haunches, ears cocked, somehow both alert and haughty at once. The word *cat* is spelled with four hieroglyphs, and the last one is the *cat* determinative (by happy coincidence the first is a jug of milk). The hieroglyphs are pronounced *meow*, a discovery that must have bolstered Champollion's confidence in his deciphering. In similar fashion, the determinative for *donkey* is a drawing of a donkey, and the hieroglyphs are pronounced *heehaw*.

Many determinatives offer peeks into Egyptian culture. A drawing of hair, for instance, means not only *hair* but also *widow* and the verb *to mourn*, presumably because mourners tore their hair out in grief.

Some of those glimpses reveal darker scenes. The determinative for *enemy*, for instance, shows a man on his knees with his arms tied behind his back. The same determinative also means *rebel*. The hard-to-miss message of that pairing was that in the natural order of things, it was *everyone's* role to bow down to Egypt.

In similar telltale fashion, the same determinative could mean either *teach* or *hit*. ("A boy's ears are on his back," an Egyptian proverb asserted, "and he listens when he is beaten.")

But it is best to be wary about using determinatives to draw conclusions about everyday Egyptian life. Every language divvies up the world into pigeonholes, many of them surprising or bewildering to outsiders. (One famous book on linguistics bears the title *Women, Fire, and Dangerous Things* because all three are pigeonholed together in an Australian Aboriginal language called Dyirbal.) To move from rules of grammar to insights into a culture is a perennial temptation—countless books have noted, for instance, that different cultures divide the rainbow up in different ways and concluded that they *see* the world differently—but this is a temptation probably best resisted.

In German *fork* is feminine, *spoon* is masculine, and *knife* is neuter. *Maiden* is neuter and *turnip* is feminine. Does this tell us anything about life in Germany? Or take Navajo. Objects that are long and rigid (like pencils and sticks) call for a particular verb stem. Long but flexible objects (like snakes and strings) require a different stem. Grainy objects (like salt or sugar) have a stem of their own. So do gloopy ones (mud and pudding). All this makes learning Navajo terribly difficult for outsiders, but it hardly offers a window into Navajo culture.

The moral, for Champollion and other decipherers, was that, in ever-so-different Egypt, determinatives were better memorized than analyzed.

Little to do with Egyptian determinatives was simple. Determinatives for verbs were often harder to decode than those for nouns, for instance, because actions were hard to capture in pictures. A determinative that showed a pair of walking legs meant *hunt* and *go* and *hurry* (and also *linger* and even *stop*). Ideas were harder still. Even so, there was a determinative—a picture—for things that cannot be pictured. A drawing of a rolled-up papyrus scroll signaled an abstraction, like *writing*.

This might seem like a peculiar and complicated system. And so it was. But some cuneiform scripts made use of similar strategies, and although English has nothing directly comparable, a handful of typographic rules come close.

When foreign terms like *coup d'état* or *jihad* first turn up in English, they're written in italics as a sort of determinative, until they grow familiar and the italics are dropped. Capital letters (to distinguish the *White House* from a *white house*, for instance, or the name *Frank* from the word *frank*) can play a similar role.

A "silent *E*" serves as a kind of determinative, too—it looks like an ordinary letter but it is not pronounced, and its role is to indicate how *other* letters are pronounced. That tiny bit of code transforms *hat* into *hate*. Spoken English has something like determinatives, too. *Do you mean* funny ha ha *or* funny peculiar?

Young had been the first to spot a determinative (*divine female*, after the name of a goddess or a queen), as he had been the first to recognize that many hieroglyphs stood for sounds. But he had not followed up, and it was Champollion who saw that every hieroglyphic text was thick with determinatives.

The system is easy enough to understand once someone explains it. But think of what Champollion had managed to see. (Neither he nor Young had ever encountered another script that made use of determinatives.)

He had found years earlier that hieroglyphs could stand for a sound, like the *p* in *Ptolemy* or the *l* in *Cleopatra*. He had shown that hieroglyphs could stand for the objects they depicted, as with *sun* or *arm*. He had shown that they could be rebuses, as in *duck* for *son*.

Now he had proposed yet another usage. A hieroglyph might look exactly like any other hieroglyph but function solely as a silent guide to the meaning of *other* hieroglyphs.

And, if Champollion had it right, determinatives were not exotic features that turned up only in rare settings. They were everywhere, and until you had made sense of them, every text you looked at would trip you up.

This was a remarkably bold proposal. "Silent *E*" is a kind of add-on, fun to have but hardly essential, like tail fins on a vintage car. Now along came Champollion claiming that determinatives were vital parts of the Egyptian engine.

Think again of some of the determinatives we have encountered— an old man signifying *old*, for instance, or a cat signifying *cat*. Until you had come up with the notion of determinatives, the hieroglyph of the old man or the cat would seem superfluous, extra symbols that cluttered up a text that, mostly, made sense without them. And if they did stand for sounds—as most hieroglyphs did—then those sounds had turned up in a place where they didn't belong. *What's that cat doing there?*

For the decipherer floundering in midstream, such examples seemed to offer disheartening proof that something was off. But once the code was broken, yesterday's mystery changed into today's confirmation. The determinative of a cat at the end of the word *cat* now seemed to call out encouragement—*Yes, cat! Don't you see it? Cat, for God's sake! How much clearer can I make it?*

Studies by modern-day Egyptologists have pinned down just how vital determinatives are. About one hieroglyph in five, it turns out, is a determinative. But determinatives had another gift to offer, beyond showing what category a word belonged to.

Having identified determinatives in the first place, Champollion now looked at *where* they turned up. He quickly saw that they came at the end of words. That was a breakthrough.

Knowing where one word ended and the next began was absolutely basic, but hieroglyphs hid that crucial information because there were no spaces between words and no punctuation marks.

The rationale for not leaving spaces was partly aesthetic. The visual appeal of hieroglyphic carvings was nearly as important as the message they conveyed. To Egyptian eyes, randomly placed gaps in an inscription were like missing teeth in a smile.

With determinatives sorted out, progress was coming fast. After century upon century of muddle and mysticism, this was all the more remarkable. Before Young and Champollion had set to work, another nineteenth-century Egyptologist marveled, everything to do with deciphering hieroglyphs "had been laid aside as a problem apparently hopeless to solve, or taken up as a toy for the amusement of pedantry."

Now the picture was nearly complete.

# CHAPTER THIRTY

# Clean Robes
# and Soft Hands

By 1824 Champollion had moved far beyond his *Letter to Monsieur Dacier*. Rather than a booklet, he put together a fat new book packed with illustrations and carrying a grand title, *A Summary of the Hieroglyphic System of the Ancient Egyptians*.

This time he put coyness aside. Thousands of years before the first Greek or Roman visitors had stumbled ashore in Egypt, he showed, Egyptian scribes had already devised an elaborate system of writing that could take on any task whatever, including depicting sounds in symbols.

The system is complicated but manageable, and in many ways not much stranger than English. At its heart are twenty-six hieroglyphs that each stand for a single sound. Here are the ☐ that stands for the sound *p* in *Ptolemy*, the 🦁 that sounds the *l* in *Cleopatra*. An owl has the sound *m*, a viper is *f*, a hand is *d*, and several hieroglyphs correspond to sounds that don't turn up in English (a ball of twine is the *ch* sound in *Loch Ness*).

Look at this cartouche that spells out the name *Tutankhamun*. (Cartouches could run vertically as well as horizontally. The choice was a matter of design, just as a restaurant or a bar today might run its name vertically down a wall. Vertical cartouches were read from top to bottom.)

In the middle right is a quail chick flanked by a pair of semicircles (which were meant to depict loaves of bread). The bread loaf stands for *t*, as it does in *Ptolemy*, the quail for *u*. *T-u-t. Tut!*

Egypt's two dozen–plus hieroglyphs, with their lions and owls and loaves of bread, form an alphabet of sorts. Today, in classes and museum programs around the world, students pick and choose among them and laboriously write their names in hieroglyphs. With pens clutched between nervous fingers, they trace *Grace Newman* and *Lee Crawford* and other names that would have bewildered any Egyptian scribe.

But those twenty-six hieroglyphs are not the whole story (even if we put determinatives aside for the time being). Another eighty-odd hieroglyphs stand for *two* consonants. A hieroglyph that looks like a bowl, for instance, stands for the letters *nb* (pronounced, by convention, as *neb*). That is decidedly odd, because the alphabet already has perfectly fine hieroglyphs for *n* and *b*. Why not use those two rather than a third, redundant symbol?

(If English worked this way, we would have not only an alphabet but also another collection of symbols. The character Υ might stand for the letters *dg*, for instance, and you could write the word *dog* either as *dg* (with the vowel omitted, Egyptian style) or, for variety's sake, as Υ.)

This business of symbols standing for a pair of consonants was so odd that Champollion missed it. One of his great breakthroughs was deciphering the hieroglyphs ⬭, which spelled out *Ramesses*. But Champollion thought that the symbol 🐾 was an *M*. It wasn't; it was *MS*. (The symbol depicted three fox skins tied together; the skins were a good-luck charm, like a rabbit's foot, and protected women in childbirth.) Champollion's mistake didn't throw him off because, by good fortune, the next two hieroglyphs stood for the sound *s*, so he ended up with the consonants of *Ramesses* despite having gone wrong along the way.

Nor is that the end of the story. Some hieroglyphs stand for *three* consonants. (The *ankh* symbol—☥—is one. Look again at the *Tutankhamun* cartouche. Now, reading right to left in the middle of the cartouche, we can see the first half of the pharaoh's name—*Tutankh*.) By good fortune, three-consonant hieroglyphs are not quite as common as two-consonant ones, but, even so, would-be scribes had to master not just the two dozen hieroglyphs of an alphabet but hundreds upon hundreds of signs beyond those.

To Western eyes, accustomed as we are to a script based on a small and tidy alphabet, all this sounds almost perversely complex. We know, though, that Egyptians didn't somehow miss the possibility of an alphabet. They saw exactly what it was, and they turned up their noses and walked away.

The first known alphabet was invented, in Egypt, around 1900 BC, near the city of Thebes. There, on a site whose name means the Gulch of Terror, archaeologists have found inscriptions scratched into limestone cliffs. The carvings are hieroglyphs, but in a simplified, easy-to-master form. The finds are recent, from 1999.

The writers who scratched those ancient signs into the rocks were not Egyptians but outsiders who happened to find themselves in Egypt. Soldiers according to some historians, traders according to others, they saw firsthand the benefits of writing and devised an alphabet based on hieroglyphs.

"It was too much to expect them all to learn Egyptian and the complex hieroglyphic writing system that few people knew well, even among native Egyptians," writes the historian Amalia Gnanadesikan. "So they created their own bare-bones set of uniconsonantal signs, modeled after the Egyptian ones. This was the 'For Dummies' version of writing, stripped of all complexity and redundancy, pared down to something an illiterate soldier could learn in a few sessions."

This was a colossal achievement, a way of grabbing one of the most powerful tools ever devised, wrestling it out of elite hands, and turning it over to ordinary men. By most historians' accounts, every alphabet that ever followed—from Phoenicia to Greece and Rome and then across the globe—descends from that first patchwork, hieroglyph-based ancestor. (As we have seen, Champollion made this very claim in his *Dacier* lecture, and today it is generally accepted.)

Egypt's scribes scarcely paused to sneer. Certainly they did not bother to take up anything so slipshod. "It must have looked funny to the Egyptian scribes," Gnanadesikan continues. "To write any word at all required several signs—how inefficient! The letters did not have to be grouped into boxes, but could just straggle after each other in a line—how ugly! And there was nothing in the spelling of a word that pointed directly to the meaning of the word—no pictographic clue, no determinative—but the word had to be laboriously sounded out before it made any sense—how cumbersome!"

More than a thousand years later, Egypt experimented with an alphabet once again. The experiment seems to have been spurred by Egypt's first encounter with the Greeks and their alphabet. Following the Greek example, Egyptian scribes set aside nearly all their hieroglyphs and retained only those that corresponded to single sounds. But this reform, too, was short-lived.

This was not simply a matter of stubbornness. Surprisingly, as one modern historian remarks, Egyptian script was "much more easily readable" when written in the traditional, inefficient way than in the new, sleeker style. An alphabet "sacrificed legibility to simplicity." The new system was easy to learn but hard to read.

How could that be? Because the same features that made hieroglyphs so difficult to decipher—that different signs could stand for the same sound, for instance, or that a single sign could have different meanings in different settings—eventually made reading *easier*, because you had a variety of handholds to grab.

If you missed one clue, you might not miss the next. (If English worked in the same way, the word *today* might sometimes be written as *2day*. A reader who could not work out the letters might nonetheless find her way, if she scoped out the role of *2*.)

Take an odd but crucial feature of Egyptian writing, called "sound complements." These were hints that helped you deal with two-sound hieroglyphs. Look at the name *Ramesses* again. As we have seen, the

🪶 sign stood for *MS*. Immediately after 🪶, the scribes added the sign ⌐,

which was the hieroglyph for the sound *s*. The ⌐ wasn't essential, and it wasn't pronounced, but in this context it meant, *See where I just wrote*

*MS? I meant it. Don't forget that there's an s sound in* 🪶. Then came an identical hieroglyph for the sound *s*, and this second one *was* pronounced. Put all those puzzle pieces together and you had *Ramesses*, but it is no wonder that even Champollion didn't quite see it.

English takes advantage of redundancy, too, although not usually in such a conspicuous way. In the word *inn*, for instance, the second *N* is not pronounced; its role is simply to tell the reader that the word she is reading is not the familiar *in*. Street signs use redundancy, too, and in a more heavy-handed way. Stop signs deliver the identical message in *three* ways (with the word *stop*, the sign's red color, and its octagon shape), even though any of the three would work on its own. Similarly for yield signs, where the triangular shape itself means *yield* and the signs often include the word *yield* as well.

"At first redundancy is confusing," says the Coptic scholar Amir Zeldes, "because your natural, knee-jerk impulse is to expect that one thing has one meaning. But once you get past that and you crack the system, then it's like a floodgate."

Hieroglyphs were not only redundant, as it turned out, but extravagantly and outlandishly redundant. Hieroglyphic writing is one of those intellectual structures, like subatomic physics, that grow ever stranger as you delve deeper. The word for *cat*, as we have seen, requires several hieroglyphs including one that *is* a cat. Why bother with the others? Why not just draw the cat?

Similar examples turn up everywhere. The word *snake* consists of five signs, and *three* of them are snakes. This seems silly and self-defeating, as if the English word *shortcut* were spelled *shooorrrtttcut*.

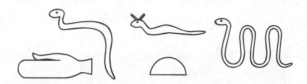

The word *snake* in hieroglyphs. The first four signs stand for sounds. The long, bent snake represents the sound *j* (as in *jail*), the hand is *d*, the horned viper is *f*, and the half-loaf of bread stands for *t*. (The word was pronounced, roughly, *djedfet*.) The third, wriggly snake is a determinative, a silent reminder that the entire string of symbols represents *snake*.

But complexity and inefficiency are features of many scripts, though perhaps they are seldom as conspicuous elsewhere as in Egyptian. In English, for instance, a single sound—*oo*—can take more than half a dozen different forms (as in *noodle, new, neutral, gnu, you, lute, fruit, shoe, blue,* and *to*). *Cat* and *kitten* start with the same sound written in different ways, and so do *feather* and *phone*.

Nobody really minds. Familiarity breeds complacency, and we cope happily—at least native speakers do—with far worse than strange spellings. A once-popular nonsense poem described an unusual winter when, "although there was no snough / The weather was a cruel fough." The poem went on to chronicle the misadventures of an unfortunate little girl who caught a chill and "coughed until her hat blough ough."

It would be easy to design a more efficient system—in Italy and Finland there are no such things as spelling bees, because words are spelled just as they sound—but when it comes to scripts, efficiency is not a priority. Egypt ruled the world for thirty centuries, and hieroglyphs served it supremely well through all those years. China built one of the richest, most sophisticated cultures the world has ever known, and—for thirty centuries and counting—has never seen any reason to discard its dazzlingly complex way of writing.

We tend to think of the alphabet as the ultimate in writing systems. The hard-to-shake notion is that the history of writing is a long saga of crude ideas culminating in the alphabet, in much the way of those evolutionary charts that show an awkward creature heaving itself ashore and then a series of misshapen, hairy ape-men gradually straightening themselves up on the long climb to . . . us.

Evidently that's wrong. Though writing was invented independently several times—in China, the Middle East, and the New World—scholars believe that the alphabet was invented only once and then spread across the globe. But the rise of the alphabet had little to do with its peculiar merits and a great deal to do with the rise and fall of empires. If history had taken a different turn and the Maya or the Chinese had conquered Europe, they would have imposed their character-based scripts on the locals (along with their language and their customs). Alphabets, whatever their virtues, would have sunk into disuse.

So the hieroglyphic system of writing, which was indeed complicated, redundant, and inconsistent, flourished even so. Partly, as we have seen, because hieroglyphs turned out to have merits that compensated for the drawbacks.

One merit stood above all the others. Hieroglyphic script was beautiful, and people will endure a great deal for the sake of beauty. In hieroglyphic writing more than in many scripts, aesthetics were crucial. Appearance trumped convenience.

Signs were sometimes written out of order, for instance, for design reasons. Because symmetry was always desirable, a short sign might be placed between two taller ones. Or words might be stretched out or compressed to fit a given space, by rearranging hieroglyphs or even by leaving some out.

And though determinatives typically came at the end of words, the rule could be broken for appearance's sake. If a determinative was small—like ⊗, which meant *town*—it might look better tucked tidily in a gap between several other hieroglyphs than dangling at the end like an afterthought.

Rearranging a few signs for the sake of appearance was a small matter, though, akin to a modern writer's fiddling with fonts. But considerations of beauty were central to the broadest questions to do with Egypt's writing system, too, like *why so many hieroglyphs?*

Here, too, the answer was aesthetic. In order to entice the eye, hieroglyphs needed the lure of variety. "If we only had 26 hieroglyphs," writes the Egyptologist Bill Manley, "then hieroglyphic monuments would look increasingly dull and repetitive." Egyptians bothered with "extra" hieroglyphs for the same reason that piano-makers bother with "extra" keys.

For still another reason—and this last factor was vital—the complexity of the hieroglyphic system never counted against it in the minds of its Egyptian users. The reason was that ease was never the point. Reading and writing were specialized skills in ancient Egypt, and those who had mastered those arts saw no reason to hand down a ladder so that others might climb to the same heights. The difficulty of the hieroglyphic script was a feature, not a bug.

Throughout the ancient world, no matter the language or the script, literacy was a rare and valuable skill. Until the Middle Ages, all but the most experienced scholars struggled through even brief texts, murmuring aloud as they labored to find the recognizable bits in a jumble of letters. When Alexander the Great read a letter from his mother, silently, his soldiers looked on in amazement.

Every advance that made reading easier took centuries to gain a foothold. (Neither Greece nor Rome bothered with punctuation or with spaces between words.) Each innovation—the use of periods to mark the ends of sentences, commas to mark pauses, question marks, exclamation points, paragraph breaks, capital letters to indicate names and the beginning of sentences—was a battle in a Many-Hundred-Years' War.

Even so simple an idea as alphabetical order took forever to catch on. As late as Shakespeare's day, readers found the notion difficult to grasp. In 1604, the author of a new dictionary had to include a note of encouragement. "If thou be desirous (gentle Reader) rightly and readily to understand, and to profit by this Table," he wrote, "then thou must learn the Alphabet, to wit, the order of the Letters as they stand."

The great virtue of alphabetical order—that it put all words on an equal footing—was considered a profound drawback. A *commoner* might come before a *king*! Other ways of making lists seemed far more natural. Until the late 1700s, Harvard and Yale listed their students' names not in alphabetical order but according to their social rank and wealth.

Why did all these changes take so long? Partly because it is a universal law that challenges often seem impossibly difficult until the moment they seem utterly simple. This is true even of ideas that are blindingly obvious once someone has come up with them. (Fifty years passed between the invention of the can and the invention of the can opener. *Thousands* of years went by between the invention of the wheel and the invention of the wheelbarrow.) But a failure of imagination was only part of the story, and not the largest part.

A bigger reason that change came so slowly to writing was that no one especially wanted it. Hints to the reader were in bad taste, like laugh tracks in a comedy. Experts disdained the idea of anything so vulgar.

This was true in general and especially true in Egypt, where scribes delighted in their elite status. Though Egyptian scribes were craftsmen, which meant that they did not share the exalted status of those who did no work at all, they led a privileged existence nonetheless. An ancient text called the "Satire of the Trades" (which few but scribes could read) spelled out their enviable place in the pecking order.

Other jobs involved endless, thankless labor. The "Satire" gleefully described the plight of the soldier, who is overworked and perpetually in danger ("dead while yet alive"), and the potter, smeared with mud like a creature in a bog, and the cobbler, reeking with the stink of chemicals used to treat animal hides. Carpenters, barbers, and embalmers had it bad, and farmers had it worst of all.

But while others sweated and suffered, scribes sat quietly and took notes. "You won't have to march in the army, your robes will be clean, you won't have to work the fields in the heat of the day." Best of all, "there is no profession free of a boss, except for that of scribe—he *is* the boss."

• • •

For years the eccentricities of the hieroglyphic system tormented would-be decipherers. By 1824 Champollion had fought his way through nearly all the snarls. That June he set out to Turin, Italy, to examine a vast collection of Egyptian antiquities that the king of Sardinia had newly purchased. In all the world no one but Champollion could read the hieroglyphs in that stash of treasures.

The king's collection included hundreds of statues, mummies, and coffins, and endless inscriptions on papyrus. In one small room in the royal palace, Champollion found a table piled high with scraps of papyrus. He gasped. "The coldest imagination would be shaken," he told his brother. So small were some of the fragments that when anyone opened the door to the room, papyrus scraps fluttered into the air.

"How can I describe the sensations I experienced in studying the shreds of this great body of history?" Champollion wrote. ". . . No chapter of Aristotle or Plato is as eloquent as that pile of papyrus . . . I have seen in my hands the names and years of those whose history is completely lost, the names of gods that had offering tables for more than fifteen centuries."

Caught between the thrill of reading words and names that had not been spoken aloud for millennia and the frustration of knowing that the scraps could never be fit back together, Champollion took up one tiny puzzle piece after another. "Barely breathing, for fear of reducing it to powder, I collected a small piece of papyrus that is the last and only refuge of the memory of a king who, in his lifetime, had, perhaps, outgrown the immense Palace of Karnak!"

# CHAPTER THIRTY-ONE

# Out of a Job

Champollion had been obsessed with Egypt before Young ever gave it a thought. Then Young made the first breakthrough, but Champollion passed him and, from then on, had the field nearly to himself.

In the centuries since, partisans of the two men have been fighting a long and unresolvable war. Does credit go to the first to see the big picture or to the one whose diligence and creativity move the story from inspiration to proof? Do we honor the detective who is first to name the culprit or the one who makes the case that sends him to prison?

At its peak, the rival camps assaulted each other with Punch-and-Judy fervor. Champollion was a "villain" whose "effrontery" and "charlatanry" and "dishonesty" were impossible to ignore; Young was "a man with a grievance," fueled by envy of Champollion and resentful of a world that had failed to value his talent as highly as he himself did.

Even when it came to assessing the value of Young's first insight, scholars violently disagreed. It was, in the judgment of François Chabas, the breakthrough of breakthroughs, "the 'Let There Be Light' of Egyptology." On the contrary, sneered an English Egyptologist named Peter Renouf, Young's big idea was a fluke, a happy thought but an isolated, sterile one. "We are reminded of the fable of the Hare and Tortoise," Renouf wrote, "with the curious additional facts that on being distanced the Hare became paralyzed, whilst the Tortoise acquired more than a fifty-Hare-power of speed."

In a sense, the bad blood between Champollion and Young was almost inevitable. Though titans in every field are prone to fits of envy and jealous rage—genius and towering self-regard make a volatile mix—rivalries in science and deciphering tend to be even fiercer than elsewhere. The problem is that everyone is racing toward a single goal. (Shakespeare had to look over his shoulder at Marlowe, but at least the two geniuses were not in a race to see who would be first to write *Hamlet*.)

But in one important respect, the rivalry between Champollion and Young was not like that of other intellectual enemies, like Newton and Leibniz. Those two had no need for each other. If Newton had never existed, Leibniz would have invented calculus on his own. And vice versa. For Champollion and Young, the case was markedly different.

What Thomas Young could do was get things started, by showing that for centuries everyone had approached hieroglyphs in a way that was all wrong. "In scientific discovery, the conceptual framework is the all-important first step," writes the Egyptologist John Ray. "It is knowing what you are looking at, and it is the equivalent of Cortez standing on his alleged peak in Darien. In Egyptology, that framework was the achievement of Thomas Young. Put simply, Young stripped away the mystery which had accumulated round Egyptian hieroglyphs and showed that they too obeyed rational rules."

Young was, in Ray's judgment, "probably the most brilliant problem-solver that Britain ever produced." But a genius for solving puzzles wasn't enough. What you needed as well was a knowledge of Coptic and Egyptian history that ran so deep that intuition and experiment could take you beyond the limits of logic. That was Champollion's role, and no one else could have played it.

It was as if the two rivals made ideal colleagues. Young, who had been first off the blocks in every race he had ever run, was almost bound to have drawn first blood. Champollion, who had been obsessed with Egypt and its culture and its language since his boyhood, was almost bound to have stuck with the riddle longer than anyone else and to have seen farther into its depths.

As time passed, both men seemed more inclined to make peace than their backers did. Young never stopped insisting on his priority, but he conceded early on (at least in private) that Champollion had likely passed him by. "With the hieroglyphs I have done little or nothing since I saw you," he wrote to his friend Hudson Gurney in 1817. ". . . I suppose they might furnish employment for an academy of forty members for half a century, and it will be enough for me to have discovered a mine by which others may enrich themselves."

Young's problem was partly that he had run out of ideas, and partly that so many subjects fascinated him. In the winter of 1816, he sent a note to the editor of the *Encyclopedia Britannica*, who had asked Young if he would write an essay on acoustics. Young took that assignment and added some ideas of his own. "I would also suggest Alphabet, Annuities, Attraction, Capillary Action, Cohesion, Colour, Dew, Egypt, Forms, Friction, Halo, Hieroglyphic, Hydraulics, Motion, Resistance, Ship, Strength, Tides, and Waves," and "anything of a medical nature." Over the next half-dozen years, Young wrote sixty-three articles for the *Britannica*, including his groundbreaking "Egypt" essay.

He never grew tired of deciphering, but he shifted his focus from hieroglyphs to demotic, the shorthand form of Egyptian script. This was a concession of sorts, for hieroglyphs were the glamorous prize, but Young labored away until almost his dying day. In his last published work, written on his deathbed in 1831, he paid a public, handsome tribute to "the ingenious and successful investigation of the justly celebrated Jean François Champollion."

Champollion proved generous, too, at least fitfully. Young had visited him in Paris, in 1828, several years after their first encounter at the *Dacier* lecture. They met at the Louvre, where Champollion had been named the first-ever curator of Egyptian antiquities. Young described the visit to his friend Gurney with delight and surprise. Champollion had "shown me far more attention than I ever showed or could show, to any living being; he devoted *seven* whole hours at once to looking over with me his papers and the magnificent collection which is collected to his care."

Young was working on a dictionary, a collection of all the demotic words he had managed to decipher. This was a remarkable achievement but a limited one. Young had largely confined himself to identifying entire words; he had not truly understood how those words were put together. (It was as if someone had managed to identify the words *United States* on various official documents but had not recognized that the same letters could be rearranged to form a multitude of other words, like *untied* and *seats*.)

*Here is the word* king *as it is written in demotic,* Young had announced. *Here is* strength. *Here is* Caesar. Champollion had taken on a different, and far harder, challenge. His goal was not merely to identify words but actually to *read* them. In effect, Young had compiled a stack of flash cards. Champollion had put together a user's manual that taught you how to read any words whatever.

One mark of science is that its great innovators put themselves out of a job. Newton's laws are public property, the intellectual counterpart of the power tools available for rent at hardware stores. They don't require Newton himself at the controls. Anyone can set to work and figure out for herself when the moon will next block the sun or where a cannonball will crash into a fortress wall.

Champollion did not especially care for science and he actively disliked mathematics, which struck him as dry and soulless. But in his scorn for fact-free flights of imagination and his eagerness to demonstrate precisely how he had come to his conclusions, he placed himself firmly in the scientific camp. He declared proudly that he never *guessed*—he put the dreaded word in italics—but relied instead on heaps of solid, painstakingly gathered observations.

The belief that know-how should be shared is new, at least as measured by history's calendar. It came into the world with the Scientific Revolution. Before that time, insights into the world's workings had always come from sages who hoarded their secrets and claimed powers unknown to all their peers. When Joseph interpreted the pharaoh's dreams for him, he relied on his private intuitions and insights. No one else could see what Joseph did. But Champollion had built a machine that anyone could operate.

# CHAPTER THIRTY-TWO

# The Lost Pharaoh

Since his boyhood, Champollion had dreamed of seeing Egypt with his own eyes. Young, though happy to visit Paris or Rome, never gave it a thought. On the contrary, he prided himself on explaining the world without ever venturing from his desk.

One of the great scientific quests of the era was to determine the precise shape of the Earth. Did it bulge at the equator, or perhaps at the poles? Large, expensive expeditions had been mounted to find the answer, one team setting off to the Arctic, another to South America. Young was fascinated with the question, but he preferred to stay put.

"It is my pride and pleasure as far as I am able to supersede the necessity of experiments and especially of expensive ones," he wrote his friend Gurney. "I have been inventing a mode of determining the figure of the earth from two points in sight of each other, without going either to Lapland or to Peru." This was the rough equivalent of studying the craters on the moon without bothering with NASA or rocket ships, and it was precisely the sort of project that Young liked best.

Despite his yearning, Champollion had never been able to afford an Egyptian trip. (His enemies delighted in mocking him for posing as an expert on a land where he had never set foot.) Finally, in 1828, he made it. By this point the best-known and the most accomplished of Egyptian decipherers, he had managed to cajole a group of wealthy and well-placed backers into financing an expedition to Egypt. Champollion would lead the group. He was thirty-seven years old and almost frantic with excitement.

Champollion's team set sail on July 31, 1828. They neared Alexandria on August 18. Champollion stood at the railing, spyglass in hand, scanning the horizon for a first glimpse of land.

Soon he had grown a thick beard, traded in his European clothes for robes like those the locals wore, and reported with delight that he could pass for Egyptian. He gulped down cup after cup of strong black coffee and puffed happily away at a hookah. No one could ignore the heat ("we melt like candles"), but Champollion claimed to enjoy it.

On October 8, he wrote a letter to his brother and proudly noted his location. "In camp, at the foot of the pyramids," he wrote, and he noted that you had to be next to the pyramids, close enough to touch the stone blocks, to understand just how colossal they are. But humble sights, too, set Champollion to marveling. Every street dog in Egypt "carried its tail raised like a trumpet," he observed gleefully, excited because those strays looked exactly like the dogs in hieroglyphs from thousands of years before. He drew a hieroglyphic dog in the margin of his journal.

Champollion was not starry-eyed—Egypt was desperately poor and flamboyantly corrupt—but his focus was far more on the past than the dismaying present. "I am Egypt's captive—she is my be-all," he wrote his brother, from Luxor, in November 1828.

Champollion celebrated New Year's Day 1829 with a note to Dacier, the head of the Academy of Inscriptions in Paris and the scholar whose name had featured in the title of Champollion's breakthrough paper. He wrote to pass along his best wishes for the coming year, Champollion began his note, but then he got to the point.

He had followed the Nile along most of its length, all the way from Alexandria in the north to the feared "Second Cataract" near Egypt's southern border. At every juncture along the way he had read inscriptions carved into temples, tombs, and monuments. The newest dated from Greek and Roman times, the earliest from thousands of years before that, when the pharaohs had reigned in glory. In every case, Champollion wrote proudly, his system had worked perfectly. "There is nothing to change in our *Letter on the Hieroglyphic Alphabet.*"

"Notre alphabet est bon," he concluded. *Our alphabet is valid.*

• • •

Then, in June 1829, Champollion made one of the most extraordinary discoveries in the history of archaeology. Or, more accurately, almost made. While reading inscriptions at the site called Deir el-Bahri, near the Valley of the Kings—he was, it is always worth bearing in mind, the only person in the world who could have done so—he found himself bewildered.

To his surprise, he wrote in his journal, he found mentions of a king he had never heard of. But "still more astonished was I to find upon reading the inscriptions that wherever they referred to this bearded king in the usual dress of the Pharaohs, nouns and verbs were in the feminine, as though a queen were in question. . . . I found the same peculiarity everywhere."

An obelisk carried a dedication to the god Amun-Ra. "For I am his daughter in very truth," the inscription proclaimed, "who glorifies him and who knows what he has ordained."

A message carved into a temple wall carried a warning: "He who shall do her homage shall live, he who shall speak evil in blasphemy of Her Majesty shall die." That confident, intimidating assertion of power might have come from any pharaoh. That wasn't a surprise. The surprise was the forthright declaration of just who was issuing the warning—*Her* Majesty.

Champollion looked on, goggle-eyed. What "astonished" him was, at first glance, merely an odd bit of grammar, but grammar has seldom had such high stakes.

Egypt had had female rulers—Cleopatra would be the most famous—but nearly all of them had been married to a pharaoh or ruled in the name of a royal prince too young to take the throne. *Who was this unknown ruler?*

The mystery would not be solved until a century after Champollion's death. He had unearthed the first evidence of what proved to be a completely unknown chapter of Egyptian history. For nearly twenty years, Egypt had been ruled by a female pharaoh—not just the wife of a ruler but a pharaoh in her own right—whose existence later rulers had tried to delete from history. This was Hatshepsut (pronounced Hat-SHEP-sut), who was, in the words of the eminent Egyptologist James Breasted, "the first great woman in history of whom we are informed."

The clues that Champollion had spotted were so subtle that they might well have been overlooked altogether, but by this point he had come to a deep understanding of Egyptian grammar.

Egyptian, Champollion had found, took great pains with gender distinctions. Some languages do, some don't. English makes a fuss over verb tenses (*I would have been having a better time if I'd known more people at the party*), for instance, but doesn't bother much with gender. English speakers make do with the same article for *the king* and *the queen*, or the same pronoun for *his brother* and *his sister*. French, say, distinguishes between *le roi* and *la reine*, or *son frère* and *sa soeur*.

Egyptian goes further—not only do masculine and feminine nouns call for different articles and different pronouns, but the nouns themselves have masculine and feminine suffixes. Egyptian had no word for *queen*; the phrase often translated as *queen* was *the king's chief wife*. But in Hatshepsut's temple, Champollion had seen that the word for *king* was followed by a feminine marker, the bread loaf hieroglyph that stood for the sound *t*. That tiny change transformed the familiar word *king* to something bizarre, on the order of *kingette*, and it startled Champollion.

(The royal scribes never settled on a consistent way of referring to Hatshepsut. Scribes adopted the word *pharaoh* at just this point in history, according to the Egyptologist Toby Wilkinson, precisely because it let them dodge the issue. From here on, the word *pharaoh* would refer to the royal palace, as it always had, and also to the ruler who presided there.)

Hatshepsut's story finally emerged in the 1920s. At Deir el-Bahri, near Luxor, archaeologists from the Metropolitan Museum of Art found two pits filled with countless broken bits of statues. As the archaeologists reconstructed the scene, the statues had reigned in splendor in a magnificent temple that Hatshepsut had built. Ancient workmen had toppled them and dragged them to the edge of a pit. There they attacked the statues with sledgehammers and rocks. Then they dumped the broken fragments into the pit.

The workmen had assaulted countless inscriptions and carvings, too, chiseling out Hatshepsut's name and image. But they missed some, and they seemed to concentrate their fury on Hatshepsut's name and face, and not on inscriptions that described the events of her reign.

"They did erase her memory," says the Egyptologist Bob Brier. "It worked. It really did. For instance, she doesn't appear on any of the kings' lists, the ancient records of all the pharaohs and their dynasties. If you'd asked Cleopatra, 'Who was Hatshepsut?,' she wouldn't have had a clue. She'd never have heard of her.

"They never thought we'd figure it out," Brier goes on. "The guys who were sent to Deir el-Bahri were told, 'Find every mention of her name and every image and get rid of it.'" (This was *defacing* in its original, frightening sense—*de-facing*—rather than the watered-down meaning we give the word today. Similarly, the attacks on Hatshepsut's statues were *iconoclastic* in the original, violent sense; the attacks involved the literal breaking of icons.)

This erasing from history was an ancient precursor of the Stalinist technique of rewriting history by cropping political figures from photos when they fell from favor. But in a society where the illiteracy rate was between 95 and 99 percent, it was inevitable that some mentions of Hatshepsut would slip by. "A lot of these sculptors, these carvers, these low-level guys who were sent into the temple to carve out Hatshepsut's name," Brier says, "they're lazy, they're not going to look hard, they're not going to get them all."

The surviving inscriptions told a remarkable story. Hatshepsut took the throne in around 1478 BC, in a period that historians call the Eighteenth Dynasty. (The same dynasty would later include some of the best-known names in Egyptian history, including Akhenaten, the "heretic king," and his son Tutankhamun.)

She had impeccable bloodlines—Hatshepsut was the daughter of a pharaoh and then the principal wife of that pharaoh's son (who was her own half brother). Then her husband died, leaving a young son by a secondary wife. Hatshepsut served as co-regent with the toddler for a short time. Then she took the throne in her own name.

She reigned nearly two decades. She thrived, and Egypt thrived.

Hatshepsut organized a massive trading expedition to the far-off Land of Punt (perhaps it was Ethiopia, but no one truly knows), and her ships returned laden with incense, and myrrh, and ivory, ebony, silver, malachite, lapis lazuli, and gold, and cattle, apes, and monkeys.

She built monuments across the length of Egypt, most notably in Thebes. There she commissioned obelisks and statues and her master-piece, the immense temple that Champollion explored. Cut from cliffs above the Nile, it featured colonnades on three different levels. The final approach was by way of a grand avenue lined with sphinxes, more than a hundred in total, stretching for a third of a mile.

How to explain the violence directed against her images? The order to remove all evidence of Hatshepsut's existence came from her stepson, Tuthmosis III, who succeeded her on the throne. It was his name—or sometimes the name of Hatshepsut's father, Tuthmosis I—that replaced Hatshepsut's in her cartouches.

But experts divide into two camps when it comes to motive. In the view of Bob Brier and his intellectual allies, Hatshepsut had to be erad-icated because the very notion of a female pharaoh violated the natu-ral order. Such an aberration had to be denied as if it had never been.

Other scholars insist that the explanation had more to do with dynas-tic politics than with revulsion. They point out that Tuthmosis III reigned for twenty years before he issued his anti-Hatshepsut decree. That seems a long time to put a vendetta on hold. The real issue, according to these skeptics, was who would rule next. Some historians believe there were rival candidates. One was Tuthmosis's son; the others were more closely related to Hatshepsut and therefore boasted better bloodlines. What bet-ter way for Tuthmosis to smooth the way for his own son to succeed him than by ensuring that no rival could stake a claim of his own?

Even if all Hatshepsut's statues had survived intact, we would not know what she looked like. In Egyptian art, the modern notion of a "portrait" did not apply. Rulers were depicted as idealized types rather than indi-viduals. Kings who had grown old and feeble were portrayed as young and imposing; so were little boys who happened to have inherited the throne. To ponder a pharaoh's image in search of clues to his character, the art historian E. H. Gombrich observed, would have been as "if someone inquired the age or mood of the king on the chessboard."

In search of history, though, archaeologists have devoted endless hours to piecing together Hatshepsut's vandalized statues. From thousands of broken pieces, they have rescued, or partly rescued, dozens and dozens of statues.

Hatshepsut is depicted sometimes as male, sometimes as female, and sometimes as a female with the traditional trappings of male authority, including a royal goatee as unmissably false as Groucho's painted-on mustache. (The name *Hatshepsut* means "She Is First Among Noble Women," so none of this had to do with hiding her identity.)

The best of the statues are treasures of world art. Perhaps the most striking of all is an eleven-foot-long, seven-ton granite sphinx with Hatshepsut's face (and royal headdress and beard) and a lion's body. Reassembled from countless fragments, it now gazes serenely at visitors to New York's Metropolitan Museum of Art.

That breathtaking statue was created more than three and a half millennia ago, at a site six thousand miles from its present home. Much of its story remains a mystery. But what we do know, we owe to Champollion's chance observation of a tiny letter *T*, in a place where it did not belong.

# Epilogue

The rest of the story is quickly told. Champollion had made immense progress, but he had taken on a vast and varied subject, and he left whole areas murky or misunderstood. Given time, he would surely have sorted things out. But he didn't have time.

Champollion had published his first and best-known work, the *Letter to Monsieur Dacier*, when he was thirty-one. He would be dead a decade later.

The task of carrying on would be left to a series of successors, most notably a scholar named Richard Lepsius who styled himself "the German Champollion." It was Lepsius who found ironclad proof that Champollion's deciphering was correct.

In 1866 Lepsius was part of an archaeological team working in Egypt. In the ruins of the ancient city of Tanis, near Alexandria—Tanis was the sand-buried city in *Raiders of the Lost Ark*—Lepsius discovered a counterpart of the Rosetta Stone.

Until Lepsius unearthed it, no one had any idea that it existed. This new stone contained a long passage in Greek and the same passage written out in demotic and in hieroglyphs. The message, which was composed a few decades earlier than the Rosetta Stone, is nothing special—it praises the pharaoh and talks about fixing glitches in the calendar. But the message wasn't the point.

The point of the Canopus Stone (it was named for the city where it was written) was that its text differed from that of the Rosetta Stone. Why was that crucial? Because, before the discovery of Canopus, it would have been possible to reject Champollion's deciphering work as an elaborate self-delusion.

That would have required a high degree of orneriness—Champollion's translations relied on rules and a system rather than inspiration;

he had written a primer, not gazed into a crystal ball. Still, it was *possible* that the message he read in a set of hieroglyphs had never occurred to the Egyptians who had written the message in the first place. How could you be sure? Champollion's learned predecessors, after all, had confidently proclaimed Egyptian "translations" that had nothing in common with his.

And early on, some thinkers rejected Champollion on philosophical grounds. Their problem wasn't that Champollion's translations didn't make sense but that they made *too much* sense. Where were the mystic depths in these worldly messages?

Ralph Waldo Emerson, for instance, felt sure that Champollion had missed the essence of the hieroglyphs. He hailed Champollion's achievement—indeed, he proclaimed him a peer of Aristotle, Leibniz, and Goethe—but he felt obliged to put Champollion's breakthroughs into perspective. No doubt Champollion had "discovered the names of all the workmen and the cost of every tile" in ancient Egypt, Emerson scolded, but he had not captured the true wisdom of the Egyptians.

But then came Canopus, and all such carping became irrelevant. Until Lepsius's find, Champollion had been in the position of some early genius who had announced a theory of arithmetic when no one else could manage such a feat. Give this brilliant thinker numbers to add or multiply or divide, and he could explain how to compute the answer. He claimed to be right each time, but who could know? Canopus provided the equivalent of an arithmetic textbook with an answer key in the back.

Now you could put Champollion directly to the test—start with the hieroglyphic text on the Canopus Decree and translate it à la Champollion, and compare the result with the Greek translation on Canopus itself.

Experts did just that. The match was nearly perfect.

"It is," one scholar at the time marveled, "as if an ancient Egyptian had suddenly emerged from his bandages to talk with us and to observe that we speak his language."

Neither Young nor Champollion lived long enough to learn of the Canopus Decree. Young died more than three decades before Lepsius made his discovery. He spent his last days too weak to rise from his bed but still at work, correcting the proofs of his *Rudiments of an Egyptian Dictionary*. (He wrote his corrections in pen until he could no longer manage ink and inkwell, and then he switched to pencil.)

In his introduction to the dictionary, Young hailed Champollion's discoveries. But, to the last, he rejected Champollion's most important conclusion. Champollion had shown that, in ordinary words and not just in spelling out foreign names, hieroglyphs stood for sounds. With almost his last breath, Young denied it. Champollion's "phonetic characters" might serve as a kind of shorthand "in assisting the memory," but that was all.

He told Gurney, his lifelong friend, that this final work was one "which if he should live it would be a satisfaction to him to have finished," but he knew that was not to be. Doctors could not offer much help and barely even a diagnosis, beyond "something extremely wrong in the action of the heart."

Young managed to reach page 96 in his dictionary before putting down his pencil for the final time. As always, he kept his emotions in check. A medical man to the end, Young contented himself with noting with mild surprise that "he had never witnessed a complaint which appeared to make more rapid progress." He died in May 1829, at the age of fifty-five.

Champollion outlived Young by only three years. He had never been robust, and the fainting fits that had marked his youth had continued into his adulthood. So did the zigs and zags that sent him careening between ecstatic highs and despondent lows. Some biographers have tried to link the physical symptoms with the emotional ones, portraying Champollion as a bit like one of those maidens in Victorian melodramas who were notoriously prone to swooning. (English writers especially favored this view of the flighty French.) But medical historians who have tried to interpret Champollion's symptoms—the family chose not to have an autopsy—tend toward down-to-earth diagnoses. The problem was likely some sort of blood vessel disease rather than a temperament too fragile for the hurly-burly of the world.

Champollion returned to France from his Egyptian trip at the end of 1829 and took a post as professor of Egyptology—the world's first—at the College of France.

Like Young on *his* deathbed, Champollion worked on a monumental Egyptian text until virtually his last breath. "Only one month more—and my 500 pages would be finished," he wrote to his brother in November 1831, "but one must resign oneself and be content with what is possible."

A page of Champollion's deathbed work, *Egyptian Grammar*

He would never finish his monumental *Egyptian Grammar*, which his loyal brother would publish posthumously. In early December 1831, Champollion collapsed while giving a lecture. A week later, a stroke left him partially paralyzed.

On December 23, his forty-first birthday, he asked to be helped to the room on rue Mazarine where, a decade before, he'd had his *Eureka!* moment. "It is there," he recalled emotionally, "that my science was born."

The end was very near. Ten years earlier, John Keats had lamented that death had snatched him far too young, "before my pen has gleaned my teeming brain." Now Champollion confronted the same fate. "So soon," he cried in January 1832. He raised his hand to his forehead. "There are still so many things inside!" It was Keats's anguished howl, shorn of art and bursting with grief.

In the same month, able to speak but scarcely able to move, Champollion struggled to hand the unfinished manuscript of his *Egyptian Grammar* to his brother.

Here was his final account, incomplete but nearly done, a clear and elegant exposition of a lifetime's discoveries. He had done his best. "Whatever happens," he said, "I will have left my calling card for posterity."

From its earliest days, Egypt had been obsessed with immortality. The endlessly repeated message was that death could be conquered and life could rise again. The towering stone mountains to safeguard the pharaohs, the elaborate mummification rituals, the encyclopedic books of spells, all rested on the belief that death was not the end.

Priests rattled off long, formal prayers in the certain knowledge that they had found the passwords to eternity. Pharaohs filled their tombs with board games and hunting spears, for entertainment in the afterlife, and stashed away slabs of beef and jugs of wine, for heavenly banquets.

For an unbeliever like Champollion, such rites were no more than time-honored superstitions. Despite his fervent devotion to Egypt, he remained a true son of revolutionary France—the notion of life after death held no appeal.

But, in a sense, Champollion's lifework honored Egyptian beliefs even so. Not by affirming ancient religious views, it goes without saying. Instead, his work demonstrated a deeper but related truth—personal immortality was not the only sort. In his too-short life, Jean-François Champollion brought a dead language, and a buried culture, back to life.

# Acknowledgments

For twenty years I had a postcard of the Rosetta Stone on my bulletin board. It served as a souvenir of a trip to London and an emblem of sleuthing genius, like Sherlock Holmes's deerstalker cap. I never examined it closely. I knew the stone's story but only in vague outline, and in all that time it never occurred to me to wonder precisely how anyone had ever managed to decipher its arcane symbols.

That question finally took shape in a Thai restaurant on Seventh Avenue, in Brooklyn. I scanned the menu. Here was *pad Thai* and *pad see ew*. It dawned on me that I ought to be able to find *pad* lurking in the menu's lovely, cryptic Thai script. *But then what?*

So began a multiyear quest to learn how geniuses of a bygone century had deciphered the Rosetta Stone. I relied for guidance on accounts and letters by the two heroes of the story, Thomas Young and Jean-François Champollion, and on a host of scholars who have devoted their careers to assessing the contributions of those two rivals.

I am grateful to a legion of librarians and researchers at the British Museum, the Metropolitan Museum of Art, the Brooklyn Museum, and the New York Public Library. Above all, I owe an immense debt to two generous scholars. One is Amir Zeldes, a Georgetown University linguist who innocently answered a stranger's narrow question about homonyms in Coptic and found himself besieged, over the course of months, with endless follow-ups. The second is Bob Brier, a renowned Egyptologist, the author of a shelf of books on ancient Egypt, and a scholar so enthusiastic and knowledgeable about every aspect of Egyptian history and culture that his collection of books and artifacts has outgrown his apartment and fills an apartment of its own. He scrutinized drafts, tracked down obscure references, and unraveled hundreds of riddles. Above all, he learned that there is, indeed, such a thing as a foolish question. The mistakes that remain are all my doing and not his.

Marion Leydier helped me with translations. Adam Okrasinski endlessly drew and redrew hieroglyphs and cartouches. Carl Berke, Barbara Berke, and Michael Golden proved the best of traveling companions. Daniel Loedel provided enthusiastic support from the book's earliest days. Colin Harrison and Sarah Goldberg provided wise counsel and guidance in matters great and small. Aja Pollock copyedited with a meticulous and thoughtful eye. Flip Brophy, my agent and my friend, has more energy and ideas than any dozen people.

Both my sons are writers, and I call on them, and lean on them, at every opportunity. No one could have better allies.

Lynn deserves more thanks than I can put in words.

# Notes

Sources for quotations and for assertions that might prove elusive can be found below. To keep these notes in bounds, I have not documented facts that can be quickly checked in standard sources. Publication information is provided only for books and articles not listed in the bibliography.

Several books and articles that I've cited often are difficult to find in print (because they're old, or obscure, or not in English). They are readily available, in full, online. These include:

Leon de la Brière, ed., *Champollion Inconnu* (Paris: Librarie Plon, 1897). Online at https://tinyurl.com/y65ylw7s.

Jean-François Champollion, *Letter to Monsieur Dacier* (Paris: Firmin Didot, Ather & Sons, 1822). In English and in French. Online at https://tinyurl.com/y6mrk2my.

Hermine Hartleben, ed., *Lettres et Journaux de Champollion le Jeune*, tome 1 (Paris: Ernest Leroux, 1909). Online at https://tinyurl.com/y65hd5e8.

Hermine Hartleben, ed., *Lettres et Journaux de Champollion le Jeune*, tome 2 (Paris: Ernest Leroux, 1909). Online at https://tinyurl.com/y3bv9rlu.

Thomas Young, *An Account of Some Recent Discoveries in Hieroglyphical Literature, and Egyptian Antiquities* (London: John Murray, 1823). Online at https://tinyurl.com/y5tz6vsf.

Thomas Young, "Egypt" (from the 1819 *Encyclopedia Britannica*) in *Miscellaneous Works of the Late Thomas Young, Volume 3: Hieroglyphical Essays and Correspondence* (London: John Murray, 1855). Online at https://tinyurl.com/y68yvwmw.

### Epigraph

vii  *"Here we are then, in Egypt"*: This is from a letter Flaubert wrote to a friend at age twenty-eight. Online at https://tinyurl.com/yykrlfks.

### Chapter One: The Stakes

1  a *"climate unlike any other"*: Herodotus, *The Histories*, book 2, chapter 35. Online at https://tinyurl.com/y4ftjero.

2 *"Gold is in Egypt"*: The passage occurs in "Amarna Letter EA26" to Queen Tiye, who was the grandmother of Tutankhamun. Online at https://tinyurl.com/y4ehho3l.

2 *"wondrous and strange things"*: The traveler was Evliya Çelebi, quoted in Hornung, *The Secret Lore of Egypt*, p. 189.

3 *Napoleon presented his wife*: Brier, *Egyptomania*, p. 63.

3 *"I saw the Nile"*: Seyler, *The Obelisk and the Englishman*, p. 89.

4 *an "infinity of hieroglyphs"*: This was a Frenchman named Paul Lucas (1664–1737), quoted in Thompson, *Wonderful Things: A History of Egyptology*, vol. 1, Kindle location 1489.

4 *"There is hardly the space"*: Thompson, *Wonderful Things*, vol. 1, Kindle location 924.

6 *"an outstanding example of how wrong"*: Pope, *Decipherment*, 88.

6 *"masons' marks"*: Fox, *The Riddle of the Labyrinth*, p. 16.

7 *"Each separate sign is in itself"*: Pope, *Decipherment*, p. 21.

7 *(The penalty for worshipping)*: Pharr et al., eds., *The Theodosian Codes*, p. 472.

7 *"The Greeks and Romans had respected"*: Mertz, *Temples, Tombs and Hieroglyphs*, p. 304.

## Chapter Two: The Find

9 *"('Boney' would snatch them)"*: See the fine essay "Boney the Bogeyman: How Napoleon Scared Children" by the novelist and historian Shannon Selin. Online at https://tinyurl.com/y5wl7ayo. Selin cites several memoirs, including Lucia Elizabeth Abell, *Recollections of the Emperor Napoleon, during the First Three Years of His Captivity on the Island of St. Helena* (London, 1844), 12.

9 *"I expect to be attacked"*: Solé and Valbelle, *Rosetta Stone*, p. 1.

11 *(Even the pyramids were plundered)*: Author interview, Bob Brier, April 8, 2019.

13 *it might take two weeks*: Pope, *Decipherment*, p. 62.

13 *"superstitions" and "depravity"*: Young, *Recent Discoveries*, p. 277.

## Chapter Three: The Challenge

15 *"brothers along with brothers"*: Caesar, *The Gallic War*, p. 78.

15 *the largest and grandest city*: Schiff, *Cleopatra*, p. 67.

16· *"They struggled through a life"*: This is from an essay called "Peasants" by Ricardo Caminos, in *The Egyptians*, edited by Sergio Danadoni.

17 *"meandered across the page"*: Manguel, *History of Reading*, p. 48.

## Chapter Four: Voices from the Dust

21 *The novelist Nicholson Baker*: Baker, *The Anthologist*, p. 108.

22 *"What that word was"*: Manguel, *History of Reading*, p. 6.

22 *"Without writing"*: Eiseley, *The Star Thrower*, p. 41.

23 *"If humans had existed"*: McWhorter, *The Power of Babel*, p. 254.

23   *"when an old man dies"*: Online at https://tinyurl.com/y67oarwq.
24   *stone knives so thin*: Annie Dillard, *For the Time Being* (New York: Vintage, 2000), p. 98.
24   *"a notable advance"*: Whitehead, *Science and the Modern World*, p. 20.
25   *the print of a scribe's inky finger*: Ray, *Rosetta Stone*, p. 122.
25   *"Neither rain, nor any sign of rain"*: Petrie, *Pyramids and Temples*, p. 150.
26   *a baker's thumbprints*: In an essay by the Egyptologist Richard Parkinson called "Egypt: A Life Before the Afterlife," *Guardian*, Nov. 5, 2010.
26   *"created writing in the beginning"*: Parkinson, *Cracking Codes*, pp. 193–94.
26   *"a new pair of sandals"*: In an interview with the Egyptologist Elizabeth Frood. Online at https://tinyurl.com/y5576sxh.
27   *"I am like a donkey to you"*: Romer, *Ancient Lives*, p. 33.
27   *"I am a free woman"*: Cerny, "The Will of Naunakhte," *Journal of Egyptian Archeology*. The passage can more readily be found in Mark Millmore's brilliantly curated website egyptianhieroglyphs.co.uk, in a section called "Love, Marriage, and Family."
27   *A wealthy couple sent a thousand roses*: At the University of Oxford's Oxyrhynchus Online site, https://tinyurl.com/yy9bw8dq.
27   *and so did an unknown play*: Parsons, *City of the Sharp-Nosed Fish*.
27   *"My beloved is on yonder side"*: This translation is by the Egyptologist Barbara Mertz, from her book *Crocodile on the Sandbank*. The book is a novel set in Egypt (cited as one of the 100 best mysteries ever written!) that Mertz wrote under the pen name Elizabeth Peters. She translated the poem slightly differently in her *Red Land, Black Land: Daily Life in Ancient Egypt*, p. 51.
28   *"Would I had phrases"*: Peet, *Literatures of Egypt, Palestine, and Mesopotamia*, p. 120. John Barth quoted the passage in an *Atlantic* essay and made the point about Homer: John Barth, "Do I Repeat Myself?", *Atlantic*, August 2011.

*Chapter Five: So Near and Yet So Far*

29   *"The beer-swilling artisans"*: Green, "Tut-Tut-Tut," *New York Review of Books*, Oct. 11, 1979.
31   *"as if they were packing for a trip"*: Brier, *Murder of Tutankhamen*, p. 28.
31   *"You are young again"*: Ibid., p. 9.
31   *"The Egyptians relished their life"*: Wilson, *Ancient Egypt*, p. 148.
31   *"a very distorted view"* [FN]: Parkinson, "Egypt," *Guardian*, Nov. 5, 2010.
32   *Saint Augustine explained*: Nightingale, *Once Out of Nature*, p. 51.
32   *cures for gray hair*: Romer, *Ancient Lives*, p. 75.
32   *"If you are a guest"*: David, *Religion and Magic*, p. 131.
32   *distraught king who sent messengers*: The Greek philosopher Strabo, who lived at roughly the time of Christ, tells the story in his *Geography*, book XVII. Online at https://tinyurl.com/y4a8t2ql.
32   *"From the early centuries"*: Mertz, *Red Land, Black Land*, p. 55.
32   *"Tut's sandals are decorated"*: "Tutankhamun for the Twenty-first Century: Modern Misreadings of an Ancient Culture." This was a talk by Robert K. Ritner, delivered at the Field Museum of Natural History, Thursday, Oct. 26, 2006.

33   *"the Michelangelo of the Nile"*: The eminent historian is Richard Parkinson, an Egyptologist at the British Museum and the author of *The Painted Tomb Chapel of Nebamun.*

34   *two million stone blocks*: Wilkinson, *Ancient Egypt.* Wilkinson discusses the building of the pyramids in Chapter Four, "Heaven on Earth."

35   *The laborers were free men* [FN]: Berman, "Was There an Exodus?", *Mosaic,* March 2, 2015. Berman is a biblical scholar at Bar-Ilan University in Israel. Online at https://tinyurl.com/yyj7slhs.

35   *Egyptians knew about wheels*: Bulliett, *Wheel,* p. 41.

36   *"they repeated the same thing"*: Author interview April 8, 2019.

36   *"These animals performed the same function"*: Ikram, *Death and Burial,* p. 89.

37   *"ten to twenty cats deep"*: Williams, "Animals Everlasting," *National Geographic,* Nov. 2009.

37   *"grotesque" proportions*: Frankfort, *Ancient Egyptian Religion,* p. 8.

38   *"a depressing light on human nature"*: Mary Renault, "Living for ever," *London Review of Books,* Sept. 18, 1980.

38   *The "poetry of history"*: Schama was paraphrasing G. M. Trevelyan. Online at https://tinyurl.com/y3yytdyk.

39   *"the excitement of the chase"*: Parsons, *Sharp-Nosed Fish.*

40   *The serial killer called the Zodiac*: Michael Levenson, "Fifty-one Years Later, Coded Message Attributed to Zodiac Killer Has Been Solved, FBI Says," *New York Times,* Dec. 11, 2020. See also a YouTube video by the team that cracked the code. Online at https://tinyurl.com/y2bymlp6.

41   *"The supreme spirit and archetype"*: Ray, *Rosetta Stone,* p. 20.

41   *"It is easy to trace"*: Diffie and Fischer, "Decipherment versus Cryptanalysis," in Parkinson, *Cracking Codes.*

*Chapter Six: The Conquering Hero*

43   *"Nature exhausted all her powers"*: Roberts, *Napoleon,* p. 158.

44   *Napoleon spent two weeks*: Ibid.

44   *"Tiny Europe has not enough"*: Strathern, *Napoleon in Egypt,* p. 3.

44   *The Dead Sea scrolls*: John Allegro, "The Discovery of the Dead Sea Scrolls," in Brian Fagan, ed., *Eyewitness to Discovery,* p. 151.

44   *an English aristocrat named Lord Carnarvon*: Fagan, *Lord and Pharaoh,* p. 57.

45   *"The first world war"*: Ray, *Rosetta Stone,* p. 25.

47   *"The country that had once built the pyramids"*: Strathern, *Napoleon in Egypt,* p. 113. My accounts of the Battle of the Pyramids and the Battle of the Nile draw heavily on Strathern's thrilling and meticulously researched history.

48   *"Let the Franks come"*: Roberts, *Napoleon,* p. 171.

48   *"the last great cavalry charge"*: Moorehead, *Blue Nile,* p. 89.

49   *"Donkeys and savants"*: Strathern, *Napoleon in Egypt,* p. 100.

## Chapter Seven: The Burning Deck

51 *close combat in wooden ships*: Keegan, *Intelligence in War*.
51 *"I am killed"*: Strathern, *Napoleon in Egypt*, p. 100.
52 *"Victory is not a name strong enough"*: Warner, *Battle of the Nile*, p. 95.
52 *"It seems you like this country"*: Roberts, *Napoleon*, p. 178.
52 *"The French army is in a scrape"*: Strathern, *Napoleon in Egypt*, p. 174.
52 *"The boy stood on the burning deck"* [FN]: Strathern, *Napoleon in Egypt*, p. 165.
53 *"Bonaparte, Member of the Institute"*: Gillispie and Dewachter, eds., *The Monuments of Egypt*, p. 5.
53 *(what had been the palace harem)*: Roberts, *Napoleon*, p. 179.
53 *"these granite pages"*: Solé and Valbelle, *Rosetta Stone*, p. 5.
54 *"the better to enjoy their torments"*: Strathern, *Napoleon in Egypt*, p. 335.
54 *(the loss of his nose, an eye, and an ear)*: Roberts, *Napoleon*, p. 192.
55 *a brand-new branch of the French army*: Gillispie, *Science and Polity in France*, p. 372; Solé and Valbelle, *Rosetta Stone*, p. 3.
55 *Bouchard sent news of the find*: Parkinson, *Cracking Codes*, p. 20.
55 *"the youthful king who has arisen"*: Ray, *Rosetta Stone*, p. 164.
56 *a "young degenerate"*: Bevan, *The House of Ptolemy*. This passage is from chapter VII, "Ptolemy IV, Philopator (221–203 BC)." Online at https://tinyurl.com/yy7jsx49.
56 *the stone's inscription hailed*: This translation is from Ray, *Rosetta Stone*, p. 164.
56 *"the Great Revolt"*: Urbanus, "In the Time of the Rosetta Stone," *Archaeology*, Nov./Dec. 2017.
56 *"A small class of Greek officials"*: Wilkinson, *Rise and Fall*, Kindle location 7493.
56 *They married other Greeks*: Brier, *Ancient Egypt*, p. 41.
56 *Greek to him*: Ray, *Rosetta Stone*, p. 137.
56 *the speech fell flat* [FN]: Wilkinson, *Rise and Fall*, Kindle location 7565.
57 *"He released those who were in prison"*: This translation is from Ray, *Rosetta Stone*, p. 164.

## Chapter Eight: Monsieur Smith Makes His Exit

59 *a "discovery at Rosetta"*: Herold, *Bonaparte in Egypt*, p. 191.
59 *the savants' presentations ranged all over*: Gillispie, "Scientific Aspects of the French Egyptian Expedition," *Proceedings of the American Philosophical Society*, Dec. 1989.
59 *"So many words for a single fish?"*: Solé and Valbelle, *Rosetta Stone*, p. 7.
59 *The first newspaper description*: The newspaper is online at https://tinyurl.com/yyhzfuvk.
60 *"The news from Europe has caused me"*: *Courier de l'Egypte*, Sept. 15, 1799. Online at https://tinyurl.com/yyhzfuvk.
60 *The chest bore a bland label*: Burleigh, *Mirage*, p. 140.
61 *"Bonaparte arrived triumphantly"*: White, *Atrocities*, p. 263.
61 *("an income of 10,000 men a month")*: Strathern, *Napoleon in Egypt*, p. 36.

61 *"That bugger has deserted us"*: Roberts, *Napoleon*, p. 201.

61 *(To the soldiers' fury)*: Burleigh, *Mirage*, p. 94.

62 *re-creating "the arts of France"*: Brier, *Egyptomania*, p. 60.

62 *"stupid, miserable, and dull-witted"*: Roberts, *Napoleon*, p. 177.

62 The *most eminent, Antoine Lavoisier* [FN]: Dennis J. Duveen, "Anton Laurent Lavoisier and the French Revolution," *Journal of Chemical Education* 31 (Feb. 1954).

63 *"Every morning peasants heaved buckets"*: Burleigh, *Mirage*, p. 181.

64 *the savants "tripped on fresh corpses"*: Ibid., p. 182.

64 *He had been the Chevalier de Non*: Pierre Rosenberg, ed., "Napoleon's Eye." This was the catalog of an exhibition at the Louvre, Oct. 1999–Jan. 2000.

64 *("a diplomat, artist, and pornographer")*: Thompson, *Wonderful Things*, vol. 1, Kindle location 1875.

64 *"War, how brilliant you shine"*: Rosenberg, "Napoleon's Eye."

64 *"I have discovered in myself the willpower"*: Gillispie and Dewatchter, eds., *The Monuments of Egypt*, p. 30.

65 *"Mine is an ardent piety"*: Ibid., p. 39.

65 *one-fourth of the savants died*: Thompson, *Wonderful Things*, vol. 1, Kindle location 1879.


### Chapter Nine: A Celebrity in Stone

67 *they happened on two tantalizing finds*: Solé and Valbelle, *Rosetta Stone*, p. 27.

68 *The attacker was quickly caught*: Herold, *Bonaparte in Egypt*, p. 404; Strathern, *Napoleon in Egypt*, pp. 413–14.

68 *After Suleiman's death, his skeleton* [FN]: Simon Harrison, *Dark Trophies: Hunting and the Enemy Body in Modern War* (New York: Berghahn Books, 2012), pp. 53, 56.

68 *"the god Mars in uniform"*: Strathern, *Napoleon in Egypt*, p. 35.

69 *"I shall defend myself to the last extremity"*: Herold, *Bonaparte in Egypt*.

69 *sleeping with it under his bed*: Strathern, *Napoleon in Egypt*, p. 414. Other historians believe Menou hid the Rosetta Stone in a warehouse. See Ray, *Rosetta Stone*, p. 35, and Parkinson, *Cracking Codes*, p. 22.

69 *"Never has the world been so pillaged"*: Burleigh, *Mirage*, p. 216.

69 *Menou's tantrum "diverted us highly"*: Ibid.

69 *"When I demand the Arabic manuscripts"*: Solé and Valbelle, *Rosetta Stone*, p. 32.

70 *(Napoleon applauded "the good harvest")*: John Howard, ed., *Letters and Documents of Napoleon, Volume 1: The Rise to Power*, p. 173. Quoted by Shannon Selin in "Napoleon's Looted Art." Online at https://tinyurl.com/y3a6nqls.

70 *"I have just been informed"*: Burleigh, *Mirage*, p. 213.

70 *"You are depriving us of our collections"*: Ibid.

70 *"We shall burn our riches ourselves"*: Solé and Valbelle, *Rosetta Stone*, p. 35.

70 *The prizes included statues*: *Gentleman's Magazine* 72, pt. 2 (1802), p. 726. Online at https://tinyurl.com/y2gdpsoo.

70 *an immense sarcophagus*: See the British Museum's description. Online at https://tinyurl.com/y4cplaws.

71  *"a proud trophy of the arms of Britain"*: Fagan, ed., *Eyewitness to Discovery*, p. 89.
71  *"a lasting monument of glory"*: Delbourgo, *Collecting the World*, p. 315.
71  *"Captured in Egypt by the British Army"*: Parkinson, *Cracking Codes*, p. 23.
71  *"one of the Museum's great embarrassments"*: Richard Parkinson in a lecture on the Rosetta Stone, at the 7:30 mark. Online at https://tinyurl.com/yytufuj8.
72  *"the prize possession of the British Museum"*: Beard, "Souvenirs of Culture," *Art History* 13, no. 4 (Dec. 1992).

### Chapter Ten: First Guesses

73  *He counted 958 different symbols*: Allen, "The Predecessors of Champollion," *Proceedings of the American Philosophical Society* 104, no. 5 (Oct. 17, 1960), p. 546.
74  *(A typical five-year-old)*: Franzo Law II et al., "Vocabulary Size and Auditory Recognition in Preschool Children," *Applied Psycholinguistics* 38, no. 1 (Jan. 2017). Online at https://tinyurl.com/y2vf4hr4.
74  *"Further goals I have thought best"*: Ray, *Rosetta Stone*, p. 24.
75  *"I would treasure an exact copy"*: Picci, Ascani, and Buzi, eds., *The Forgotten Scholar*, p. 172.
75  *By the end of the Napoleonic Wars*: White, *Atrocities*, p. 259.
75  *they distributed copies of the inscription*: Parkinson, *Cracking Codes*, p. 22.
76  *a tattoo copied long ago*: Jacob Mikanowski, "Language at the End of the World," *Cabinet*, Summer 2017. Online at https://tinyurl.com/y4k6c2h7.
76  *Thomas Young sent a letter*: Young wrote to William Bankes's father and asked him to pass the note to his son. The letter is online at https://tinyurl.com/y5my4l78.
78  *"The hope I had at first entertained"*: Solé and Valbelle, *Rosetta Stone*, p. 49.
79  *"Seven years having now elapsed"*: Thompson, *Wonderful Things*, vol. 1, Kindle location 2087.
79  *"Everything now must be Egyptian"*: The writer who complained was Robert Southey, quoted in Judith Pascoe, *The Hummingbird Cabinet: A Rare and Curious History of Romantic Collectors* (Ithaca, NY: Cornell University Press, 2006), p. 112.
79  *a specially made chest of drawers*: Gillispie and Dewachter, eds., *Monuments of Ancient Egypt*, p. 1.
79  *"the immortal name of Bonaparte"* [FN]: Pope, *Decipherment*, p. 207.
80  *reproduced the stone's inscriptions "with religious care"*: Solé and Valbelle, *Rosetta Stone*, p. 44.
80  *"The stone is black granite"*: Ibid.
80  *"At its first discovery"*: Thomasson, *Life of J.D. Åkerblad*, p. 249.

### Chapter Eleven: The Rivals

81  *provided him "extraordinary pleasure"*: Glynn, *Elegance in Science*, p. 108.
81  *He was the child of an unlikely match*: Ibid., p. 42.
82  *"rather below than above the middle station"*: Hilts, "Autobiographical Sketch," p. 248. Near the end of his life, Young wrote an autobiographical essay that he hoped would appear in the *Encyclopedia Britannica* after his death. It never did,

but in 1978 a historian of science, Victor Hilts, published Young's essay along with some commentary.

82  *an inheritance of £10,000*: Peacock, *Life of Thomas Young*, p. 124.

82  *"Enthusiasm, that is the only life"*: Ray, *Rosetta Stone*, p. 59.

82  *"ridiculous deities" and "superstitious rites"*: Young, *Recent Discoveries*, p. 79.

82  *"merely men of Lilliput"*: Ray, *Rosetta Stone*, p. 56. The full letter (in French) is in Hermine Hartleben, ed., *Lettres et Journaux de Champollion le Jeune*, tome 2, p. 161.

82  *This same uncle had rebuked* [FN]: Peacock, *Life of Thomas Young*, p. 16.

83  *bakers kneaded dough with their feet*: Herodotus, *The Histories*, book 2, chapter 36. Online at https://tinyurl.com/y4ftjero.

83  *mourners shaved their eyebrows*: Herodotus, *The Histories*, book 2, chapter 66. Online at https://tinyurl.com/y4aq6fat.

83  *crocodiles were kept as pets*: Herodotus, *The Histories*, book 2, chapter 69. Online at https://tinyurl.com/y4aq6fat.

83  *"You have long since demonstrated"*: Aimé Champollion-Figeac, *Les Deux Champollion*, p. 90. The entire book (in French) is online at https://tinyurl.com/y4d6t4sg.

84  *"In 1804 he married Miss Eliza Maxwell"*: Hilts, "Thomas Young's 'Autobiographical Sketch,'" p. 252.

84  *"some poor Italian or Maltese"*: Robinson, *Cracking the Egyptian Code*, p. 83.

84  *"He shot out of the darkness"*: Jean Lacouture, "Champollion, a Hero of the Enlightenment," *UNESCO Courier*, Oct. 1989. Lacouture's biography is *Champollion: Une vie de lumières*.

84  *"Scientific investigations are a sort of warfare"*: Ray, *Rosetta Stone*, p. 51.

84  *"a virulent polemicist"*: Lacouture, "Champollion," *UNESCO Courier*.

85  *"a beak and claws"*: Thompson, *Wonderful Things*, vol. 1, Kindle location 2395.

85  *one day he would decipher*: Ibid., Kindle location 2130.

85  *In 1677 one German traveler*: Pope, *Decipherment*, p. 37.

85  *most scholars believed that Coptic and Greek*: Hamilton, *The Copts and the West*, p. 195.

85  *Johann Vansleb roamed widely* [FN]: Johann Vansleb, *The Present State of Egypt: Or, A New Relation, or Journal, of the Travels of Father Vansleb Through Egypt*, pp. 49, 63. Online at https://tinyurl.com/y6sqkdlz.

86  *Perhaps the most important collector*: Iversen, *The Myth of Egypt*, p. 91.

86  *the first to bring clay tablets*: Kramer, *The Sumerians*, p. 7.

87  *two mummies he had purchased*: Iversen, *The Myth of Egypt*, p. 91.

87  *"I give myself up entirely to Coptic"*: Adkins and Adkins, *The Keys of Egypt*, p. 87.

87  *"I dream only in Coptic"*: Ibid.

87  *letting the sounds of the Coptic mass*: Robinson, *Cracking the Egyptian Code*, p. 61.

87  *"I think there are few Coptic books"*: Adkins and Adkins, *The Keys of Egypt*, p. 83.

88  *"He knew so much"*: Humphry Davy, "Characters, by Sir Humphry Davy," *The Gentleman's Magazine* (Oct. 1837), p. 367. Online at https://tinyurl.com/y4fc9n8t.

88  *By the age of two*: Hilts, "'Autobiographical Sketch,'" p. 250.

88  *"Phenomenon Young"*: Peacock, *Life of Thomas Young*, p. 118.

88  *So far-seeing was Young*: Ray, *Rosetta Stone*, p. 41.

89  *the first person to use the word* energy: Wilson, *Signs and Wonders Upon Pharaoh*, p. 18.

89  *"a sentiment not very far from conceit"*: Hilts, "'Autobiographical Sketch,'" p. 249.

89  *"With an eye less prominent"* [FN]: David Atchison and W. Neil Charman, "Thomas Young's contribution to visual optics: The Bakerian lecture 'On the Mechanism of the Eye,'" *Journal of Vision*, Oct. 2010. Online at https://tinyurl .com/y69tymgh.

90  *"There are two kinds of geniuses"*: James Gleick, *Genius: The Life and Science of Richard Feynman* (New York: Pantheon, 1992), p. 10.

### Chapter Twelve: Thomas Young Is Almost Surprised

93  *It had been found in a tomb*: "A Letter from W. E. Rouse Boughton to the Reverend Stephen Weston Respecting Some Egyptian Antiquities" (from *Archeologia*, vol. XVIII), p. 1. Online at https://tinyurl.com/yz9l7wp4.

94  *"You tell me that I shall astonish the world"*: Peacock, *Life of Thomas Young*, p. 261.

94  *One string of symbols occurred*: Young, "Egypt," in *Miscellaneous Works of the Late Thomas Young*, vol. 3, p. 130. Online at https://tinyurl.com/y68yvwmw.

94  *"marking, on a straight ruler"*: Ibid., p. 132.

95  *"Certainly the labour of a few days"*: Peacock, *Life of Thomas Young*, p. 261.

95  *"intolerably provoking"*: Ibid.

95  *"The difficulties have been far greater"*: Ibid., p. 264.

95  *"I am very anxious to know"*: Solé and Valbelle, *Rosetta Stone*, p. 65.

95  *he had "always entertained grave doubts"*: Wood, *Thomas Young*, p. 211.

95  *"I ought to add"*: Ibid.

96  *"I am always working"*: Robinson, *Cracking the Egyptian Code*, p. 76.

96  *"I am convinced that I would already"*: Ibid., p. 84. Young tells the story of the accidental letter in his *Recent Discoveries*, 40. Online at https://tinyurl.com/ y6p2q8t4.

96  *"Your first letter disturbed my rest"*: Peacock, *Life of Thomas Young*, p. 262.

97  *"I am not a little anxious"*: Ibid., p. 264.

97  *Ninety years later, an Oxford historian*: Charlotte Higgins, "How to Decode an Ancient Roman's Handwriting," *New Yorker*, May 1, 2017.

97  *A colleague of the great decipherer Michael Ventris* [FN]: Chadwick, *Decipherment of Linear B*, p. 4.

98  *"a dozen or more pieces"*: Damrosch, *Buried Book*, p. 30.

98  *Simply teasing the sheets apart*: Tyndall, *Thomas Young*, p. 23. This was a lecture presented at the Royal Institution of Great Britain in 1886 by the physicist John Tyndall. Online at https://tinyurl.com/y2rhqkmz.

98  *"Those who have not been in the habit"*: Robinson, *Cracking the Egyptian Code*, p. 86.

99  *"row upon row of agitated commas"*: Mertz, *Red Land, Black Land*, p. 132.

99  *no "very striking analogy"*: The remark appears in "Egypt," Young's 1819 essay in the *Encyclopedia Britannica*, p. 135. Online at https://tinyurl.com/y3h7o7bv.

100  *"If you wish to know my 'secret'"*: Robinson, *Cracking the Egyptian Code*, p. 89.

### Chapter Thirteen: Archimedes in His Bathtub, Thomas Young in His Country House

102   *"That's funny"*: Kevin Brown, *Penicillin Man: Alexander Fleming and the Antibiotic Revolution* (Stroud, Gloucestershire, UK: The History Press, 2017), p. 2.

102   *"It is in the negligible"*: Nicholas Wroe, "Jonathan Miller: A Man of Many Talents," *Guardian*, Jan. 9, 2009.

102   *"The Chinese article is by Barrow"*: Peacock, *Life of Thomas Young*, p. 272fn.

102   *Fleming happened to be a skilled shot* [FN]: Siang Yong Tan and Yvonne Tatsumura, "Alexander Fleming (1881–1955): Discoverer of Penicillin," *Singapore Medical Journal* 56, no. 7 (July 2015). Online at https://tinyurl.com/mytskgr.

103   *The ambassador arrived bearing gifts*: Fleming discusses the ill-fated visit briefly in *Barrow's Boys*. Alain Peyrefitte provides a full and fascinating look at British and Chinese cultures in collision, in *The Immobile Empire* (New York: Vintage, 2013).

103   *"We have never valued ingenious articles"*: Fleming, *Barrow's Boys*, p. 4.

106   *"Long live the king!"*: Adkins and Adkins, *Keys of Egypt*, p. 294.

108   The Last Man Who Knew Everything: The two biographies are *The Last Man Who Knew Everything: Thomas Young, the Anonymous Polymath Who Proved Newton Wrong, Cured the Sick and Deciphered the Rosetta Stone* by Andrew Robinson, and *The Last Man Who Knew Everything* by Mike Hockney. Robinson is a brilliant writer, and I have drawn repeatedly on this biography and his other marvelous books on the Rosetta Stone, language, and writing.

108   *"When one . . . compares one's own small talents"*: Matthew Stewart, *The Courtier and the Heretic: Leibniz, Spinoza, and the Fate of God in the Modern World* (New York: Norton, 2007), p. 12.

### Chapter Fourteen: Ahead of the Field

109   *"My fate is clear"*: Adkins and Adkins, *Keys of Egypt*, p. 109.

109   *"You will tell me that it is like a priest"*: Ibid., p. 134. The quote first appears in Aimé Champollion-Figeac, *Les Deux Champollion*, p. 88. The entire book (in French) is online at https://tinyurl.com/y4d6t4sg.

109   *"Every day my Coptic dictionary is getting thicker"*: Ceram, *Gods, Graves, and Scholars*, p. 115.

111   *"Never woman gave man so great delight"*: This is *Idyll* 17 by Theocritus. Online at https://tinyurl.com/y2lryxwh.

111   *"There is no royal road to geometry"* [FN]: The anecdote is ancient and seems to have appeared first in a history of mathematics written by the Greek philosopher Proclus sometime in the 400s AD. See Glenn Morrow, ed., *Proclus: A Commentary on the First Book of Euclid's Elements* (Princeton, NJ: Princeton University Press, 1970), p. 57. Online at https://tinyurl.com/y5nvv97q.

112   *(leaving out one bad fit as "superfluous")*: Young, "Egypt," in *Miscellaneous Works of the Late Thomas Young*, vol. 3, p. 159. Online at https://tinyurl.com/y68yvwmw.

112   *"The warmest advocates of Dr. Young"*: Peacock, *Life of Thomas Young*, p. 314.

114  *"everybody whose approbation is worth having"*: Ibid., p. 254.
114  *"Young had by far exceeded"*: Adkins and Adkins, *Keys of Egypt*, p. 154.

### Chapter Fifteen: Lost in the Labyrinth

115  *"there were no books piled"*: Peacock, *Life of Thomas Young*, p. 119.
115  *"patient of unintermitted labour"*: Ibid., p. 486.
115  *"Don't be discouraged about the Egyptian text"*: Solé and Valbelle, *Rosetta Stone*, p. 56.
116  *"Ventris would set course"*: Fox, *Riddle of the Labyrinth*, p. 218. The story is from Leonard Cottrell, "Michael Ventris and his Achievement," *Antioch Review* 25, no. 1, Special Greek Issue (Spring 1965).
116  *"a desk job really"*: This is from a BBC documentary on Ventris, *A Very English Genius*. Online at https://tinyurl.com/y2ymnykv.
116  *"the door burst open"*: BBC, *A Very English Genius*, part 5. Online at https://tinyurl.com/y4w9qdvh.
117  *"intended to preserve the memory"*: Thompson, *Wonderful Things*, vol. 1, Kindle location 1653.
117  *"I have understood nothing"*: Robinson, *Cracking the Egyptian Code*, p. 67.
117  *"It is my conviction"*: Ibid., p. 76.
117  *"the years of anxious searching in the dark"*: Einstein's remark is from a 1933 lecture called "About the Origins of the Theory of General Relativity" that he delivered at the University of Glasgow.
117  *"an almost infinite tolerance for drudgery"*: Budiansky, *Battle of Wits*, p. 136.
118  *"In no other science"*: This is from an essay called "An Introduction to Methods for the Solution of Ciphers." William F. Friedman is listed as the sole author, but the essay was co-authored by Elizebeth Friedman.
118  *"Not 'paranoid' in the sense"*: Budiansky, *Battle of Wits*, p. 136.
118  *"a light of centuries to come"*: Robinson, *Cracking the Egyptian Code*, p. 33.
118  *he vowed that someday*: Andrew Robinson examines this story in characteristically clear and careful fashion and proves that it was "almost certainly false." *Cracking the Egyptian Code*, pp. 49–53.
119  *(a "complete contempt for public opinion")*: Hilts, "Autobiographical Sketch," p. 249.
119  *"miserable boarding school"*: Ibid., p. 250.
119  *he "had the good sense to leave"*: Ibid.
119  *"as little assistance as possible"*: Young, "On the Mechanism of the Eye."
119  *the best crossword puzzle solvers in Britain*: Budiansky, *Battle of Wits*, p. 137.
119  *"we can all become code-breakers"*: Beard, "What was Greek to Them?"
119  *"By thinking on it continually"*: Richard Westfall, *Never at Rest: A Biography of Isaac Newton* (New York: Cambridge University Press, 1983), p. 105.
119  *Newton never joked*: Ibid., p. 192.
119  *The Nazis, also, used crossword puzzles* [FN]: Kahn, *Codebreakers*, p. 241.
120  *"Newton could hold a problem in his mind"*: John Maynard Keynes, "Newton, the Man." Online at https://tinyurl.com/y9lmmwj3.
120  *a grandmaster can burn*: This is from a TED Talk by Sapolsky titled "The Uniqueness of Humans." The remark on chess grandmasters is at the ten-minute mark. Online at https://tinyurl.com/y53vj2ua.

120 *"an extraordinary memory and excellent health"*: Adkins, *Empires of the Plain*, p. 61.

121 *"For a charmed few"*: Fox, *Riddle of the Labyrinth*, p. 207.

121 *Ventris corresponded with Swedish scholars*: Chadwick, *Linear B*, p. 2.

121 *Ventris was handsome and charming* [FN]: Margalit Fox discusses the arguments surrounding Ventris's death in *The Riddle of the Labyrinth*, pp. 212, 261.

122 *"I am the first man to read that"*: E. A. Wallis Budge, *The Rise and Progress of Assyriology* (London: Clay & Sons, 1925), p. 153. The entire book is online at https://tinyurl.com/ollt3vt.

123 *"The thrill of your life"*: Fagone, *The Woman Who Smashed Codes*, p. 75.

### Chapter Sixteen: Ancient Wisdom

125 *He even compiled a table*: Robinson, *Cracking the Egyptian Code*, p. 121.

126 *"We are all tattooed in our cradles"*: Oliver Wendell Holmes Sr., *The Poet at the Breakfast Table*. Online at https://tinyurl.com/yyzmhfrx.

127 *not discovered until 1419*: Dieckmann, "Renaissance Hieroglyphics."

127 *regarded with "sacred awe"*: Iversen, *The Myth of Egypt*, p. 49.

127 *"they draw a hawk"*: Alexander Turner Cory (translator), *Hieroglyphics of Horapollon* VI: "What They Signify by Delineating a Hawk," p. 13. Online at https://tinyurl.com/y48afn26.

127 *a vulture meant* mother: Ibid., XI: "What They Imply By Depicting a Vulture," p. 23.

127 *A goose meant* son: Ibid., LIII: "How They Represent A Son," p. 73.

128 *A hare meant* open: Ibid., XXVI: "How An Opening," p. 48.

128 *"a man with a donkey's head"*: Pope, *Decipherment*, p. 18. (Pope's translation is slightly different from Cory's.)

128 *"men walking on water"*: Cory (translator), *Hieroglyphics of Horapollon*, LXVIII: "How an Impossibility," p. 79.

128 *A vulture meant not only* mother: Ibid., XI: "What They Imply by Depicting a Vulture," p. 23.

129 *"Poor old Horapollo got discredited"*: The Egyptologist John Ray participated in a History Channel documentary called *The Rosetta Stone*. Ray discussed Horapollo at about the 22-minute mark. Online at https://tinyurl.com/yx wucubh.

129 *A crocodile stood for* evil: Pope, *Decipherment*, p. 17.

129 *a fish symbolized* hatred: Ibid., p. 25.

130 *"the symbolic and occult teachings"*: Iversen, *The Myth of Egypt*, p. 45.

130 *"All things that shine through a veil"*: Ibid.

131 *"chronicles of ancient Egyptian Wisdom"*: Glassie, *Man of Misconceptions*, p. 46.

131 *"All the secrets of the Hieroglyphic Art"*: Pope, *Decipherment*, p. 31.

131 *"virtues and gifts in the sidereal world"*: Ray, *Rosetta Stone*, p. 20.

131 *the discovery of America*: Glassie, *Man of Misconceptions*, p. 135.

131 *"Nothing is more beautiful than to know all"*: Bauer, *Unsolved*, p. 35.

131 *"formerly the Pharaonic language"*: Iversen, *The Myth of Egypt*, p. 92.

132 *"strange glimpses of genius"*: Ibid., p. 96.

132  *"veils of allegory and enigma"*: Ucko and Champion, eds., *The Wisdom of Egypt*.

133  *"deliberately disregarded all evidence"*: Iversen, *The Myth of Egypt*, p. 49.

134  *"his duty of leading the dead"*: Coe, *Breaking the Maya Code*, Kindle location 2527.


*Chapter Seventeen: "A Cipher and a Secret Writing"*

137  *Egyptian mathematics was rudimentary*: Dirk J. Struik, *A Concise History of Mathematics* (New York: Dover, 1967), p. 26.

137  *threw brains into the trash*: Brier, *Ancient Egypt*, p. 61.

137  *The heart was special*: Ibid.

137  *"not as other men"*: Ray, *Rosetta Stone*, p. 19.

138  *They had known the law of gravitation*: Haycock, *Science, Religion, and Archaeology in Eighteenth Century England*, especially chapter 4, "The Macrocosm." Available online at the marvelous website called "The Newton Project," https://tinyurl.com/y37nbd92.

138  *"The Egyptians," Newton wrote*: Westfall, *Never at Rest*, p. 434.

139  *"The past was always better than the present"*: Yates, *Giordano Bruno and the Hermetic Tradition*, p. 1.

139  *"the earliest thinkers walked more closely"*: Ibid., p. 5.

139  *"Egypt was the original home"*: Ibid.

139  *"To 'dis-cover' was to pull away"*: McMahon, *Divine Fury*, p. 4.

139  *"Until about the year 1649"*: John Aubrey, *The Natural History of Wiltshire* (London: Nichols, 1847). Originally published in 1685. Aubrey's remark is from his preface.

141  *"the grandest symbols of authoritarian rule"*: Toby Wilkinson, "The Tradition of the Pharaohs Lives On," *Wall Street Journal*, Feb. 5, 2011.

141  *the shriveled mummy at the core*: Brier, *Murder of Tutankhamen*, p. 6.

141  *"clapped their hands with delight"*: Vivant Denon, *Travels in Upper and Lower Egypt*, vol. 2 (London: Longman, 1803), p. 84.

141  *("I shall never forget")*: Geoffrey Wall, *Flaubert: A Life* (New York: Farrar, Straus and Giroux, 2007), p. 176.

142  *to decipher that "strange Cryptography"*: William P. Dunn, *Sir Thomas Browne: A Study in Religious Philosophy* (Minneapolis: University of Minnesota Press, 1950), p. 95.

142  *"a cipher and a secret writing"*: Steven Levy, *Crypto: How the Code Rebels Beat the Government—Saving Privacy in the Digital Age* (New York: Penguin, 2002), p. 7.

143  *"The mother of love emulates"*: Holly Haworth, "The Fading Stars: A Constellation," *Lapham's Quarterly* (Winter 2019). Online at https://tinyurl.com/y7t9tw7a.

143  *"hieroglyphics painted invisible objects"*: Hugh Blair, *Lectures on Rhetoric and Belles Lettres* (London: Lockwood and Son, 1857), Lecture 7: "Rise of Progress of Language, and of Writing," p. 57. The entire book, which was originally published in 1783, is online at https://tinyurl.com/yxogepvm.

*Chapter Eighteen: The Exile*

145   *sprawled across sixty thousand acres*: Sebba, *Exiled Collector*, p. 17.

145   *"very dull, very meddling, very silly"*: Ibid., p. 114.

145   *"laughed for two hours"*: Ibid., p. 115.

146   *"the father of all mischiefs"*: This is from a letter written in 1820. George Gordon Byron, *Byron's Letters and Journals: The Complete and Unexpurgated Text*, vol. 1 (Cambridge, MA: Harvard University Press, 1973), p. 110fn9.

146   *"not wholly unlike a shrimp"*: Finati, *Life and Adventures*, vol. 2, p. 78.

146   *A dash of risk*: Finati tells the story of the snake charmer in his memoirs. Finati, *Life and Adventures*, vol. 2, p. 99.

147   *orchestrated by Laurel and Hardy*: We have eyewitness accounts from two different memoirs, one by Belzoni and the other by Giovanni Finati, who traveled with Bankes for four years.

148   *"All hands were at work"*: Ibid., p. 308.

148   *"Alas!" recalled Belzoni*: Belzoni, *Travels in Egypt and Nubia*, p. 295.

148   *"stiff as a post"*: Ibid., p. 296.

149   *"If the boat touched the stones"*: Ibid., p. 299.

149   *"the great boat wheeling and swinging"*: Finati, *Life and Adventures*, vol. 2, p. 309.

149   *(his aim was to "combine much comfort")*: Sebba, *Exiled Collector*, p. 174.

151   *a single word in pencil*: Patricia Usick, "William John Bankes' Collection of Drawings and Manuscripts Relating to Ancient Nubia," p. 40. This is a University of London PhD thesis from 1998. Online at https://tinyurl.com/y6hhdqrq.

151   *these early decades of the 1800s were terrible times*: As noted in the text, the last execution for sodomy on English soil took place in the year 1835. Naomi Wolf caused a tremendous stir in 2019 when she wrote, mistakenly, that England continued carrying out executions for sodomy until the middle 1800s.

151   *A conviction for "sodomy"*: Morrison, *The Regency Years*, p. 161.

152   *"more executions for sodomy than for murder"*: A. D. Harvey, "Prosecutions for Sodomy in England at the Beginning of the Nineteenth Century," *Historical Journal* 21, no. 4 (1978)

152   *England executed more than fifty men*: Ibid.

152   *the typical sentence was ten years*: Sebba, *Exiled Collector*, p. 177.

152   *abolished for piracy, slave-trading, and rape*: Ibid., p. 157.

152   *"they laugh instead of burning"*: Ibid., p. 188.

152   *Bankes was put on trial*: Anna Sebba tells the story of Bankes's two arrests and his exile in compelling detail in chapters 7 and 8 of her biography.

152   *In one notorious case in 1811* [FN]: Morrison tells the story briefly in *The Regency Years*, pp. 161–62, and Lilian Faderman examines it at book length in *Scotch Verdict: The Real-Life Story that Inspired "The Children's Hour"* (New York: Columbia University Press, 1983). The remarks about "physical impossibility" and "God save the King" can be found on page 233.

153   *"he was writing daily instructions"*: Sebba, *Exiled Collector*, p. 231.

## Chapter Nineteen: Here Comes Champollion

155 *"the Englishman knows no more Egyptian"*: LaBrière, ed., *Champollion Inconnu*, p. 65. The entire book is online at https://tinyurl.com/y65ylw7s.

156 *"I did certainly expect to find"*: Young, "Discoveries in Hierographical Literature," in *Miscellaneous Works of the Late Thomas Young*, vol. 3, p. 292. Online at https://tinyurl.com/y68yvwmw.

156 *Champollion called it a "sparrow hawk"*: Champollion, *Letter to Monsieur Dacier*, p. 4. Online at https://tinyurl.com/y6mrk2my.

158 *Then "a shallow teacup"*: These descriptions of hieroglyphs are Champollion's own, from his *Letter to Monsieur Dacier*, pp. 4–5.

159 *(the amusing blunders of "this English scholar")*: Ibid., p. 30fn22.

160 *"As I had not leisure"*: Young, *Recent Discoveries*, p. 49.

160 *"the great tragedy of science"*: Thomas Huxley, *Collected Essays*, vol. 8, p. 229. Online at https://tinyurl.com/y9mcunw7.

160 *"Ninety Percent of the Universe"*: *New York Times*, Dec. 29, 1960.

## Chapter Twenty: "A Veritable Chaos"

161 *a down-to-earth explanation*: Manlio Simonetti, ed., *Ancient Christian Commentary on Scripture: Matthew 14–28* (Westmont, IL: InterVarsity Press, 2002), p. 102.

162 *a mistake of a single letter*: Author interview with Dr. Benjamin Solomon, National Human Genome Research Institute, Feb. 24, 2020.

162 *notorious for countless cruelties*: Daniel Luckenbill, *Ancient Records of Assyria and Babylonia*, vol. 2 (Chicago: University of Chicago Press, 1927), p. 319.

162 *"Day and night we shall strain"*: Andrew George (trans. and ed.), *The Epic of Gilgamesh* (New York: Penguin, 2003), p. xxii.

163 *"In their death agonies"*: Greenblatt, *Adam and Eve*, p. 42.

163 *Carsten Niebuhr, a Danish explorer*: Hansen, *Arabia Felix*, p. 114; Guichard, Jr., *Niebuhr in Egypt*, p. 1.

164 *"the drawings were a mishmash"*: Wilson, *Signs and Wonders*, p. 31.

164 *"the habits of a schoolboy"*: Hilts, "Autobiographical Sketch," p. 254.

164 *a publication called* The Nautical Almanac: Peacock, *Life of Thomas Young*, p. 356.

165 *"reducing his dignity in the scale of existence"*: Hilts, "Autobiographical Sketch," p. 253.

165 *the largest military force*: Daniel Mendelsohn, "Arms and the Man," *New Yorker*, April 28, 2008.

165 *Champollion recognized its hieroglyphs*: Pope, *Deciphering*, p. 74.

165 *"It is abundantly clear"*: Ibid.

165 *"a veritable chaos"*: Champollion, *Précis du Système Hiéroglyphique*, p. 255. (Pope translates the passage in *Deciphering*, p. 75.)

166 *"Inevitably [it would be] very obscure"*: Ibid.

### Chapter Twenty-One: The Birth of Writing

168  *"A hard-hat symbol means"*: Man, *Alpha Beta*, p. 19.

168  *chosen to add captions*: I owe this observation to Michael Cook. See his *Brief History of the Human Race* (New York: Norton, 2005), p. 45.

170  *"jars, loaves, and animals"*: Tim Harford, "50 Things That Made the Modern Economy," BBC World Service, "Cuneiform" episode, broadcast April 30, 2017.

170  *a French Sherlock Holmes*: Schmandt-Besserat, "The Evolution of Writing," p. 9. Online at https://tinyurl.com/y72ynmqz.

171  *"the Rosetta Stone of the inscription system"*: Schmandt-Besserat, *How Writing Came About*, p. 9.

171  *Paul Revere used lanterns*: Michael Coe cites Paul Revere in *Breaking the Maya Code*, Kindle location 274.

171  *"it has taken great men to discover simple things"*: D'Arcy Wentworth Thompson, *On Growth and Form* (New York: Dover, 1972), p. 13.

172  *only "some god or some divine man"*: The phrase is from Plato's "Philebus," quoted in Hornung, *The Secret Lore of Egypt*, p. 21.

172  *it took a thousand years*: Ludwig Morenz, "The Origins of Egyptian Literature" in Manley, ed., *Seventy Great Mysteries*, p. 211.

172  *"His Majesty burst after them"*: James B. Pritchard, *Ancient Near Eastern Texts Relating to the Old Testament with Supplement* (Princeton, NJ: Princeton University Press, 2016), pp. 245 and 245fn12.

173  *"the hero without equal"*: Ian Shaw, ed., *The Oxford History of Ancient Egypt* (Oxford, UK: Oxford University Press, 2003), pp. 118–20.

173  *"I cut their throats like lambs"* [FN]: Erika Belibtreu, "Grisly Assyrian Record of Torture and Death," *Biblical Archeological Society*, Jan./Feb. 1991.

### Chapter Twenty-Two: The Paduan Giant

175  *"signs of things and not sounds"*: Jean-François Champollion, *De l'écriture hiératique des anciens Égyptiens*, p. 2. This is the fourth and last item in a list Champollion made of his major findings. (The first was that hieroglyphs were "not in any way alphabetical.") Online at https://tinyurl.com/y5p2ek2w.

176  *(there were 166 different hieroglyphs)*: Champollion, *Précis du système hiéroglyphique des anciens Égyptien*, p. 266. Online at https://tinyurl.com/y2cbjcqz.

177  *endured a miserable childhood*: François Pouillion, ed. *Dictionaire des Orientalistes de langue Française* (Paris: IISMM, 2008), "Rémusat," p. 810.

177  *"without a teacher, without a textbook"*: Ibid.

177  *France's reigning authority on Chinese*: Pope, *Deciphering*, p. 76.

177  *"they constituted a good half"*: Ibid.

178  *tourists wrenched off a hand or an arm*: Jill Sullivan, *Popular Exhibitions, Science and Showmanship, 1840–1910* (Abingdon-on-Thames, Oxfordshire, UK: Taylor & Francis: 2015), p. 202.

178  *eleven men at a time*: Mayes, *Belzoni*, p. 20.

178  *Shelley never set foot in Egypt* [FN]: Guy Davenport, "Ozymandias," *New York*

*Times*, May 28, 1978; John Rodenbeck, "Travelers from an Ancient Land: Shelley's Inspiration for 'Ozymandias,'" *Alif: Journal of Comparative Poetics* 24 (2004), pp. 124–25.

179 *"But what a place of rest!"*: Belzoni, *Travels in Egypt and Nubia*, p. 132.
180 *"a thousand generations of tomb robbers"*: Mertz, *Temples, Tombs, and Hieroglyphs*, p. 72.

### Chapter Twenty-Three: Abu Simbel

181 *motivated almost solely by curiosity*: Moorehead, *Blue Nile*, p. 145.
182 *"the bonnets only appear"*: Burckhardt, *Travels in Nubia*, p. 91. The entire book is online at https://tinyurl.com/y5l5tkso.
184 *used the same stones to rebuild in his name*: Wilson, *Ancient Egypt*, p. 252.
184 *the titan's big toe*: The toe is 14.7 inches across. Flinders Petrie, *Tanis, Part I, 1883–4* (London: Trübner, 1889), p. 22.
185 *it listed his occupation as "King (deceased)"*: The Egyptologist Rosalie David is the source for the "King (deceased)" story. See this 2010 interview in a University of Manchester newsletter, https://tinyurl.com/y6l7jo5z. The story may have grown through the years. In her book *Conversations with Mummies: New Light on the Lives of Ancient Egyptians*, published a decade earlier, in 2000, David wrote (on page 108) that "rumor has it" that Ramesses carried the "King (deceased)" passport.
185 *"a giant Beware of Pharaoh sign"*: "Engineering Egypt", a DVD made by *National Geographic*. Peter Brand, an Egyptologist at the University of Memphis, appears at about the 77-minute mark.
186 *Ramesses seated on his throne is sixty-seven feet*: Brier, *Ancient Egypt*, p. 37.
187 *"The whole is like a chaos"*: Belzoni, *Travels in Egypt and Nubia*, p. 167.
187 *Sandstorms "tear over the ground"*: Petrie, *The Pyramids and Temples of Gizeh*, p. 151.
187 *Petrie labored away under the desert sun*: Petrie, *Seventy Years in Archeology*, p. 21.
187 *Kilroy was here [FN]*: Green, "Tut-Tut-Tut."
188 *"a flavour of its own"*: Drower, *Petrie*, p. 319.
188 *"a table so excruciatingly bad"*: Stiebing, *Uncovering the Past*, p. 80.
188 *"if a can did not explode"*: Adams, *Millionaire and the Mummies*, pp. 97–8.
188 *"like making a hole in the water"*: Belzoni, *Travels in Egypt and Nubia*, p. 68.
189 *He never saw Abu Simbel*: Thompson, *Wonderful Things*, vol. 1, Kindle location 2565.
189 *The only light came*: Sebba, *Exiled Collector*, p. 99.
189 *"What treasure have they found?"*: Seyler, *The Obelisk and the Englishman*, p. 176.

### Chapter Twenty-Four: Eureka!

191 *that "dirty scoundrel"*: Thompson, *Wonderful Things*, vol. 1, Kindle location 2197.
193 *the complicated intellectual machinery*: Ray, *Rosetta Stone*, p. 88.
194 *Socrates recounts a story*: The passage occurs in "Phaedrus." Online at https://tinyurl.com/yxafzdpj.

194   *"the author of every work"*: Budge, *The Gods of the Egyptians*, vol. 1, p. 414.
195   *the royal couple were themselves*: Wilkinson, *Rise and Fall*, Kindle location 3442.
195   *Hanging upside down*: Darnell and Manassa, *Tutankhamun's Armies*, p. 18.
197   *"I dream in Coptic"*: Adkins and Adkins, *Keys of Egypt*, p. 87.


### Chapter Twenty-Five: The Unveiling

201   *he hailed him as the Oedipus*: Aimé Champollion Figeac, *Les Deux Champollion*, p. 41.
201   *Champollion bursts into the room*: Ibid., p. 57.
202   *unresponsive for "five full days"*: Hartleben, *Champollion: Sein Leben und Sein Werk*, p. 422.
202   *Young had arrived in Paris*: Young, *Recent Discoveries*, p. 38.
202   *"acknowledged with the most scrupulous justice"*: Ibid., p. 39.
203   *"step by step and very briefly"*: Champollion, *Letter to Monsieur Dacier*, p. 7.
203   *"why the Egyptians decided"*: Ibid., p. 12.
203   *The same principle held*: Ibid., pp. 12–13.
203   *Look closely at the modern alphabet*: Ibid., p. 15.
203   *"We can finally read"*: Ibid., p. 16.
203   *"higher than the towers of Notre Dame"*: LaBrière, ed., *Champollion Inconnu*, p. 71.
204   *"Now anything is possible"*: Hartleben, ed., *Lettres de Champollion le Jeune*, tome 1, p. iv.
204   *"many things that I should like to show"*: Peacock, *Life of Thomas Young*, p. 322.
204   *"a junior coadjutor in my researches"*: Young, *Miscellaneous Works*, vol. 3, p. 222.
204   *Champollion had done "gigantic" things*: Ibid., p. 220.
205   *"if he did borrow an English key"*: Ibid.
205   *used in "pure hieroglyphic writing"*: Champollion, *Letter to Monsieur Dacier*, p. 15.
206   *"getting into long drawn-out details"*: Ibid.


### Chapter Twenty-Six: A Duck May Be Somebody's Mother

208   *"I had long suspected"*: Young, *Miscellaneous Works*, vol. 3, p. 77.
208   *"it is possible that we may at some future time"*: Ibid.
209   *But Caligula and Nero had no sons*: Pope, *Decipherment*, p. 82.
210   *Jerome had the bright idea*: James Geary, *Wit's End: What Wit Is, How it Works, and Why* (New York: Norton, 2018), p. 5.
210   *a clock makes a bad wedding gift*: Fallows, *Dreaming in Chinese*, p. 44.
210   *Voilà, thirty-two thousand cattle*: Gardiner, *Egyptian Grammar*, p. 7.
212   *"The mystery of language was revealed"*: Helen Keller, *The Story of My Life* (New York: Dover, 2012), p. 12.
213   *many hieroglyphs were "dead metaphors"*: Parkinson, *Cracking Codes*, p. 63.
214   *"Hieroglyphic writing is a complex system"*: Champollion, *Précis du Système Hiéroglyphique*, p. 327. (Robinson translates the passage in *Cracking the Egyptian Code*, p. 15.)

*Chapter Twenty-Seven: Straining to Hear*

215  *"a want of liberality"*: Young, *Recent Discoveries*, p. 39.

215  *"any intentions actually dishonourable"*: Ibid.

215  *"It may not be strictly just"*: Ibid., p. 42.

216  *"three words in a row"*: LaBrière, ed., *Champollion Inconnu*, p. 66.

216  *"discoveries" were in fact fantasies*: Ibid.

216  *"one stone on top of another."* Ibid.

216  *"ridiculous boasting"*: Ibid., p. 65.

216  *"Dr. Young did some work*: Champollion, *Letter to Monsieur Dacier*, p. 30fn22.

216  *"this English scholar thought"*: Ibid.

217  *archaeologists clashed angrily*: Baruch A. Levin, "Notes on an Aramaic Dream Text from Egypt," *Journal of the American Oriental Society* 84, no. 1 (Jan.–Mar. 1964).

218  *(That slack in the system)*: Author interview with Amir Zeldes, Oct. 20, 2018.

218  *"the mutilated and imperfect fragment"*: The remark is from a note by Simon Wilken, the editor of an 1852 edition of Thomas Browne's *Vulgar Errors*. See "Of the Hieroglyphical Pictures of the Egyptians," book V, chapter XX. Online at https://tinyurl.com/y6dgljst.

219  *creepy subliminal messages*: Jeffrey Bloomer, "Why Everyone Thought *Aladdin* Had a Secret Sex Message," *Slate*, May 24, 2019. Online at https://tinyurl.com/yxu3jgdo.

219  *The phrase to recognize speech*: Dave Tompkins, *How to Wreck a Nice Beach: The Vocoder from World War II to Hip Hop, The Machine Speaks* (Chicago: Stop Smiling Books, 2010).

220  *a poet who ate a lion*: Fallows, *Dreaming in Chinese*, p. 40.

220  *friend and enemy are identical*: Everett, *Don't Sleep, There Are Snakes*, p. 185. Both words are the same three syllables, but *friend* has two high tones and *enemy* has only one.

220  *he boiled his mother-in-law*: Gleick, *The Information*, p. 23.

220  *we will never hear*: Perhaps "never" is too strong. The *New York Times* reported in January 2020 on a team of scientists who had tried to re-create the voice of a mummified Egyptian priest named Nesyamun. For the past two hundred years, Nesyamun's mummy has been at the Leeds City Museum in England. Nesmayun died some three thousand years ago, in around 1100 BC. (An inscription on his coffin called him "Nesmayun, Sound of Voice.") Much of the mummy's mouth and throat remain intact, and the recent experiments involved printing a 3-D copy of Nesmayun's voice box and trying to reproduce the sounds of his speech. So far the scientists have managed to synthesize a single sound akin to "ah." This was a difficult task, and a difficult one to evaluate as well. Was this a jump into the air or the earliest stage of a voyage to the moon? (See Nicholas St. Fleur, "The Mummy Speaks: Hear Sounds from the Voice of an Ancient Egyptian Priest," *New York Times*, Jan. 23, 2020.)

221  *perhaps clocks could announce*: Library of Congress webpage, "History of the Cylinder Phonograph." Online at https://tinyurl.com/zcbn7jh.

221  *"This tongueless, toothless instrument"*: Richard Osborne, *Vinyl: A History of the Analogue Record* (Abingdon, UK: Routledge, 2012), p. 23.

221  *we can hear it to this day*: Online at https://tinyurl.com/y5trmalz.
221  *A voice that had been silent*: Presumably this resurrection was one of a kind, though a few optimistic scientists have held out hope that some ancient conversations were recorded by accident. Their scenario starts with a bygone potter who held a sharp stick to a pot as it spun around on his potter's wheel, to inscribe a design. Could he have unknowingly recorded the sounds in the room? At least one archaeologist claims to have carried out promising experiments on those lines.

    The American philosopher Charles S. Peirce seems to have been the first to imagine such after-the-fact eavesdropping. "Give science only a hundred more centuries of increase in geometrical progression," he wrote around 1902, "and she may be expected to find that the sound waves of Aristotle's voice have somehow recorded themselves."
222  Our Father, who art in heaven: Quoted in Parkinson, *Cracking Codes*, p. 42.
222  *just about incomprehensible today*: Gerald Davis, *Beowulf: The New Translation* (Bridgeport, CT: Insignia, 2013), p. 13.
222  *The Old English for* body: Josephine Livingstone, "Old English," *New York Times Magazine*, Jan. 6, 2019.
222  *"'Hickory, Dickory, Dock'"*: John McWhorter, "Don't Use the Word 'Emolument,'" *Atlantic*, Oct. 24, 2019. Online at https://tinyurl.com/y3rkm8c8.

### Chapter Twenty-Eight: Strength in Numbers

223  *(the origin of the* ankh *symbol)*: Author interview with Bob Brier, April 8, 2019.
224  *Next in the Ptolemy cartouche*: Budge, *Rosetta Stone*, p. 14. This is a booklet published by the British Museum in 1913. Online at https://tinyurl.com/y6s92hbr.
224  *"You need big, important words"*: Author interview Oct. 20, 2018. All the quotations from Zeldes in this chapter are from this interview. Zeldes is an associate professor of computational linguistics at Georgetown and co-editor of a Coptic dictionary.
227  Give us this day our daily bread: John Hennig, "Our Daily Bread," *Theological Studies* 4, no. 3 (Sept. 1, 1943).
228  *"balk'd in their own blood"*: The phrase is from *Henry IV, Part One*.
228  *Mark Twain complained*: In "The Awful German Language," which is an appendix to *A Tramp Abroad*.
228  *The word* alligator: See the Online Etymology Dictionary, at https://www.etymonline.com/word/alligator.
229  *in the judgment of the Egyptologist John Ray*: Ray, *Rosetta Stone*, p. 90.

### Chapter Twenty-Nine: A Pair of Walking Legs

231  *He named these special signs "determinatives"*: The first "déterminatif" that Champollion identified was a star symbol that marked a division of time. See Hartleben, ed., *Lettres et Journaux de Champollion*, tome 2, p. 117.
232  *The hieroglyphs are pronounced* meow: Parkinson, *Cracking Codes*, p. 65.
232  *mourners tore their hair in grief*: Ibid., p. 62.

232   *The determinative for* enemy: Darnell, *Tutankhamen's Armies*, p. 59.

232   *("A boy's ears are on his back")*: Breasted, *History of Egypt*, p. 99.

232   *Or take Navajo*: Kahn, *The Codebreakers*, p. 290.

233   *cuneiform scripts made use of similar strategies*: Chadwick, *Linear B*, p. 32.

233   *About one hieroglyph in five*: Parkinson, *Cracking Codes*, p. 59.

235   *"a toy for the amusement of pedantry"*: Ebers, *Egypt: Historical, Descriptive, and Picturesque*, p. 8. The remark appears in the Introduction, which was written by the Egyptologist Samuel Birch.


### Chapter Thirty: Clean Robes and Soft Hands

239   *The finds are recent*: John Noble Wilford, "Discovery of Egyptian Inscriptions Indicates an Earlier Date for Origin of the Alphabet," *New York Times*, Nov. 13, 1999.

240   *"the 'For Dummies' version of writing"*: Gnanadesikan, *Writing Revolution*, p. 145.

240   *"It must have looked funny"*: Ibid.

240   *"much more easily readable"*: Battiscombe Gunn, "Notes on the Naukratis Stela," *Journal of Egyptian Archaeology* 29 (Dec. 1943), p. 56.

240   *"sacrificed legibility to simplicity"*: Ibid.

241   *"At first redundancy is confusing"*: Author interview Jan. 22, 2019.

243   *the alphabet was invented only once*: Cook, *A Brief History of the Human Race*, p. 45.

244   *"If we only had 26 hieroglyphs"*: Bill Manley, *Egyptian Hieroglyphs for Complete Beginners* (London: Thames & Hudson, 2012), p. 21. Learning hieroglyphs outside a classroom is terribly difficult. The two best primers are Manley's book and Bridget McDermott's *Decoding Egyptian Hieroglyphs: How to Read the Secret Language of the Pharaohs* (New York: Chartwell, 2016).

244   *When Alexander the Great read a letter*: Manguel, *History of Reading*, p. 43.

244   *alphabetical order took forever*: Lynch, *You Could Look It Up*.

245   *(the wheel and the invention of the wheelbarrow)*: The historian Joel Mokyr cites this example in James Fallows, "The Fifty Greatest Inventions Since the Wheel," *Atlantic*, Nov. 2013. Online at https://tinyurl.com/ybnnnzp6.

245   *"Satire of the Trades"*: The complete text is online at https://tinyurl.com/y5gz3tef.

245   *"he is the boss"*: Mertz, *Red Land, Black Land*, p. 127.

246   *The king's collection included*: Romer, *History of Ancient Egypt*, vol. 2, p. 34.

246   *"The coldest imagination would be shaken"*: LaBrière, ed., *Champollion Inconnu*, p. 83. This translation can be found in Romer, *History of Ancient Egypt*, vol. 2, p. 36.


### Chapter Thirty-One: Out of a Job

247   *Champollion was a "villain"*: Renouf, "Young and Champollion," p. 189. Renouf was quoting John Leitch, the editor of Young's *Miscellaneous Works*.

247   *Young was "a man with a grievance"*: Pope, *Deciphering*, p. 67.

247   *"the 'Let There Be Light' of Egyptology"*: Ray, *Rosetta Stone*, p. 45.

247   *"the Hare and Tortoise"*: Renouf, "Young and Champollion," p. 189.

248   *"the all-important first step"*: Ray, *Rosetta Stone*, p. 54.

248 *"the most brilliant problem-solver"*: Ray appeared as a talking head in a History Channel documentary called "Secrets of the Rosetta Stone." The remark is at about the 29-minute mark.

248 *"I have done little or nothing"*: Peacock, *Life of Thomas Young*, p. 450.

249 *"I would also suggest"*: Ibid., p. 253.

249 *"the ingenious and successful investigation"*: Young, *Rudiments of an Egyptian Dictionary*, p. v.

249 *"the justly celebrated Jean François Champollion"*: Young, *Rudiments of an Ancient Egyptian Dictionary*, p. v. Online at https://tinyurl.com/yyqqvcpb.

249 *"shown me far more attention"*: Wood, *Thomas Young*, p. 247. Andrew Robinson points out in *The Last Man Who Knew Everything* that Young's first biographer, George Peacock, quoted the identical letter but for some reason omitted the phrase "shown me far more attention than I ever showed or could show, to any living being." Robinson suggests that Peacock deleted the phrase to avoid wounding Young's wife.

250 *he never* guessed: Champollion, *Précis du Système Hiéroglyphique*, p. 252.

## Chapter Thirty-Two: The Lost Pharaoh

251 *"It is my pride and pleasure"*: Peacock, *Thomas Young*, p. 477.

252 *puffed happily away at a hookah*: Hartleben, ed., *Lettres et Journaux de Champollion*, v. 2, 34.

252 *("we melt like candles")*: Ibid., p. 39.

252 *"at the foot of the pyramids"*: Ibid., p. 123.

252 *close enough to touch*: Ibid., pp. 120, 123.

252 *Every street dog in Egypt*: Ibid., p. 27.

252 *"I am Egypt's captive"*: Ibid., p. 150.

252 "Notre alphabet est bon": Ibid., p. 181.

253 *"as though a queen were in question"*: Ibid., pp. 329–30. This translation is from Joyce Tyldesley's *Hatchepsut: The Female Pharaoh*.

253 *"For I am his daughter"*: Wilkinson, *Rise and Fall*, Kindle location 3610.

253 *"he who shall speak evil"*: Ian Shaw, ed., *The Oxford History of Ancient Egypt* (Oxford, UK: Oxford University Press, 2000), p. 233.

254 *"the first great woman in history"*: Breasted, *A History of Egypt*, p. 271.

254 *on the order of* kingette: Author interview with Bob Brier, March 4, 2019.

254 *Scribes adopted the word* pharaoh: Wilkinson, *Rise and Fall*, Kindle location 3588.

254 *Hatshepsut's story finally emerged*: Arnold, "The Destruction of the Statues of Hatshepsut," pp. 270, 273.

255 *"They did erase her memory"*: Author interview with Bob Brier, March 4, 2019.

255 *a society where the illiteracy rate*: Wilkinson, *Rise and Fall*, Kindle location 749.

255 *"A lot of these sculptors"*: Author interview with Bob Brier, March 4, 2019.

256 *her ships returned laden*: Tyldesley, *Hatchepsut*, p. 153.

256 *by way of a grand avenue*: Arnold, "The Temple of Hatshepsut."

256 *Hatshepsut had to be eradicated*: Brier, *Ancient Egypt*, p. 331.

256 *Other scholars insist*: Dorman, "The Proscription of Hatshepsut," p. 267.

256  *"the king on the chessboard"*: E. H. Gombrich, *Art and Illusion* (New York: Phaidon, 1977), p. 114.

257  *Hatshepsut is depicted sometimes*: Roth, "Models of Authority," p. 9.


### Epilogue

259  *"the German Champollion"*: Romer, *History of Ancient Egypt*, vol. 2, p. 52.

260  *"the cost of every tile"*: The passage is from Emerson's "History," an essay from 1841. Online at https://tinyurl.com/yxjv3krx.

260  *"as if an ancient Egyptian had suddenly emerged"*: François Chambas, *Voyage d'un Egyptien: en Syrie, en Phenicie, En Palestine* (originally published in Paris: Dejussieu, 1866. Reprinted Whitefish, MT: Kessinger, 2010), p. viii. This translation is by Solé and Valbelle, *Rosetta Stone*, p. 107.

261  *until he could no longer manage*: Gurney, "Memoir," included in Young's *Rudiments of an Egyptian Dictionary*, p. 41.

261  *"in assisting the memory"*: Ibid., p. vi.

261  *"if he should live"*: Gurney, "Memoir," p. 42.

261  *"something extremely wrong in the action of the heart"*: Ibid., p. 41.

261  *managed to reach page 96*: Robinson, *Last Man*, p. 235.

261  *some sort of blood vessel disease*: Nadim Nasser and David Savitzki, "What Caused Jean-François Champollion's Premature Death?", *Medical Case Reports*, Dec. 21, 2015.

262  *"Only one month more"*: Robinson, *Cracking the Egyptian Code*, p. 235.

263  *"my science was born"*: Hartleben, *Champollion*, p. 522.

263  *"There are still so many things inside"*: Ibid.

263  *"my calling card for posterity"*: Ibid., p. 516.

# Bibliography

A'Beckett, G. A. "Bonaparte at Miss Frounce's School." *The Illuminated Magazine* 1 (May to October 1843).

Adams, John M. *The Millionaire and the Mummies: Theodore Davis's Gilded Age in the Valley of the Kings*. New York: St. Martin's, 2013.

Adkins, Lesley. *Empires of the Plain: Henry Rawlinson and the Lost Languages of Babylon*. New York: Thomas Dunne, 2004.

Adkins, Lesley, and Roy Adkins. *The Keys of Egypt: The Race to Crack the Hieroglyph Code*. New York: HarperCollins, 2000.

Allegro, John. "The Discovery of the Dead Sea Scrolls." In Brian M. Fagan, ed., *Eyewitness to Discovery: First-person Accounts of More Than Fifty of the World's Greatest Archeological Discoveries*. New York: Oxford University Press, 1996.

Allen, Don Cameron. "The Predecessors of Champollion." *Proceedings of the American Philosophical Society* 104, no. 5 (Oct. 17, 1960).

Arnold, Dieter. "The Temple of Hatshepsut at Deir el-Bahri." In Catherine H. Roehrig, ed., *Hatshepsut: From Queen to Pharaoh*. New York: Metropolitan Museum of Art, 2005.

Arnold, Dorothea. "The Destruction of the Statues of Hatshepsut from Deir el-Bahri." In Catherine II. Roehrig, ed., *Hatshepsut: From Queen to Pharaoh*. New York: Metropolitan Museum of Art, 2005.

Baker, Nicholson. *The Anthologist*. New York: Simon & Schuster, 2009.

Bauer, Craig P. *Unsolved: The History and Mystery of the World's Great Ciphers from Ancient Egypt to Online Secret Societies*. Princeton, NJ: Princeton University Press, 2017.

BBC documentary about Michael Ventris, "A Very English Genius." 2006. Online in seven parts at https://tinyurl.com/y2ymnykv.

Beard, Mary. "Souvenirs of Culture: Deciphering in the Museum." *Art History* 13, no. 4 (Dec. 1992).

———. "What Was Greek to Them?" *New York Review of Books*, Dec. 5, 2013.

Belzoni, Giovanni. *Travels in Egypt and Nubia*. London: J. Murray, 1822.

Berman, Joshua. "Was There an Exodus?" *Mosaic*, March 2, 2015.

Bevan, Edwin. *The House of Ptolemy*. London: Methuen, 1927.

Blair, Hugh. *Lectures on Rhetoric and Belles Lettres*. Dublin, 1783.

Breasted, James Henry. *A History of Egypt from the Earliest Times to the Persian Conquest*. New York: Scribner's, 1912.

Brier, Bob. *Ancient Egyptian Magic*. New York: Quill, 1981.

———. *Egyptomania: Our Three Thousand Year Obsession with the Land of the Pharaohs*. New York: Palgrave Macmillan, 2013.

————. *The Murder of Tutankhamen: A 3,000-Year-Old Murder Mystery*. New York: Putnam's, 1998.

Brier, Bob, and Hoyt Hobbs. *Ancient Egypt: Everyday Life in the Land of the Nile*. New York: Sterling, 2013.

Brooks, Peter. "Napoleon's Eye." *New York Review of Books*, Nov. 19, 2009.

Budge, E. A. Wallis. *The Gods of the Egyptians: Or, Studies in Egyptian Mythology*, vol. I. London: Methuen, 1904.

————. *The Rise and Progress of Assyriology*. London: Clay & Sons, 1925.

————. *The Rosetta Stone*. London: British Museum, 1913.

Budiansky, Stephen. *Battle of Wits: The Complete Story of Codebreaking in World War II*. New York: Simon & Schuster, 2002.

Bulliet, Richard. *The Wheel: Inventions and Reinventions*. New York: Columbia University Press, 2016.

Burckhardt, John Lewis. *Travels in Nubia*. London: J. Murray, 1819.

Burleigh, Nina. *Mirage: Napoleon's Scientists and the Unveiling of Egypt*. New York: Harper Perennial, 2008.

Camino, Ricardo. "Peasants." In Sergio Danadoni, ed., *The Egyptians*. Chicago: University of Chicago Press, 1997.

Ceram, C. W. *Gods, Graves, and Scholars: The Story of Archaeology*. New York: Knopf, 1951.

Cerny, Jaroslav. "The Will of Naunakhte and the Related Documents." *Journal of Egyptian Archeology* 31 (1945).

Chadwick, John. *The Decipherment of Linear B*. Cambridge, UK: Cambridge University Press, 2014.

Champollion, Jean-François, *Grammaire Égyptienne*. Paris: Fermin-Didot Frères, 1836.

————. *Lettre à M. Dacier. (Letter to Monsieur Dacier.)* Paris: Firmin Didot, Ather & Sons, 1822.

————. *Précis du Système Hiéroglyphique des Anciens Égyptiens*. Paris: Treuttel et Würtz, 1824.

Champollion-Figeac, Aimé, *Les Deux Champollion: Leur Vie et Leurs Oeuvres*. Grenoble, France: Drevet, 1887.

Coe, Michael D. *Breaking the Maya Code*. New York: Thames & Hudson, 1992.

Damrosch, David. *The Buried Book: The Loss and Rediscovery of the Great Epic of Gilgamesh*. New York: Henry Holt, 2006.

Darnell, John Coleman, and Colleen Manassa. *Tutankhamun's Armies: Battle and Conquest during Ancient Egypt's Late 18th Dynasty*. Hoboken, NJ: John Wiley & Sons, 2007.

David, Rosalie. *Conversations with Mummies: New Light on the Lives of Ancient Egyptians*. New York: Morrow, 2000.

————. *Religion and Magic in Ancient Egypt*. New York: Penguin, 2003.

Delbourgo, James. *Collecting the World: Hans Sloane and the Origins of the British Museum*. Cambridge, MA: Harvard University Press, 2019.

Dieckmann, Liselotte. "Renaissance Hieroglyphics." *Comparative Literature* 9, no. 4 (Autumn 1957).

Diffie, Whitfield, and Mary Fischer. "Decipherment versus Cryptanalysis." In Richard Parkinson, *Cracking Codes: The Rosetta Stone and Decipherment*. Berkeley: University of California Press, 1999.

Dorman, Peter F. "The Proscription of Hatshepsut." In Catherine H. Roehrig, ed., *Hatshepsut: From Queen to Pharaoh*. New York: Metropolitan Museum of Art, 2005.

Drower, Margaret. *Flinders Petrie: A Life in Archeology*. Madison: University of Wisconsin Press, 1995.

Ebers, George. *Egypt: Historical, Descriptive, and Picturesque*. Jazzybee Verlag: 2017. (Originally published 1886.)

Eiseley, Loren. *The Star Thrower*. New York: Random House, 1979.

Everett, Daniel. *Don't Sleep, There Are Snakes: Life and Language in the Amazonian Jungle*. New York: Vintage, 2009.

Fagan, Brian. *Lord and Pharaoh: Carnarvon and the Search for Tutankhamun*. London: Routledge, 2016.

———. *The Rape of the Nile: Tomb Robbers, Tourists, and Archeologists in Egypt*. New York: Basic Books, 2004.

Fagone, Jason. *The Woman Who Smashed Codes: A True Story of Love, Spies, and the Unlikely Heroine Who Outwitted America's Enemies*. New York: HarperCollins, 2017.

Fallows, Deborah. *Dreaming in Chinese: Mandarin Lessons in Life, Love, and Language*. New York: Walker, 2010.

Finati, Giovanni. *Narrative of the Life and Adventures of Giovanni Finati*, vol. 2. Edited by William Bankes. London: J. Murray, 1830.

Findlen, Paula. *Athanasius Kircher: The Last Man Who Knew Everything*. New York: Routledge, 2004.

Fleming, Fergus. *Barrow's Boys*. Boston: Atlantic Monthly Press, 2000.

Fox, Margalit. *The Riddle of the Labyrinth: The Quest to Crack an Ancient Code*. New York: Ecco, 2013.

Frankfort, Henri. *Ancient Egyptian Religion: An Interpretation*. New York: Columbia University Press, 1948.

Friedman, William. "An Introduction to Methods for the Solution of Ciphers." In *Publication No. 17*. Geneva, IL: Riverbank Laboratories, Dept. of Ciphers, 1918.

Gardiner, Alan. *Egyptian Grammar*. Oxford, UK: Griffith Institute, 1927.

George, Andrew, ed. *The Epic of Gilgamesh*. New York: Penguin, 2003.

Gillispie, Charles C. *Science and Polity in France: The Revolutionary and Napoleonic Years* Princeton, NJ: Princeton University Press, 2004.

———. "Scientific Aspects of the French Egyptian Expedition 1798–1801." *Proceedings of the American Philosophical Society* 133, no. 4 (Dec. 1989).

Gillispie, Charles C., and Michel Dewachter, eds. *The Monuments of Egypt: The Complete Archeological Plates from* La Description de l'Égypte. Princeton, NJ: Princeton Architectural Press, 1987.

Glassie, John. *A Man of Misconceptions: The Life of an Eccentric in an Age of Change*. New York: Penguin, 2012.

Gleick, James. *The Information: A History, A Theory, A Flood*. New York: Vintage, 2012.

Glynn, Ian. *Elegance in Science: The Beauty of Simplicity*. New York: Oxford University Press, 2010.

Gnanadesikan, Amalia. *The Writing Revolution: Cuneiform to the Internet*. Hoboken, NJ: Wiley-Blackwell, 2009.

Gordon, John Steele. *Washington's Monument: And the Fascinating History of the Obelisk*. New York: Bloomsbury, 2016.

Green, Peter. "Tut-Tut-Tut." *New York Review of Books*, Oct. 11, 1979.

Greenblatt, Stephen. *Swerve: How the World Became Modern*. New York: Norton, 2012.

———. *The Rise and Fall of Adam and Eve*. New York: Norton, 2017.

Guichard Jr., Roger H. *Niebuhr in Egypt: European Science in a Biblical World*. Cambridge, UK: Lutterworth Press, 2014.

Gunn, Battiscombe. "Notes on the Naukratis Stela." *Journal of Egyptian Archaeology* 29 (Dec. 1943).

Gurney, Hudson, "Memoir." In Thomas Young. *Rudiments of an Ancient Egyptian Dictionary in the Ancient Enchorial Character*. London: J. & A. Arch, 1831.

Hansen, Thorkild. *Arabia Felix: The Danish Expedition of 1761–1767*. New York: Harper & Row, 1962.

Harrison, Simon. *Hunting and the Enemy Body in Modern War*. New York: Berghahn, 2012.

Hartleben, Hermine, ed. *Lettres et Journaux de Champollion le Jeune*, 1, 2. Paris: Leroux, 1909.

———. *Champollion: Sein Leben und Sein Werk*. Weidmannsche Buchhandlung: Berlin, 1906.

Haycock, David Boyd. *William Stukeley: Science, Religion and Archaeology in Eighteenth-Century England*. Woodbridge, Suffolk, UK: Boydell Press, 2002.

Herodotus. *The Histories*. London: Penguin, 1954.

Herold, J. Christopher, *The Age of Napoleon*. New York: Mariner Books, 2002.

———. *Bonaparte in Egypt*. Tucson, AZ: Fireship Press, 2009.

Higgins, Charlotte. "How to Decode an Ancient Roman's Handwriting." *New Yorker*, May 1, 2017.

Hilts, Victor L. "Thomas Young's 'Autobiographical Sketch.'" *Proceedings of the American Philosophical Society* 122, no. 4 (Aug. 18, 1978).

Horapollo, *The Hieroglyphics of Horapollo Nilous*. London: W. Pickering, 1840.

Hornung, Erik. *The Secret Lore of Egypt: Its Impact on the West*. Ithaca, NY: Cornell University Press, 2001.

Hume, Ivor. *Belzoni: The Giant Archeologists Love to Hate*. Charlottesville: University of Virginia Press, 2011.

Ikram, Salima. *Death and Burial in Ancient Egypt*. Cairo: American University in Cairo Press, 2015.

Iversen, Erik. *The Myth of Egypt and its Hieroglyphs*. Princeton, NJ: Princeton University Press, 1961.

Kahn, David. *The Codebreakers: The Story of Secret Writing*. London: Sphere Books, 1973.

Keegan, John. *Intelligence in War: Knowledge of the Enemy from Napoleon to al-Qaeda*. New York: Knopf Doubleday, 2003.

Kember, Joe, John Plunkett, and Jill Sullivan, eds. *Popular Exhibitions, Science and Showmanship, 1840–1910*. New York: Routledge, 2012.

Kramer, Samuel Noah. *The Sumerians: Their History, Culture, and Character*. Chicago: University of Chicago Press, 1971.

LaBrière, Leon de la. *Champollion Inconnu: Lettres Inédites*. Paris: Plan, 1897

Leal, Pedro Germano. "Reassessing Horapollon: A Contemporary View on *Hieroglyphica*." *Emblematic* 21 (2014).

Livingstone, Josephine. "Old English." *New York Times Magazine*, Jan. 6, 2019.

Luckenbill, Daniel. *Ancient Records of Assyria and Babylonia*, vol. 2. Chicago: University of Chicago Press, 1927.

Lynch, Jack. *You Could Look It Up: The Reference Shelf from Ancient Babylon to Wikipedia*. New York: Bloomsbury, 2016.

Man, John. *Alpha Beta: How 26 Letters Shaped the Western World*. New York: Barnes & Noble, 2005.

Manetho. *History of Egypt*. Translated by W. G. Waddell. Cambridge, MA: Harvard University Press, 1940.

Manguel, Alberto. *A History of Reading*. New York: Penguin, 2014.

Mayes, Stanley. *The Great Belzoni: The Circus Strongman Who Discovered Egypt's Ancient Treasure*. London: Tauris Parke, 2006.

McDowell, Andrea. *Village Life in Ancient Egypt: Laundry Lists and Love Songs*. New York: Oxford University Press, 1999.

McMahon, Darrin. *Divine Fury: A History of Genius*. New York: Basic Books, 2013.

McWhorter, John. *The Language Hoax: Why the World Looks the Same in any Language*. New York: Oxford University Press, 2014.

———. *The Power of Babel: A Natural History of Language*. New York: Henry Holt, 2001.

Mertz, Barbara. *Red Land, Black Land: Daily Life in Ancient Egypt*. New York: William Morrow, 2008.

———. *Temples, Tombs and Hieroglyphs: A Popular History of Ancient Egypt*. New York: Morrow, 2009.

Moorehead, Alan. *The Blue Nile*. New York: Harper Perennial, 2000.

Morenz, Ludwig. "The Origins of Egyptian Literature." In Bill Manley, ed., *The Seventy Great Mysteries of Ancient Egypt*. London: Thames & Hudson, 2003.

Morrison, Robert. *The Regency Years: During Which Jane Austen Writes, Napoleon Fights, Byron Makes Love, and Britain Becomes Modern*. New York: Norton, 2019.

Nightingale, Andrea. *Once Out of Nature: Augustine on Time and the Body*. Chicago: University of Chicago Press, 2011.

Parkinson, Richard. "Egypt: A Life Before the Afterlife." *Guardian*, Nov. 5, 2010.

———. *Cracking Codes: The Rosetta Stone and Decipherment*. Berkeley: University of California Press, 1999.

———. *The Painted Tomb Chapel of Nebamun*. London: British Museum Press, 2008.

Parsons, Peter. *City of the Sharp-Nosed Fish: The Lives of the Greeks in Roman Egypt*. London: Orion, 2012.

Peacock, George. *Life of Thomas Young, M.D., F.R.S. , & C.* London: J. Murray, 1855.

Peet, T. Eric. *A Comparative Study of the Literatures of Egypt, Palestine, and Mesopotamia: Egypt's Contribution to the Literatures of the Ancient World*. Eugene, OR: Wipf and Stock, 1997.

Petrie, Flinders. *Seventy Years in Archeology*. London: Low, Marston, 1931.

———. *The Pyramids and Temples of Gizeh*. London: Field & Tuer, 1883.

Pharr, Clyde, Theresa Sherrer Davidson, and Mary Brown Pharr, eds. *The Theodosian Codes and Novels and the Sirmondian Constitutions*. Princeton, NJ: Princeton University Press, 1952.

Picchi, Daniela, Karen Ascani, and Paola Buzi, eds. *The Forgotten Scholar: Georg Zoëga (1755–1809): At the Dawn of Egyptology and Coptic Studies*. Leiden, Netherlands: Brill, 2015.

Pope, Maurice. *The Story of Decipherment: From Egyptian Hieroglyphs to Maya Script*. London: Thames and Hudson, 1975.

Ray, John. *The Rosetta Stone and the Rebirth of Ancient Egypt.* Cambridge, MA: Harvard University Press, 2007.

Reid, Donald Malcolm. *Whose Pharaohs?: Archeology, Museums, and Egyptian National Identity from Napoleon to World War I.* Berkeley: University of California Press, 2003.

Renouf, Peter Le Page. "Young and Champollion." *Proceedings of the Society of Biblical Archeology* 19 (May 4, 1897).

Ritner, Robert K. "Tutankhamun for the Twenty-first Century: Modern Misreadings of an Ancient Culture." Talk delivered at the Field Museum of Natural History, Chicago, on Oct. 26, 2006. Online at tinyurl.com/4z6vh60h.

Roberts, Andrew. *Napoleon: A Life.* New York: Penguin, 2015.

Robinson, Andrew. *Cracking the Egyptian Code: The Revolutionary Life of Jean-François Champollion.* New York: Oxford University Press, 2012.

———. *Lost Languages: The Enigma of the World's Undeciphered Scripts.* New York: McGraw-Hill, 2002.

———. *Sudden Genius?: The Gradual Path to Creative Breakthroughs.* New York: Oxford University Press, 2010.

———. *The Last Man Who Knew Everything: Thomas Young, the Anonymous Genius Who Proved Newton Wrong and Deciphered the Rosetta Stone, Among Other Surprising Feats.* New York: Plume, 2007.

———. *The Man Who Deciphered Linear B: The Story of Michael Ventris.* London: Thames & Hudson, 2012.

———. *The Story of Writing: Alphabets, Hieroglyphs, and Pictograms.* London: Thames & Hudson, 1995.

Roehrig, Catharine H., ed., *Hatshepsut: From Queen to Pharaoh.* New York: Metropolitan Museum of Art, 2005.

Romer, John. *A History of Ancient Egypt, Volume 2: From the Great Pyramid to the Fall of the Middle Kingdom.* New York: Thomas Dunne, 2017.

———. *Ancient Lives: Daily Life in Egypt of the Pharaohs.* New York: Holt, Rinehart and Winston, 1984.

Roth, Ann Macy. "Models of Authority: Hatshepsut's Predecessors in Power." In Catharine H. Roehrig, ed., *Hatshepsut: From Queen to Pharaoh.* New York: Metropolitan Museum of Art, 2005.

Salt, Henry. *Essay on Dr. Young's and M. Champollion's Phonetic System of Hieroglyphics.* Cambridge, UK: Cambridge University Press, 2014. (Originally published 1823.)

Schiff, Stacy. *Cleopatra: A Life.* Boston: Little, Brown, 2010.

Schmandt-Besserat, Denise. "The Evolution of Writing." Online at https://tinyurl.com/y72ynmqz.

———. *How Writing Came About.* Austin: University of Texas Press, 1992.

Sebba, Anne. *The Exiled Collector: William Bankes and the Making of an English Country House.* Dovecote, UK: Dovecote Press, 2009.

Selin, Shannon. "Boney the Bogeyman: How Napoleon Scared Children." Online at https://tinyurl.com/y5wl7ayo.

Seyler, Dorothy U. *The Obelisk and the Englishman: The Pioneering Discoveries of Egyptologist William Bankes.* Amherst, NY: Prometheus Books, 2015.

Shaw, Ian, ed. *The Oxford History of Ancient Egypt.* New York: Oxford University Press, 2003.

Solé, Robert, and Dominque Valbelle. *The Rosetta Stone: The Story of the Decoding of Hieroglyphics.* New York: Four Walls Eight Windows, 2002.

Stiebing Jr., William H. *Uncovering the Past: A History of Archeology.* New York: Oxford University Press, 1993.

Strabo. *Geography.* Cambridge, MA: Harvard University Press, 1932.

Strathern, Paul. *Napoleon in Egypt.* New York: Bantam, 2009.

Thomasson, Fredrik. *The Life of J. D. Åkerblad: Egyptian Decipherment and Orientalism in Revolutionary Times.* Leiden, Netherlands: Brill, 2013.

Thompson, Jason. *Wonderful Things: A History of Egyptology, Volume 1: From Antiquity to 1881.* Cairo: American University in Cairo Press, 2015.

———. *Wonderful Things: A History of Egyptology, Volume 2: The Golden Age: 1881–1914.* Cairo: American University in Cairo Press, 2016.

———. *Wonderful Things: A History of Egyptology, Volume 3: From 1914 to the Twenty-first Century.* Cairo: American University in Cairo Press, 2018.

Tyldesley, Joyce. *Hatchepsut: The Female Pharaoh.* London: Penguin, 2008.

———. *Myths and Legends of Ancient Egypt.* New York: Viking, 2010.

Tyndall, John. "Thomas Young. A Discourse." Lecture delivered at the Royal Institution in London on Jan. 22, 1886. Online at https://tinyurl.com/y2rhqkmz.

Ucko, Peter, and Timothy Champion, eds. *The Wisdom of Egypt: Changing Visions Through the Ages.* Abingdon, UK: Routledge, 2003.

Urbanus, Jason. "In the Time of the Rosetta Stone." *Archaeology,* Nov./Dec. 2017.

Usick, Patricia. *William John Bankes' Collection of Drawings and Manuscripts Relating to Ancient Nubia.* University of London PhD thesis from 1998. Online at https://tinyurl.com/y6hhdqrq.

Walker, C. B., and James Chadwick. *Reading the Past: Ancient Writing from Cuneiform to the Alphabet.* Berkeley: University of California Press, 1990.

Warner, Oliver. *The Battle of the Nile.* New York: Macmillan, 1960.

White, Matthew. *Atrocities: The 100 Deadliest Episodes in Human History.* New York: Norton, 2012.

Wilkinson, Toby. *The Rise and Fall of Ancient Egypt.* New York: Random House, 2010.

———. *Writings from Ancient Egypt.* New York: Penguin, 2017.

Williams, Ann. "Animals Everlasting." *National Geographic,* Nov. 2009.

Wilson, John A. *Signs and Wonders Upon Pharaoh: A History of American Egyptology.* Chicago: University of Chicago Press, 1964.

Wood, Alexander. *Thomas Young: Natural Philosopher.* Cambridge, UK: Cambridge University Press, 1954.

Yates, Frances. *Giordano Bruno and the Hermetic Tradition.* Abingdon, UK: Routledge, 1999.

Young, Thomas. "Egypt." *Encyclopedia Britannica,* supplement vol. 4, 1819. In John Leitch, ed., *Miscellaneous Works of the Late Thomas Young.* London: J. Murray, 1855.

———. "On the mechanism of the eye." *Philosophical Transactions of the Royal Society of London* 91 (Part I, 1801).

———. *An Account of Some Recent Discoveries in Hieroglyphical Literature and Egyptian Antiquities including the Author's Original Alphabet as Extended by Mr. Champollion with a Translation of Five Unpublished Greek and Egyptian Manuscripts.* London: J. Murray, 1823.

———. *Rudiments of an Ancient Egyptian Dictionary in the Ancient Enchorial Character.* London: J. & A. Arch, 1831.

# Photo Credits

*Photo Insert*

1. Lent to Belvedere by Kunsthistorisches Museum
2. Copy by Henry Briggs of Thomas Lawrence's portrait of Thomas Young
3. Portrait of Jean-François Champollion, 1831, by Léon Cogniet. Louvre
4. North Wind Picture Archives / Alamy Stock Photo
5. Courtesy of the author
6. © RMN-Grand Palais / H. Lewandowski / Art Resource, NY
7. © 2020 Bridgeman Images
8. Dan Breckwoldt / Alamy Stock Photo
9. Calin Stan / Alamy Stock Photo
10. Jan Adam Kruseman, 1824, Fitzwilliam Museum
11. © National Trust Images / Derrick E. Witty
12. © National Trust Images / John Hammond
13. © National Trust Images / John Hammond
14. National Archives
15. New-York Historical Society
16. © President and Fellows of Harvard College
17. Danita Delimont / Alamy Stock Photo
18. Design Pics / Alamy Stock Photo
19. © The Metropolitan Museum of Art. Image source: Art Resource, NY

# Index

Page numbers in italics refer to photographs.

# About the Author

Edward Dolnick is the author of *The Clockwork Universe*, *The Forger's Spell*, *Down the Great Unknown*, and the Edgar Award–winning *The Rescue Artist*, among other books. A former chief science writer at the *Boston Globe*, he has written for the *Atlantic*, the *New York Times Magazine*, and many other publications. He lives with his wife near Washington, DC.